Mother Jones

WOMEN'S
BIOGRAPHY *series*

A volume in the Women's Biography Series

SERIES EDITORS: Kristie Miller, Melanie S. Gustafson, and Pamela Reeves

Mother Jones
Raising Cain and Consciousness

———)(———

Simon Cordery

University of New Mexico Press | Albuquerque

opposite: Mother Jones outside the White House (1924), courtesy Library of Congress Prints and Photographs Division

© 2010 by the University of New Mexico Press
All rights reserved. Published 2010
Printed in the United States of America
15 14 13 12 11 10   1 2 3 4 5 6

Library of Congress Cataloging-in-Publication Data
Cordery, Simon, 1960–
Mother Jones : raising Cain and consciousness / Simon Cordery.
p. cm.
Includes bibliographical references and index.
ISBN 978-0-8263-4810-4 (pbk. : alk. paper)
1. Jones, Mother, 1843?–1930. 2. Women labor leaders—United States—
Biography. 3. Women social reformers—United States—Biography. 4.
United Mine Workers of America—History. 5. Coal miners—Labor unions—
Organizing—United States—History. 6. Labor—United States—History. I.
Title.
HD8073.J6C67 2010
331.88092—dc22
[B]
2009045999

Contents

Illustrations

————————)(————————

Acknowledgments

IT IS A PLEASURE TO THANK the individuals and institutions without whose help writing this book would have been impossible. I have spent many enjoyable hours at the Newberry Library in Chicago researching and participating in the Labor History seminar, and I want to thank Leon Fink of the University of Illinois at Chicago and Toby Higbie, now at the University of Illinois at Urbana-Champaign, for encouraging me to attend and present my research. I would also like to acknowledge the Mellon Foundation for a research grant administered through the Associated Colleges of the Midwest, which allowed me to do some crucial early work on this project. A faculty development grant and a sabbatical from Monmouth College enabled me to complete the writing of this book, and I am grateful for that support.

Several colleagues at Monmouth College deserve recognition for their assistance with this project. Ira Smolensky and Steve Buban read the manuscript and provided suggestions for improvements that strengthened the final product, and Craig Vivian suggested the subtitle. Katherine Blackmer and Andrea Crum provided timely and much-needed help, while Richard Sayre, our indefatigable librarian, supplied invaluable assistance in locating newspapers. Thank you as well to the students in my U.S. history surveys who helped me think about how to analyze Mother Jones and American labor history. At the University of New Mexico Press it is a great pleasure to thank Kristie Miller, Melanie Gustafson, and Pamela

Reeves Kilian, the series editors, for their very useful comments on an earlier incarnation of this project, and to thank Clark Whitehorn, my editor, for his support and patience. It is a joy to thank Elisabeth A. Graves and Elizabeth Albright, Karen Mazur, Nancy Woodard, and Elise M. McHugh of the press for their excellent work to improve the manuscript. My friend and colleague Brad Brown, whose advice and suggestions I have long valued, has been a great sounding board for my ideas.

Last but not least, this book could not have been written without the enduring support of my family. My parents, Ned and Mary Cordery, and my father-in-law, Jim Rozek, have provided inspiration for my professional career and my personal life, and I thank them for that. For Stacy and Gareth words cannot express how much you mean to me, but I hope you know. With the two of you all is possible, but adequate thanks are impossible.

Introduction

Mother Jones and the American Labor Movement

ON A CLOUDY AND COLD December morning in 1930, thousands of people gathered in the small town of Mount Olive, Illinois, to mourn the death of a woman who had fought to improve life for working families for thirty years. Worn out after decades of union organizing and ill-health, ninety-three-year-old Mary Harris "Mother" Jones had died a week before in a suburb of Washington, D.C. A funeral service in St. Gabriel's Catholic Church in the nation's capital had drawn an overflow crowd, with union dignitaries and government officials among the honorary pallbearers. Afterward a special train brought her coffin to Mount Olive, arriving on 4 December. Her body lay in state in the Oddfellows Hall for three days as mourners from around the country filed slowly past to pay their last respects, demonstrating the affection in which Mother Jones was held by the great and the lowly.

Those who came to Mount Olive, a small mining community situated halfway between Springfield and St. Louis, remembered Mother Jones for educating workers about their rights and agitating for a better future. Once called "the most dangerous woman in America" because of her ability to inspire working people to demand higher wages, safer working conditions, and a fair share of the wealth they created, her withered and lifeless body lay in peace at last. On 7 December the Rev. J. W. R. McGuire delivered his eulogy in the Church of the Ascension to a crowd of more than four thousand people, most of whom had to listen to his tribute on speakers mounted outside the hall. Thousands more heard the service live over Chicago radio station WCFL, owned by the Chicago Federation of Labor, and the next day newspapers across the country reported the event.

In his tribute Father McGuire made no attempt to hide the fighting qualities of Mother Jones, born into a family of Irish radicals and raised into the labor movement by marriage and experience. He told the assembled crowd, "Wealthy coal operators and capitalists throughout the United States are breathing sighs of relief while toil-worn men and women are weeping tears of bitter grief. The reason for this contrast of relief and sorrow is apparent. Mother Jones is dead."[1] For many Americans, the priest asserted, "she represented all that was finest in womanhood. Armed with only the weapons of a burning mother's love, a flaming tongue, and indomitable spirit, she went forth to convince a cold, money-glutted world of [the need for] justice, mercy, and love."[2] Afterward survivors of the "Virden Massacre," a deadly clash between striking miners and mine guards in 1898, carried her coffin from the church to the burial plot accompanied by a human chain exceeding a mile in length. At the cemetery union representatives placed floral tributes on her grave. A folk song, penned anonymously soon after she passed away, began:

> The world today is mourning
> The death of Mother Jones;
> Grief and sorrow hover
> Over the miners' homes;
> This grand old champion of labor
> Has gone to a better land,
> But the hard-working miners,
> They miss her guiding hand.[3]

That hand had guided them into and out of conflicts for the best part of thirty years. The gentle rolling hills and the thickets of trees across central Illinois hid a land that had witnessed open warfare between coal miners and the operators hired by mining corporations as managers. Mother Jones had asked to be buried in Mount Olive at the only cemetery in the country owned by a labor union, to be near "her boys" when the end came. The burial ground stood as mute testimony to a new wave of violence in Gilded Age workplaces and city streets. Mother Jones had witnessed some of those battles, radicalizing her and bringing her into sustained contact with the labor movement. At Virden, on 12 October 1898, seven miners and four guards died when gunfire erupted as strikers turned away replacement workers. The Miners' Cemetery opened in September 1899 after local churches refused to bury miners killed in the Virden Massacre.

Mother Jones organized workers into unions at the height of this brutal age, heedless of her personal safety and contemptuous of the many threats against her. She made herself into a national symbol of resistance to tyranny, a celebrity the world over. She became widely recognized as the grandmotherly figure with white hair who wore silk dresses and stood up to private detectives and federal troops to advocate class war and proclaim the labor theory of value, the idea that the wealth of the nation should go to those who produce it. Mother Jones understood that class did not just happen and that class consciousness was not the inevitable or natural consequence of earning a wage. Class had to be made, and her agitation sought to bring working people to an awareness of social inequality as a reason for collective action. She organized to show working people that their interests were fundamentally opposed to those of capitalists and only through class war could they obtain what was rightfully theirs, the fruits of their labor.

The journey that ended at Mount Olive in 1930 began with the birth of Mary Harris in Cork, Ireland, in 1837. When she was eight the country was devastated by the potato famine, a blight that destroyed the crop more than half the nation's population relied on for survival. To escape, her family emigrated to Canada. After qualifying as a teacher in Toronto Mary moved briefly to Michigan and then Illinois before marrying an iron molder named George Jones and starting a family in Memphis, Tennessee. In 1867, however, her husband and their four children died in a yellow fever epidemic, and she returned to Chicago, where she established a dressmaking business. Misfortune followed her there, too: her shop was destroyed in the Great Fire of 1871. After this she took to the road and wandered for over a decade until she found a home in the labor movement in the 1890s. Before then she left virtually no trace in the historical record, and what she said or thought was undocumented. By 1897 Mary Jones had transformed herself into "Mother Jones" and embarked on a high-profile career in the labor movement stretching all the way to 1926.

Mother Jones became famous for her fiery speeches. Her name was most closely associated with bitter conflicts between owners and workers in Colorado and West Virginia, though she traveled across the country and participated in strikes everywhere she went. During the course of her career she was intimidated by private detectives, imprisoned by court-martial, and deported from strike zones for speaking out against low wages and dangerous working conditions. She violated all the norms for women in the early twentieth century by swearing, drinking, traveling alone, and resisting authority. She never remarried. Driven by her desire for social justice and the ghosts of her own past she journeyed at great personal risk into isolated valleys and up treacherous mountainsides to meet working people and convince them to join labor unions. She spent sleepless nights on cold floors and in prison beds. She faced down gunmen hired by coal companies to threaten and kill union organizers. She walked through pouring rain and icy blizzards to converse with working-class families. In between two stints as a mine-union organizer she spent six years working as a speaker for the Socialist Party, telling voters not to throw away their ballot on the Democrats and the Republicans but to join the vanguard of a movement leading to what she and many others at the time saw as a new dawn. And she did all this in her sixties, seventies, and eighties.

By 1915 Mother Jones had become a celebrity who could no longer travel anonymously. Her life had taken on mythical qualities, a transformation she encouraged by inventing stories about her role in the labor movement. She claimed to have attended important early strikes when there was no chance she could have done so. After she became a paid organizer around 1900 the newspapers followed her movements in great detail, interpreting her arrival in troubled areas as a sign of the seriousness of the unrest. Her physical appearance called to mind a sweet and docile octogenarian, but she railed against capitalism in earthy language. A journalist who interviewed her for the *Brooklyn Daily Eagle* in 1913 captured this paradox, describing her as "short of stature, with a slight limp in her walk, and with curly white hair and 'specs,' [who] resembles almost my grandmother who has lived a peaceful life in the bosom of a happy family." This demeanor deceived, for "when she talks, you forget the happy grandmother simile. You think that grandmother is cross. Mother [Jones] is very cross." She retained traces of her roots, one journalist detecting a "touch of the Irish, in brogue and oratorical flourish."[4] This carefully crafted image served Mother Jones well, but she arrived at it only after a life of trauma and sadness.

Mother Jones drew on her traumatic past as she traveled through the isolated valleys of West Virginia, up craggy peaks in Colorado, crossing and re-crossing the country by train. Union organizing was difficult, dangerous, and often futile, but she loved talking to "my boys," as she called the miners, and excoriating "the pirates," as she labeled capitalists. Because of the intensity of her experiences and her self-belief, Mother Jones had a tendency to see the world in black and white terms, often ignoring or criticizing those who suggested alternative strategies to her own. Unlike many in the union movement, however, she refused to discriminate against African Americans, though she took a more conventional attitude toward women, arguing that they should remain in the home to raise children.

Her origins remained with her and conditioned who she was and how she saw the world. But what precisely did she achieve? Like all union organizers, and indeed like all radicals seeking to overturn an entire social system, she failed on her own terms. Her efforts did not lead to the overthrow of capitalism, and people continued to work for wages in corporations controlled by a wealthy few or in small businesses employing a handful of family members. But, in tandem with hundreds of other dedicated organizers and socialists, she forced the rights of labor onto the national political agenda and helped improve the lives of thousands of working people. When her career opened, federal soldiers were shooting striking workers; when it ended, organized labor had become an accepted part of the power structure of the United States. She did not forge this change by herself, but Mother Jones contributed significantly to the shift toward respectability for labor.

It is one of the ironies of her career that she would not have welcomed this respectability, implying as it did acceptance of the status quo. Mother Jones was a socialist who wanted the government to play a meaningful role in the national economy, including ownership of large industries like coal mining and the railroads. Even after leaving the Socialist Party in disgust she remained a socialist committed to democracy. She taught working people about the U.S. Constitution and the American Revolution, which together with her Catholic upbringing served as the basis for her radicalism, to convince them of the justice of socialism. She believed in a republic of equals and in gender-specific roles for men and women. Her speeches resonated: she said things that made sense or that brought into focus what many working people had been thinking and feeling but had not formulated coherently for themselves. The resonances and the paradoxes fill the pages of this book to capture the complexities, limitations, and possibilities of the life of Mother Jones.

1

An Irish Inheritance

MOTHER JONES WROTE AND SPOKE to audiences across the United States and ventured into Canada and Mexico during her three-decades-long career as a labor organizer. She often told stories drawn from her own life, filling her speeches and writings with self-revelation. Veracity was not her strong suit, however. Her oratory overflowed with references to her past, many of them elaborate exaggerations and some of them eloquent fictions. Thus she informed coal miners that she had "worked with you for years . . . [and] went into the mines on the night shift and the day shift and helped the poor wretches to load coal at times," and later that "I worked on the night shift and the day shift in Pennsylvania from Pittsburgh to Brownsville. There isn't a mine that was open in those days that I didn't go on the night shift and the day shift."[1] Though she almost certainly did descend into mine shafts, it is most unlikely that she worked in them. She told an audience in West Virginia, "I have met every President of the United States since President Lincoln down. I have had talks with them with regard to conditions in certain places."[2] In reality she met with not twelve presidents but four (McKinley, Taft, Wilson, and Coolidge), an impressive enough collection. She tried to meet Theodore Roosevelt, but he purposefully eluded her. In her *Autobiography* and in sworn congressional testimony Mother Jones recounted how she traveled to Pittsburgh, Pennsylvania, to aid striking railroaders in 1877—a journey she almost certainly could not and did not take.[3] Even in the matter of her birth she maintained one thing while the historical record reveals something else. She claimed at various times to have been born in Canada, on May Day (the international workers' holiday), in 1830.[4] In fact, she was born in the city of Cork in southwestern Ireland on 1 August 1837.[5]

The actual differences between fiction and fact are relatively unimportant compared to the significance of her decisions about how to present her life story. As she later said, "How can it change things if I am Irish from Dublin or Irish from Cork, or that I am Irish at all? It is enough that I am of the world. I'm just plain Mary Jones of the U.S.A."[6] Choosing 1830 as her year of birth enabled an elderly Mother Jones to imagine reaching the century mark; 1 May (May Day) had been designated as the workers' holiday, a day set aside for celebrating labor instead of performing it. Mother Jones wanted to be remembered as the centenarian labor leader whose life from the very day of her birth had been destined "to leave this nation a nobler manhood and greater womanhood."[7] The labor movement provided her with the means to achieve these aims, and history, the stage upon which to announce them.

History is about change and continuity, and both filled the life of Mother Jones. Change was ever present for Mary Harris "Mother" Jones: she emigrated from Ireland after the potato famine; she moved from Toronto to Chicago to Memphis, returning to the Windy City before reaching the age of forty; she was widowed by a yellow fever epidemic that also claimed her four children; she lost her business in the Great Chicago Fire; and she spent three decades constantly traveling in an attempt to help working people fight for a better life. She became an itinerant labor union organizer, claiming later in life that "I have spoken in every state in this union, and in every city." She sought neither aid nor pity for herself. As she put it, "I don't like sympathy, sympathy never got me anything, and I have no use for it. We don't want sympathy, we want to stand out straight before the world that we are fighting the battle for our own cause."[8]

Continuities abounded too. Despite occasional disclaimers, Mother Jones remained self-consciously Irish and aware of the limitations she faced as a woman. She knew the sting of stereotypes and, though a self-proclaimed patriotic American, was often represented in the press as a "daughter of Erin." One of her friends reported in 1915 how "she is impulsive . . . saying everything that comes in to her mind while she is feeling it. That's the bog temperament; that's the Irish of her."[9] A reporter for the *Washington Post* wrote of how, even in her nineties, "her Irish eyes seemed to burn with a fire born of the combustion of timid thought."[10] Her Irishness helped her identify with working people, whose hard lives she understood and whose support for unionism she sought.

Catholicism is crucial to understanding the choices Mother Jones made, particularly (but not exclusively) her decision to take on a new identity in the 1890s, when she was nearly sixty years of age. The very notion of "mother," allied with the name Mary, invoked the Blessed Virgin Mary for knowing audiences. The early influences of the Catholic Church remained with her and shaped who she was and how she saw the world. By the time she began organizing in 1897 Mother Jones had publicly repudiated the Church as an institution, dismissing it as a weapon capitalists used to oppress ordinary people. Nonetheless she continued to find inspiration in the life of Christ and spoke often of drawing solace and strength from God. She told union members in 1909, "I have a contract with God to let me stay here many more [years] to help clean up that old gang" of businessmen.[11] She employed religious imagery to inspire her listeners. To striking miners in Montgomery, West Virginia, she explained how "the star of Bethlehem has crossed the world, it has risen here; see it breaking slowly through the clouds. The Star of Bethlehem will usher in the new day and new time and new philosophy—and if you are only true you will be free—if you are only men."[12] She wanted to put the fear of God in her enemies, asking capitalists:

> Oh, men, have you any hearts? Oh, men, do you feel? Oh, men, do you see the judgment day on the throne above, when you will be asked, "Where did you get your gold?" You stole it from these wretches. You murdered, you assassinated, you starved, you burned them to death, that you and your wives might have palaces, and that your wives might go to the sea-shore.[13]

She drew her inspiration from Jesus, placing herself in a direct line from the man she called "the world's greatest agitator."[14]

Her ethnicity, religion, and gender provided the material with which Mary Harris Jones remade herself. Becoming "Mother" allowed her to join the workers' struggle at some of its most vital—and most violent—moments. Dressing as a grandmother enabled her to travel freely through strife-torn regions of the country. In all this she claimed to remain faithful to her origins, recalling that "I was born of the struggle and the torment and the pain. A child of the wheel, a brat of the cogs, a woman of the dust."[15] She grew up in a poor family committed to radical change. She maintained her devotion to the labor movement, to its heroes, and to its aims. Here again she repudiated institutions but always remained true to her long search for justice for working people, especially coal miners. She refused to become involved in the internal conflicts habitually besetting the two institutions with which she worked most closely, the United Mine Workers of America and the Socialist Party. She thus retained the freedom to act for what she saw as the welfare of working people, or, as she put it, "I am not looking for office I am looking for your interests and your children's interests."[16] In this quest Mother Jones found her calling as an educator and agitator, teaching and organizing those without political power.

Mother Jones loved fiery rhetoric, hated despotism and injustice, and despised hypocrisy, brutality, cowardice, and cant. Also significant was her decision, in an autobiography otherwise short on personal details, to write about her family members. She recalled that her own family had "for generations . . . fought for Ireland's freedom," a fight she carried with her across the Atlantic to North America.[17] She identified with and drew strength from the struggles of her radical forebears, writing while incarcerated in 1913, "I am a military prisoner. This is just what the old monarchy did [to] my grandparents 90 years ago in Ireland."[18] She learned about and sought to emulate the bravery of her ancestors and proudly wore the label "the most dangerous woman in America," bestowed upon her in 1902 by a West Virginia attorney. In this way she lived up to her heritage.

This heritage lay in a poor country with a rich legacy of suffering and resistance. Inhabiting a beautiful but poverty-stricken agrarian island, the Catholic majority in Ireland suffered under a rapacious and treacherous imperial English state. The "Emerald Isle" enjoyed an abundance of fertile land and regular rainfall, though for Mother Jones this was a mixed blessing: "Rain never means green grass to me; it always means wet babies and pneumonia."[19] English colonization of Ireland's productive farmland began in the medieval period. The defeats of two Catholic kings, Charles I in 1649 and James II in 1689, caused the pace of English settlement to accelerate. The government in London transferred land from Catholic owners to Protestants and "transplanted" English families to administer the country in what became known as the "Protestant Ascendancy." For Catholics the loss of land and political power translated into oppression. This period witnessed the struggles of her ancestors ingrained in Mother Jones's memory. Ireland became a colony producing wheat, oats, barley, and other crops tended by Catholic laborers on farms owned by Protestants for export to England to feed that country's growing population.

Protestants gained further power when Parliament enacted a series of Penal Laws to punish Irish Catholics. Anyone who openly taught Catholic doctrine risked imprisonment, and Catholics thereafter developed a network of secret "hedge schools," so called because they assembled surreptitiously under the numerous hedgerows marking field boundaries. In an attempt to defeat the hedge schools the British government established an elementary education system in 1831 to teach basic literacy. Girls were schooled in the domestic arts of sewing, knitting, cooking, and cleaning. In an attempt to destroy Gaelic, the language of instruction was English, and Mary Harris, like others of her generation, was thus inadvertently prepared for emigration to North America.

Penal Laws and political powerlessness meant that by the time of Mary Harris's birth in 1837 the Roman Catholic Church in Ireland met neither the liturgical nor the pastoral needs of its congregations. Looking back on her youthful encounters with the Church, Mother Jones ignored the constraints it faced and did not mince words condemning it. She criticized priests for "the rotten superstitious stuff that they pour down our throats" and the people because "we swallow, and we don't protest, and we go in rags." She labeled clerics "men who have walked upon the necks of the poor, who have bled money out of the working man."[20] For prayer she had little time, telling one audience: "I long ago quit praying and took to swearing. If I pray I will have to wait until I am dead to get anything; but when I swear I get things here."[21] She railed against the hypocrisy of church leaders living in wealth gained by "robbing the representatives of Jesus."[22] She called bishops "sky pilots" for what she considered their obsession with theology and their apathy toward human suffering, especially child labor. Yet her brother William rose through the ranks of the Catholic Church in Toronto to become a dean. Clearly, the two encountered Catholicism in very different ways.

When young Mary and William Harris lived in Ireland, the Catholic Church was in disarray. The country's population had doubled to 8.2 million between 1788 and 1841, exerting intense pressure on the oppressed Church. There were too few church buildings and not enough parish priests. The legal and political barriers imposed by the Penal Laws demoralized the clergy, many of whom neglected their vestments and their flocks. The Irish people maintained pagan traditions and upheld the superstitions of a popular culture steeped in folklore and magic. Belief in fairies and sprites, in holy wells, and in the power of protective charms persisted throughout Mary Harris's childhood and mingled with Catholic teachings. The shortage of churches and the relative disengagement of the people were symbolized by a practice called "stations" whereby priests held mass in the houses of wealthy parishioners. The priests received ample feasts and excessive fees in return. No wonder she turned her back on it: the Church Mary Harris knew in Ireland was incapable of meeting the needs of its people, stained by corruption, and engulfed in superstition.

Her hometown of Cork exemplified some of the worst of the practices and problems. Stations and other abuses of clerical power, particularly drunkenness, were rampant, and the Church did little to endear itself to the average Catholic. The Act of Union of 1801 making Ireland part of the new United Kingdom had stripped the province of Munster of eleven of its seventeen members of Parliament, and the number of urban seats had fallen from thirty-four to seven. A sense of powerlessness pervaded the area, a condition made worse by the inadequacies of a Church in which the ratio of priests to parishioners was about one to thirty-five hundred, higher than the national average. If Mother Jones thought the Church out of touch, perhaps the origins of her perception are to be found in the difficulties facing the priests she first encountered.

The demoralized priests of her youth presented a vivid contrast to the heroic nationalists Mary Harris claimed for her family lineage. Her radical relatives lived when small groups of Irish politicians and reformers fought a romantic but doomed struggle for independence from Great Britain. The French Revolution seemed to promise a new dawn. In 1798, Irish nationalists in an organization called the United Irishmen rebelled in expectation of assistance from France to overthrow English rule. The attempt failed, in no small measure because of the ability of the British navy to keep French soldiers from landing, but the rising entered popular memory as a moment rich with possibility. Hope was in short supply for the majority suffering under British economic and political discrimination. Things grew worse: the English government ended cloth exports from Ireland to protect the English economy after the Napoleonic Wars, destroying the Irish textile industry and forcing thousands of people back into subsistence agriculture.

Surprisingly, Republicanism remained a minor ideology, except in Cork. By the time of Mary Harris's birth the city was a center for "Irish-rights" advocates who wanted independence from London. The political world in which Mary Harris matured was torn by religious controversy as Catholics endeavored to thwart the encroaching power of the established, and Protestant, Church of Ireland. Supported by the British state, it appeared to many Catholics to be trying to create Protestant parishes and foster an anti-Catholic educational system. Though Catholic Emancipation repealed the worst of the Penal Acts and legalized Catholic worship services in 1829, a sense of betrayal persisted when the British government failed to keep its promise of full religious and political freedom for Catholics.

The failure of the Catholic Church to stand up for the people earned it the animus of Mother Jones. Archbishops, bishops, and most of the clergy spoke out against revolutionary change, considering it a sin. This had angered members of a secret organization called the Whiteboys, who, in the 1760s, defended peasants from eviction and attacked priests who upheld the status quo, even going so far as to destroy a few churches. The French Revolution, which had occurred within living memory at the time of Mary Harris's birth and had caused the exile and death of many churchmen, reinforced clerical conservatism. The defeat of the United Irishmen had been due in part to opposition by priests. All of this must have caused Mary Harris to despair of reforming society through the instrument of the Church. She complained of priests that they ignored the suffering around them and "have prostituted Christ's holy doctrine" for their personal enrichment.[23]

The fight for Irish independence became more urgent when the Great Famine of the 1840s demonstrated the weakness of Ireland's position as an English colonial possession. By then, well over half of the eight million people in Ireland depended on the potato for all or most of their nutrition, with a majority of Irish Catholic families surviving on harvests of one acre or less. Rich in minerals and protein and easy to prepare, the potato was in theory an excellent basis for a rural subsistence economy. It offered high yields from small landholdings, and its green leaves provided food for the chickens and pigs farmers sold to make rent payments. Foreign visitors in the eighteenth century commented favorably on the healthy appearance of Irish peasants compared with their English counterparts. But dependence on a single crop created the conditions for catastrophe, and an ecological disaster in the form of a national potato famine arrived in 1845. The Great Famine proved to be a turning point in Irish history, though it did not materialize out of thin air. Localized failures of the potato crop caused by disease had occurred at least three times before 1845, but the unprecedented scale of the problem in that year and again in 1847 defied belief and defeated relief.

The cause of the failure was a fungus, probably carried across the Atlantic Ocean from America. The wet climate of Ireland helped it to spread through the soil. Its presence remained unnoticed until harvest time because it attacked the crop below the surface. When the potatoes were pulled up they were rotten, emitting a noxious stench that filled the air and turned the stomach. Farmers who immediately dug up their whole crop had the best harvests, albeit in the form of puny and dangerously unappetizing yields. Many left their potatoes underground in the forlorn hope that the fungus would vanish, with disastrous consequences. Forced to sell their livestock to buy food, families were unable to make their rent payments. Landlords evicted those who could not meet their obligations and razed their houses to intimidate others. But such punitive measures were futile in the face of so enormous a catastrophe, and the disaster broadened. Selling and stealing quickly gave way to hunger and sickness.

Families faced the dire choice of emigration or starvation. As many as one and a half million people who did not or could not leave died from starvation and famine-induced diseases in the decade after the first crop failure.

The extent of the problem was soon evident, but the government in London was paralyzed by ideology and bigotry. No state assistance was forthcoming, though aid did arrive from the United States and from a religious sect called the Society of Friends, or Quakers, in England. Members of Parliament felt bound by laissez-faire ideology—the idea that the government should not intervene in the marketplace—to do as little as possible. The fact that the sufferers were mostly Irish Catholics reinforced their desire to let the laws of supply and demand prevail. Some deplored the extent of the human suffering (one English politician called the famine "a calamity unexampled in the history of the world"), but others profited. The government required all relief to be carried on British vessels, though in early 1847 that law was repealed as it became clear that thousands of Irish people were dying and more vessels were needed to bring aid to the survivors. Through it all, however, crops being grown in Ireland for export to England were not diverted for Irish consumption. Government action had its limits, and the government was, after all, in London not Dublin.

Mary Harris was eight years old when the famine began. She was ten in 1847, its worst year. She witnessed the suffering caused by famine-induced diseases, from scurvy and diarrhea to typhus and dysentery, and saw friends, relatives, and neighbors die. As she remembered later, "I've seen too many deaths ungarnished with the lily" to be romantic about it.[24] The countryside around her became unnaturally quiet. Children sat mute and fearful, their eyes blank and their heads a muddle of tufts as their hair fell out. Hopelessness compounded the problem: Irish farmers planted less than one-fifth of the land in 1846 compared with the year before. But then, why sow if the future appeared empty? Some people gave up; others planned to leave. The Harris family fell into the second of these categories.

Though Mary Harris would follow her father and eldest brother to Canada sometime around her fifteenth birthday, her experiences in Ireland defined who she would become in the New World. They shaped her decision to devote the last thirty years of her life to fighting for economic and social justice for ordinary people. Visions of the unfairness of English landlords profiting while Irish people starved to death remained with her. Her early exposure to injustice and inequality conditioned the antiauthoritarian streak that ran through her career as a labor organizer. The refusal of the Catholic Church to advocate radical change alienated her from religious institutions, while Catholic theology contributed to her rhetoric and her ideology. She matured in the politically active generation of famine survivors who carried the struggle for equality across the Atlantic Ocean. Mother Jones understood poverty not as a sin or the consequence of individual immorality but as the result of an unfair society and an unequal political system benefiting the rich. Powerful people made the rules, and the rules protected those in power. After she moved to the United States she rejected her adopted homeland's creed of individualism and tried to teach working people that they could improve their lives only by banding together. Mary Harris grew up in a culture that perceived women as naturally subordinate to men, a message the Church reinforced. She embraced the role of mother because it was one of the few ways women could exert power in a patriarchal society. That she abandoned Ireland and left the Church is significant in and of itself: along with millions of others, her family joined the Irish diaspora to find new hope and a new life in America. Once across the Atlantic Ocean her personal strength and courage carried her around the country and into the annals of the labor movement, in large measure because of how she understood and reacted to her wrenching experiences growing up in Ireland. But emigration did not end her troubles, and further tragedy awaited her as she carved a life for herself in America.

2

Leaving Homes

THE VOYAGE MARY HARRIS and the rest of her family undertook to get to the United States was unique but also typical because they were doing what millions of others had done. While there was no single immigrant story in the nineteenth century, there were patterns of movement—physical and emotional—that all immigrants traced in their individual paths. To a greater or lesser degree immigrants traveled from the decision to emigrate to slow acculturation. For Irish immigrants of the mid–nineteenth century the most important common denominator was the experience of famine and the subsequent mass exodus of families. In this case, at least, the Harris family deviated slightly from the norm by sending the two eldest members ahead.

The year the Harris men left, 1847, was marked by a rash of hasty and poorly planned departures by whole families. Two seasons of failure led to panic, and families simply gathered up as many of their belongings as they could carry and walked to the nearest port unprepared for either the voyage or their new lives across the ocean. Squalor aboard ship, poor food, and little or no money with which to survive in an unfamiliar world followed. Several innovations worsened transatlantic travel in 1847. This was the first year of autumn and winter sailings, for until then transatlantic crossings had been restricted to the summer because of the bad weather. The huge new demand among would-be emigrants encouraged shipping companies to offer risky off-season voyages. Thousands of hopeful families filled

Cork, where a lucrative business of housing them sprang up while they tried to buy tickets for passage across the Atlantic. As the year progressed the inability to find room on board ship became increasingly common, and perhaps as many as half of those who tried to leave were turned back. The successful often left with virtually no money to their names, having endured weeks or even months in dirty rooms rented at exorbitant prices.

The Harris family did not fit this mold. While most emigrant families from Ireland departed together, the Harrises appear to have made a strategic decision to send the father and eldest son, both named Richard, to Canada first. This practice, called remittance emigration, meant that those who departed worked to secure funds to bring over other members of the family. Whether because of their poverty or because of their desire to set foot in the New World on the strongest possible terms, Mary Harris, three other siblings, and her mother were forced to wait through the uncertainties and stress of seeing their primary breadwinners leave at a time of continuing calamity. For father and son the passage would doubtless have been attended by many inconveniences, though perhaps they were relatively well supplied with food. Once landed in Quebec and through quarantine they immediately traveled south to Burlington, Vermont, and we can therefore surmise they arrived in good health.

When Richard Harris and his eldest son decided to leave Ireland they joined a rising tide of voluntary transatlantic migration unprecedented in Irish, or indeed in world, history. The passage from the Old World to the New was treacherous in the 1840s because of feeble shipping regulations and because poverty and ill-health dogged the majority of immigrants. The journey took forty or more days to complete. Despite the dangers, approximately one in every seven survivors of the Great Famine left the Emerald Isle for North America. For better-off farmers, merchants, and small businessmen who departed during 1847 cabins could usually be secured to endure the crossing in moderate comfort, but the majority of Irish traveled in steerage. There, in the holds below deck, travelers lived on temporary floors made of planks that might pull apart in rough seas. Privacy was unknown, ventilation was poor, and, worst of all, cholera, typhus, and other famine diseases were unwittingly brought aboard and spread unhindered. Death rates among immigrants from Ireland to North America in 1847 proved to be the highest of the nineteenth century for voluntary transatlantic travel. One in every nine emigrants on the ships from Cork to Canada died en route or shortly after landing. Of the seventy thousand Irish who arrived in Canada in 1847 only about twenty thousand stayed, while another twenty thousand died within a year of arrival and a further thirty thousand left for the United States. Immigrants undertook this dangerous voyage in hopes of finding a life better for their health, their material well-being, and, in some cases, their revolutionary politics. America promised a future the famine seemed to have destroyed.

At first, emigrants had to travel on the only boats available, freight vessels returning to Canada or the United States after depositing lumber, cotton, or grain at their European destinations. The sailors on such vessels viewed passengers as an inconvenience, delaying departures and causing problems en route. Because most ships sailed west empty or underloaded, carrying passengers promised some profit where none might otherwise have been expected. But such was the rapid increase in the numbers of emigrants that shipping companies began to divert vessels from other routes. In the face of adverse publicity, the British government slowly strengthened regulations about berth size, sanitation arrangements, and ventilation and required permanent decks with proper bulkheads. When the rest of the Harris family followed the two Richards across the Atlantic in the early 1850s, conditions had improved and the death rate was falling, though the voyage remained uncomfortable and frightening.

Newly arrived immigrants went directly into quarantine. The elder Harris men landed at Grosse Island, near Quebec, where they waited until a government physician checked their health. Grosse Island had managed to handle the large number of immigrants who passed through in 1846, but, despite warnings, officials were woefully unprepared for the huge increase in immigrants in 1847. By June, a facility built to hold four hundred people housed twelve thousand in hastily erected tents. Medical officers began to clear people out prematurely as the scale of the influx became apparent. The result was outbreaks of typhus and cholera in Toronto, aggravating an already dangerous situation where a Protestant majority waited anxiously and angrily for the unwelcome flood of Irish Catholics.

Perhaps fearing anti-Catholic sentiment or possibly taking the most lucrative offers they found, the elder Harris men crossed, as did so many of their compatriots, into the United States. They joined the time-honored tradition of common laborers who formed an army of seemingly disposable workers building the communications infrastructure that would transport the United States into the industrial age. But for reasons unknown these two immigrants crossed back into Canada and traveled to Toronto, in the province of Ontario. Here, sometime in the early 1850s, the Harris family reunited. Canada, or British North America as it was then called, was divided into two main areas: Lower Canada (later to be known as Canada East, containing Quebec) and Upper Canada (which would become Canada West, including Ontario). Though still under the sovereignty of the British crown, Canada was far enough from England and foreign enough to feel like a separate country. Because of its French Catholic origins, Canada also lacked the virulent nativist feeling so strong in the United States. The famine refugees found sanctuary.

The mainly Catholic famine generation clustered into cities, whereas earlier Irish immigrants had settled mainly in rural areas. The pre-famine immigrants from Ireland worked as farm laborers, artisans, shopkeepers, clerks, publicans, and policemen. Into this world came some twenty thousand Irish immigrants in 1847 alone, 90 percent of them Catholic and many lacking both skills and capital. The Harris family settled in Toronto, which had a sizable Irish immigrant population and offered the familiar sound of Irish voices in streets and shops. A local subculture based in family, neighborhood, saloon, and parish smoothed the path to assimilation for many immigrants. By 1851, one-quarter of the population of Toronto was of Irish extraction, the fastest-growing ethnic group in the city. The Harris family entered a compact but expanding community defiantly different from the multilingual Protestants of Ontario and the French-speaking Catholics situated in Quebec.

At the time the Harris family arrived, Toronto was beginning to experience the stresses and strains of industrialization. The railroad entered the town in 1850, bringing with it the factory system, machine shops, foundries, and a continuing flow of migrants and immigrants, of whom the Irish formed the largest component. Looking back on her adolescence in Toronto, Mary Harris would claim that she fought the first of her many "industrial battles" there. Her father worked occasionally as a laborer on the Grand Truck Railroad, which subcontracted gangs for two months and then laid them off. She later asserted that the boss "used to hire the men and keep them two months without a penny of wages and then they would go away and never pay the men." She remembered that "I happened to be one of the victims, as the child of my father who was not paid, and I knew where the [contractor] lived, out on the edge of town, in a very comfortable place, and I organized an army of girls and we went out there, and I made that fellow pay us the money that he owed us."[1] Fanciful though this story might be, it indicates how Mother Jones read her later career back into her past and hints at a possible origin of what would become one of her most successful labor union organizing tactics: mobilizing women in strikes into "mop and broom brigades." The episode also suggests some of the uncertainties of her family's life in Canada. As an unskilled worker Richard Harris earned an irregular income and, like other casual laborers, faced exploitation by greedy bosses. Also contributing to the unease would have been a new consumer culture filling stores with inexpensive goods. Toronto was changing from a frontier outpost into a center of the new economy connected by rail and telegraph to Lower Canada, the United States, and Europe. The shift from agrarian to industrial was incomplete, however, and casual, seasonal labor remained commonplace. These innovations, and the sense of displacement they wrought, provided fertile soil for the Church.

The Catholic Church exerted a powerful influence over the Irish community in Canada, an authority strengthened by a transatlantic shift in the relationship between parishioners and priests known as the devotional revolution. As in Ireland, some parish priests in Upper Canada had harmed the Church by neglecting their duties through laziness or drunkenness, missing masses, failing to perform the sacraments, and ignoring their flocks. This changed in the 1850s as the Church entered a period of transatlantic reform centered in large measure on education. Two Catholic orders, the Sisters of Loretto and the Christian Brothers, established schools in Toronto as part of the process by which the Church sought to consolidate its hold on local congregations. The devotional revolution encouraged regular church attendance and buttressed the power of the priests. A building program increased the number of churches while encouraging the simultaneous development of voluntary associations to assist the poor. A temperance crusade endeavored to reduce drunkenness, and St. Patrick's Day became a major religious festival reminding Irish Catholics in the New World of their roots and reinforcing their sense of community.

The devotional revolution embraced the contemporary cult of domesticity urging women to make their home into a "haven in a heartless world." This put women—especially mothers—on a pedestal, but it also implied a duty to stay at home. Women were supposed to join voluntary associations connected with the Church and directed by the bishops. Following the example of Mary—the mother of Jesus—women were expected to remain passive recipients of commands from above. Mary Harris's most consistent quality was initiative, something the Church neither cultivated nor tolerated in women. Doubtless her desire for independence collided with the Church's demand for female subordination.

Though she would later assert that she enrolled in "the school of hard knocks and hunger," Mary Harris's formal education lasted longer than that of most girls at the time.[2] Her stubborn streak probably contributed to her parents' decision to send her to a public school, for though parochial schools flourished in the 1850s, Mother Jones said that she "went to the Toronto public schools, passing through them into the high school," a claim the historical record supports. Canadian schools in the mid–nineteenth century boasted a new curriculum designed to assimilate immigrants into a Protestant, royalist society. Mary Harris later recalled that after high school she entered "a convent school," though the evidence reveals that she actually enrolled in a state-funded teachers' school.[3] Teaching was one of the few careers open to women in the nineteenth century. The patience and gentleness presumed to be innate in women would make them good teachers, unlike men, who supposedly grew bored with the slow pace of the classroom.

Like all girls in a patriarchal society, Mary Harris faced few career choices, but Upper Canada was changing. Dressmakers and milliners opened shops across the region around the time of her arrival. Many Irish immigrant women worked in the clothing industry, putting in long hours for low pay on sewing machines at home. Most women remained in the house raising children after marriage, but some made careers in this limited range of occupations and operated their own businesses. These pioneers would serve as role models for Mary Harris when she began her own dressmaking business in Chicago years later.

The dramatic arrival of thousands of immigrants, combined with widespread fear of Catholics because of their devotion to the supposedly infallible Pope, generated discrimination against Catholics in Ontario. Irish accents, dress, and demeanor made them readily identifiable as foreigners, and they created their own powerful and visible subculture. Later in life Mother Jones claimed that she had been the victim of a bigoted teacher who "made some slighting remark about the Irish" that, she recalled, made her want "to 'lick' the teacher then and there."[4] In nineteenth-century Canada, religion helped to determine a person's political, economic, and social status. Religious feelings were intense, although anti-Catholic sentiment did not take root in Canada as deeply as it did in the United States. Canadian Catholics had long been settled and possessed political rights, but so sustained was conflict between Catholic and Protestant Irish settlers in Toronto that the decade of the 1850s was remembered as the "Fiery Fifties." In 1859 nativism—rejecting or discriminating against foreigners—reached its zenith as global economic depression and competition for jobs fueled a bitter election focused on the place of the Bible in education, the creation of Sunday schools, and Protestant fears of the "Celtic Irish." Conservative Protestant politicians championed by the Orange Order loyal to the British crown rode a wave of nativist rhetoric to victory at the polls.

Nativism rested on stereotypes. Most of the Irish Catholics in Toronto found respectable work and good housing soon after arrival, but memories of those first post-famine settlers ossified into a common picture of Irish immigrants as poor and ignorant. The press perpetuated the stereotype by depicting them as drunken, irascible, belligerent, criminal illiterates. A small minority provided ammunition for the nativists by appearing in the courts and the streets perpetually inebriated and habitually unemployed. On this flimsy but recurring evidence Protestant Canadians condemned all Catholics as barbarians lacking morals or sensibility, spouting superstition, and controlled by the Pope. Mary Harris would have been aware of this sentiment and perhaps, at times, its victim as she walked through the streets and visited the shops of Toronto. Experiences that reminded her bluntly and painfully of her otherness may have prompted her to depart Canada. She doubtless also felt the desire for independence teenagers regularly experience.

In 1859, Mary Harris left her family for good. The decision itself was probably a difficult one, but once made it was easy to effect. Many had gone before her, and, as with her departure from Ireland, Mary Harris joined thousands of others. The border between Canada and the United States was unregulated until the early twentieth century, and the Great Lakes region formed a transnational economy through which people moved unhindered. Her own father and eldest brother had themselves crossed and re-crossed the border in search of employment; she was metaphorically retracing their steps.

Mary Harris traveled to Monroe, Michigan, a small town on the Lake Erie shoreline with a large Irish American population. She taught for a year at St. Mary, a Catholic school for girls and boys under twelve founded in 1846 by the Order of the Immaculate Heart of Mary. Education was fast becoming the profession of choice for Irish women in America. In many states it was illegal for married women to teach, but Irish women married late in order to earn a steady income. Teaching also brought respectability and social standing for women who defined themselves by the nature of their work, as many Irish immigrants did. Indeed, one of the principal characteristics of Mary Harris's generation was their desire for economic independence. But Catholic schools in the United States faced persistent financial difficulties, and teachers occasionally took in sewing to support themselves. Contracting with local firms to embroider religious vestments, make shrouds, and even stitch baseball covers sometimes provided their only source of income. Though things might not have been quite that desperate in Monroe, it is likely that Mary Harris confronted large classes and inadequate supplies, to say nothing of facing the loneliness of life for a single woman in a small town.

The Catholic Church she encountered in the United States may have amplified her sense of isolation and difference. Nativism ran deeper in the United States than in Canada, while Americans' emphasis on personal

freedom and political democracy challenged Church teachings about submission to authority and loosened its hold on the flock. Mary Harris would
have disliked the discrimination while embracing antiauthoritarianism.
The Church in the United States nonetheless expected parishioners to pray
and obey. Catholics were to accept unquestioningly the word of priests and
bishops and submit to the power of the pulpit. Sin, the Church taught, was
omnipresent and embodied in Protestants. Worldly misfortune was divine
punishment for wicked behavior or thoughts. Many American Catholics
grew up in insular communities where they never encountered members
of other religions. The strictures of teaching at St. Mary combined with
the authoritarianism of the Church and the personal freedoms prized
by Americans would have left the worldly and inquisitive Mary Harris
unhappy and itching for change.

She moved to Chicago. Though her reasons for selecting this city
are obscure, it seems in retrospect a natural choice. At that time, the
numerical majority of Irish immigrants was shifting from families to
single women, suggesting that she would have found clusters of people
like herself. The expanding metropolis promised the young woman
anonymity, employment, and excitement. Waterways and railroads placed
the city at the center of a global transportation network. Its location on Lake
Michigan and proximity to rivers flowing east and west made it a gateway
to the interior. The national railroad network gravitated to Chicago and,
after completion of the first transcontinental in 1869, radiated out from
the Windy City. The extensive grain trade that created the city was soon
boosted by lumber, coal, iron, and meatpacking.

· Chicago developed quickly without any particular attention to either
human needs or architectural imperatives. Mary Harris entered a city of
ungainly contrasts in which builders made no effort to fit new structures
into their surroundings. Rapidly erected wooden houses backed up to
stockyards, grain elevators, railroad complexes, and factories. Placed just
a few feet above the level of the lake, the city's unpaved streets became
quagmires after the slightest rain, and dust filled the air in dry periods.
The city smelled foul because of the very waterways and railroads driving
its growth. Locomotives poured thick black smoke into the air, while
human sewage and industrial runoff flowed through the rivers. Particularly
noxious was the area around the "Back of the Yard" neighborhood, so
called because of its proximity to the packing houses that deposited animal
carcasses and waste chemicals directly into the Chicago River. Pollution,
and the ability to avoid it, segregated the city and its new suburbs into rich
and poor areas. Those who could afford to do so moved away from the
stench. Those who could not, mostly working people whose wage labor

produced Chicago's wealth, stayed. Mary Harris straddled both worlds by sewing dresses for the wealthy while living in a poor neighborhood.

The Chicago to which Mary Harris moved had the air of a frontier town. Its itinerant population, drawn by greed and the spirit of adventure, formed an "extraordinary outpost . . . at the very verge of western civilization."[5] Business claimed the attention of its 112,000 inhabitants, who seemed well aware that Chicago in 1860 was poised to become an important center of the American economy. Wealth was something of an obsession in this part of the United States; one Scottish visitor called Chicagoans "mad after money." But below the materialistic surface lay a cosmopolitan culture. It was the largest book-buying market west of the Atlantic seaboard and claimed high literacy rates. The English novelist Isabella Lucy Bishop wrote of hearing "nothing of coarseness, and not a word of bad language" while staying in what she considered a rough hotel.[6]

Into this contradictory atmosphere of refinement and raw perpetual motion Mary Harris temporarily injected herself. She did not stay long, working for a short time as a dressmaker before continuing her journey south. Perhaps she disliked the air of materialism pervading the city, perhaps she left to find employment as a teacher, or perhaps she despaired of finding a husband, but for whatever reason Chicago did not hold her. She traveled south until settling in Memphis, Tennessee. Here, she recalled, she entered into the tail end of a world marked by "chattel slavery, when the babe was torn from his mother's breast and sold." She felt keenly the pain of slave women who "wailed and mourned and pleaded with the God of justice to give her a chance to save her child."[7] Such would be her own experience, for in Memphis Mary Harris would marry, raise, and then lose her own family.

Like Chicago, Memphis was experiencing growing pains. It was a bustling port city serving as a railroad and river center, and its population had expanded dramatically during the antebellum period, while its infrastructure lagged behind. In 1840 it had some seventeen hundred inhabitants, growing to 8,841 within a decade. Despite repeated applications of gravel, the streets were little more than rivers of mud, and sanitation was nonexistent. The city had a reputation for disease, having suffered through the first of many visitations of yellow fever in 1855. The predominantly Irish neighborhood into which Mary Harris moved, called Pinch, was situated on swampland near the Mississippi River. Subject to occasional flooding, its inhabitants suffered from the epidemics besetting Memphis. Shortly after her arrival Mary Harris married George Jones, in December 1860. They had four children, three daughters and a son, and attended St. Mary's Church. We know nothing about George Jones—

Mother Jones refers to him twice in her autobiography, in both instances only as "my husband"—except that he was an iron molder and perhaps, given his surname, of Welsh extraction.

Despite his historical anonymity, George Jones had an important impact on the making of Mother Jones. Ironworking was a skilled profession, and George Jones was a member of one of the few powerful labor unions in the country at the time, the International Iron Molders Union. Iron molders worked in foundries where their skills were crucial to the manufacture of complex components for steam engines, railroad cars, and textile machines. Union members brought a specific set of skills to work and, significantly, were able to control the number of new entrants into their trade and bargain with employers to protect their wages. George Jones would have brought home the *Iron Molders' International Journal*, the union's newspaper, from which his wife, Mary, read of the need to respect the dignity of labor. She would have learned about the history of labor unions and the reasons all working people should join them. Unions meant solidarity and strength, for, as she said later, "the bosses have no answer to give when you stand up and say that you are an American, and you are not going to enslave me. Join the Union and don't be afraid of anybody."[8] The lessons had an immediate application: her family enjoyed a high standard of living because George's union membership preserved his steady income. Over the long term the lesson of union solidarity stayed with Mary Jones and informed her life as an agitator and educator of working people.

Memphis was a border town and initially split about which side to join in the looming war between the states. When the Civil War did break out its inhabitants enthusiastically embraced the Confederacy, but its strategic location made Memphis one of the first targets of Northern forces. Attacking from the river they quickly captured the city. Union occupation ironically gave Memphis citizens immunity from many of the difficulties experienced by other Southerners, and the city's inhabitants ate well while its buildings remained intact. The war economy helped Memphis industries boom, keeping George Jones and his fellow iron molders in regular work.

The conclusion of the war did not bring peace to Memphis. In 1866, a vicious race riot occurred in the city (soon to become a center of the white-supremacist Ku Klux Klan) when whites, including many Irish policemen and fire fighters, tried to intimidate newly freed blacks looking for work. In the next year disaster struck Pinch in the form of a yellow fever epidemic making its way inexorably from the Gulf Coast up the

Mississippi to Memphis. Beginning with flu-like symptoms and spreading throughout the body, the mosquito-borne fever burst blood vessels and caused internal bleeding. In Memphis, the yellow fever epidemic of 1867 killed some thirty-five hundred inhabitants, including George Jones and all four of the Jones children. Mary Jones found herself at the center of this horrible crisis, nursing and ultimately losing the five people closest to her until, she admitted in her autobiography, "I sat alone through nights of grief."[9] From this unimaginable anguish Mother Jones would remember that "children are a terrible thing to have, but a more terrible thing to lose."[10] Mary Jones was reminded once again of the injustice of a social system in which wealth meant luxury and safety while poverty resulted in discomfort, danger, and death. As she saw it, the "victims were mainly among the poor and the workers" who could not afford to escape yellow fever while the rich left the city for safer climes.[11]

Fleeing the site of her sorrows, Mary Jones returned to Chicago. In the seven years since she had left it, the city on Lake Michigan had experienced tremendous expansion. In 1860 its population had stood at around 100,000; by 1870, there were nearly three times that number, though the haphazard manner of its growth had continued. In fact, the speed of its development proved to be both Chicago's strength and its weakness. Wood and supposedly fireproof masonry buildings were easily destroyed in the fires that regularly beset the city. Chicago boasted an elaborate system of alarm bells connected to city hall, and fire fighters usually contained fires before they spread too far. Newly widowed and childless, Mary Jones opened a downtown dressmaking shop. Here she sewed "for the aristocrats of Chicago" and observed the contrast between their lives of "tropical comfort" and the condition of "the poor, shivering wretches, jobless and hungry, walking along the frozen lake front."[12]

Her business flourished until 8 November 1871. On that day a small fire broke out in a barn probably owned by Catherine O'Leary and perhaps started by her cow, though more likely by a careless cigarette smoker seeking shelter from the wind while lighting up. The conflagration spread quickly, a strong breeze pushing the flames ahead of fire fighters exhausted from an eight-hour battle the previous day. That earlier fire had raged over twenty acres; this new one would take three days to extinguish and burn over two thousand acres, destroying eighteen thousand buildings and killing more than three hundred people. At its height one eyewitness caught in the downtown maelstrom recalled how "the cinders were falling like snow flakes in every direction . . . and it looked like a snow storm lit by colored light."[13] The disaster left over 100,000 people homeless, including

The Great Chicago Fire (1871), courtesy Frank Leslie's *Illustrated Newspaper*, Library of Congress Prints and Photographs Division

Mary Jones, who spent the first night huddled by the lake and the next few days inside St. Mary's Church. Because the factory district was spared, however, the city could be rebuilt quickly. Not so the life of Mary Jones.

Her immigrant background, her early travels, and now her devastating miseries would transform Mary Harris into Mother Jones. As an Irishwoman she knew political powerlessness and the pain of discrimination. As a Catholic in an age of revived Protestant nativism she witnessed and experienced prejudice and hatred. In Memphis for a few short years she felt the joys and hardships of motherhood, a role she would reprise not in the conventional way by remarrying but by presenting herself as a maternal figure to all working people. She had tried to conform to social expectations by marrying and having children, acquiring the social status and domestic authority of the housewife and mother, but yellow fever had denied her this standing.

Her experiences with the fragility and unpredictability of human existence convinced her of the need to transcend the limited life choices open to women. Though restricted by convention and ideology to the so-called nurturing vocations of teaching, nursing, and mothering, Mary Jones developed a new identity to follow what she came to see as her mission. She possessed a strong will and a keen sense of adventure, to say nothing of an ample supply of fearlessness. Her upbringing served her well in this regard, and her verbal eloquence followed the Irish tradition of resisting oppression by telling stories about the glorious past and a better future. Her desire for mobility and her experiences moving around Upper Canada, the Midwest, and the upper South fed into the making of Mother Jones.

The character of Mother Jones was forged in rejection and resignation. She spent the first half of her life discarding old ways and, sadly, seeing the traditional roles of wife and mother taken from her. Church and nation were central to the self-image of Irish Catholics, but she abandoned both. Her experiences in Memphis and Chicago led her to preach the gospel of labor and embrace her identity as an American.

After her husband, children, and dressmaking business were taken away, she abandoned neighborhood life, preferring virtually ceaseless travel. She described herself as "always in the fight against oppression." She spoke about how, "wherever a fight is going on I have to jump there, and sometimes I am in Washington, sometimes in Pennsylvania, sometimes in Arizona, sometimes in Texas, and sometimes up in Minnesota." All this movement made her homeless, for, as she said in 1910, "I really have no particular residence. . . . no abiding place, but wherever a fight is on against wrong, I am always there."[14] Her attitude toward family was similarly complex. She abandoned her own parents and siblings in Toronto, leaving them and never looking back. The roots of this rejection may well lie in Ireland, when the elder Harris men departed for the New World at a time whole families were emigrating together. Mary Harris would have looked around and seen her friends leaving while she had to stay, perhaps interpreting her father's departure as a betrayal. She then lost everything she had been taught to expect out of life when forces beyond her control killed her husband and their children.

As a widow, she gained social approbation and a new freedom. She refused the usual path of remarriage, having learned that marriage could be unpredictable, even malevolent, and certainly not the "haven" promised by the prevailing ideology. When things were bad, as in Monroe, she left; even when life was good, as in Memphis, happiness could be taken away. Ultimately, for reasons that remain unclear but must surely include her experiences of famine, emigration, yellow fever, and fire, Mary Jones disavowed conventional expectations for women. Instead, she took hold of her destiny and made herself into Mother Jones, thereby establishing her place in history.

3

The Making of Mother Jones

RETURNING TO CHICAGO must have seemed a defeat for Mary Jones. Her young life to this point had been in forward motion, but now she was forced to retreat by circumstances beyond her control. Even in Chicago she could not escape disaster: after the deaths of her husband and children came the destruction of her dressmaking store in the Great Fire. Mary Jones was disconsolate and alone. She had abandoned her biological family in Canada, but the life she had chosen rejected her. She had doubtless hoped that conforming to conventional expectations for women would bring society's blessings, but instead she had experienced profound grief, renewed uncertainty about her future, and unbelief.

Mary Jones discarded the ideas of starting another family, returning to Canada or Ireland, or reopening her business. She was a widow; with that role came power. How she alighted on a career as a labor union organizer is unclear, though her reasons for having done so are easier to fathom in hindsight. She brought from the Emerald Isle an early and sustained interest in politics and religion along with lessons about the restrictions that society and the Roman Catholic Church placed on women. Her life with George Jones in Memphis had shown her the benefits of unionism for working people and illustrated the need for working-class solidarity. Drawing strength from her upbringing and her experiences in Memphis and Chicago, she chose a life of incessant travel and conflict with authority, committing herself to teaching working people to oppose injustice and demand better lives for themselves and their families.

How and why Mary Jones chose to style herself "Mother Jones" are a matter of conjecture. She never explained her transformation from Mary to Mother, though her choice must have been influenced by the limited range of careers open to Victorian women. Non-elite nineteenth-century women were expected to be subservient to the men in their lives—fathers, husbands, brothers, sons—while working when necessary in low-paying, often physically demanding jobs that seemed logical extensions of the domestic sphere. Women in the United States could work as seamstresses, teachers, laundresses, domestic servants, textile workers, prostitutes, and little else in the 1870s. Catholic women serving the poor gained virtually no economic or political influence and remained subordinate to men, but they did possess a kind of power by nurturing the males in their lives and teaching the young. Being an organizer for labor unions combined meaningful work with service to those who needed assistance. Constant travel must also have served as a distraction from the tragedies in her own life.

Some women were able to expand the role society assigned them by participating in reform movements. These women, usually middle class, publicly championed sanitary and electoral improvements. Women's political activism, often called municipal housekeeping, gave Mary Jones another example of how women could influence the wider society. She rejected the efforts of the middle-class reformers prominent during the Progressive Era of roughly 1901 to 1917. Mother Jones perceived them as seeking to ameliorate extant conditions rather than dramatically remaking society, as she wished to do. For her, waging class war to establish an egalitarian society and create an economy based around the labor theory of value would improve life for most people far more than electoral reform or improved diets.

For her own part, she understood that men saw women, especially those of advanced years, as sexless and harmless, enabling them to go anywhere unhindered. Being a widow could have advantages for a labor organizer: a white-haired woman in a sensible dress, looking as innocuous as a grandmother, could travel unmolested across picket lines and into the war zones of labor–management combat. Mother Jones used this freedom of movement to good effect.

Becoming "Mother," no matter how or when it happened, connected Mary Jones with the country of her birth. The heroes of Irish history were romantic rebels and clever conversationalists who could bewilder the enemy with words. Cork had a particularly rich oral tradition embedded in the popular religion of the oppressed majority. The Irish had a reputation for seeking knowledge and insight, not in a literal understanding of the world or by resort to reason and logic but through intuition and instinct. The fantastic and the miraculous played key roles in the Ireland in which Mary Harris matured, as did mythology.

Myths supply psychic comfort and strength. For Mary Jones myths may have provided sustenance after indescribable pain and loss. Mythology may also have suggested a way to define herself as a prophet and maternal figure. The persona Mary Jones created for herself closely parallels one of the local myths she would have heard growing up in the province of Munster. Munster was the home of the Cailleach Bheare, a mountain woman who had lived sinfully as a young woman (as all Catholic girls do because they can never be the Virgin Mary) and repented by becoming a wise and fearless old woman. She reared innumerable foster children, like Mother Jones and "her" miners, and outlived all of her relatives, including her husbands, another echo of the life of Mary Jones. Regardless of the connections to this particular legend, it is true that Mother Jones would spin many myths about her life when she spoke to and on behalf of the workers of America.

Mother Jones also fulfilled the role of trickster, a person who deceives in order to establish deeper truths than would otherwise be visible. Her deceptions, about her role in the early strikes and her access to presidents, for example, established her credibility as a labor leader at a time when women simply did not do what Mother Jones aspired to accomplish. Like the tricksters of African and European folklore, she changed her identity by using her courage, her sharp wit, and her quick tongue to free herself from the constraints of conventional expectations for women. Obtaining autonomy for herself not only allowed Mary Jones to travel freely and to educate working people about their rights, it also enabled her to set about freeing them from capitalism.

Her career as Mother Jones began at the end of the Gilded Age, a time of national economic, social, ideological, and political upheaval. Americans were moving from a life of republican frugality, when most people could meet only their basic needs and consumed principally what they produced themselves, to one of middle-class luxury facilitated by mass consumption. Collective ideals lost out to individualism as urban areas expanded. This was also a time of growing concentration of wealth in the hands of a few capitalists, causing conflict between those who made the new consumer goods and the owners employing them. Individual luxury and leisure replaced virtuous self-denial, with the result that many became impoverished while a few grew very rich. Social inequality, individualism, and conflict dissolved the collectivist, mutualist outlook Mother Jones sought to rekindle for working people.

This transformation provided both the context within which she lived and a set of grievances against which Mother Jones protested. She criticized the way working people were treated in this emerging new order and condemned the impersonal style of life it seemed to encourage. She found in the new conditions an opportunity to help working families. Instead of trying to turn the clock back to a nostalgically remembered past, Mother Jones wanted to move forward to a future of social justice, political equality, and, above all, a decent material life for all people.

Mother Jones could not help but glance back to the small-scale markets and face-to-face relationships of the world in which she had grown up. In that bygone age employers supposedly knew their employees by name, and shopkeepers recognized every customer; teachers met their charges' parents, and priests knew their congregations. Her own career in Chicago as a dressmaker to elite women had shown her the possibility for personal relationships in the midst of an anonymous crowd, but during her lifetime that world vanished for many Americans. In retailing, the small downtown specialty shop was being replaced by large department stores offering a variety of openly displayed goods and encouraging free movement into and out of new multi-story buildings. Mother Jones had few illusions about recent history, neither idolizing nor idealizing the world that had been lost: as she put it, "The past has never been peaceful."[1]

By the 1870s, the dressmaking skills Mary Jones had learned in childhood were less in demand because of mechanization. Factories producing for mass consumption and selling their wares to department stores undercut the prices entrepreneurs like Mary Jones could charge. Speed, diversification, and quantity changed retailing as manufacturers developed faster machinery, more product lines, and greater total output. But the world that she had known did not completely evaporate. Most people still lived in "island" communities centered around family, neighborhood, and church. Mother Jones would spend the majority of her career as a labor activist in the island communities of mining villages, trying to protect miners from exploitation in isolated, mountainous locations. She sought to defend the ethos of mutuality and cooperation from the advances of capitalism. In this sense her radicalism was backward-looking even as she anticipated progress toward a better future.

Mary Jones saw the transformation of American society proceeding unevenly and incompletely. Industrialization was largely a northern phenomenon: as late as 1900 there were still more industrial workers in the city of Cincinnati, Ohio, than in the entire state of Georgia. Factories developed not just in cities but in urban areas of all sizes; by the turn of the century, half of all Midwestern industrial workers could be found in towns. During the last third of the nineteenth century, America's Gilded Age, the United States became the world's leading economy. Before that period, American industrial production had lagged behind Britain and Germany; in just forty years, the United States came to produce more industrial goods than those two countries combined.

Ironically, even as output expanded, the United States, in common with the rest of the industrial world, experienced an economic depression lasting more or less continuously from 1873 to 1897. The cost of food fell by about 5 percent between 1873 and 1876, but wages dropped by a quarter over the same three-year period. By 1876 working families were spending half of their earnings on food, lowering their standard of living compared to the decades before 1850. Employers responded to shrinking sales and uncertainty by cutting costs and merging to eliminate competition. By 1904, 4 percent of American corporations controlled 57 percent of total industrial output. One response of working people to their loss of power at work was organizing labor unions to oppose pay cuts and deteriorating working conditions.

Hard times prompted a rise in nativism. Limiting immigration was a rational response to underemployment, albeit an intolerant and ultimately self-defeating one. Mary Jones, though herself a victim of nativist taunts while living in Toronto, seems to have participated in a movement to keep Chinese workers out of the United States. Mother Jones would later claim that she had been in California in 1876 when she "had a hand in that Chinese agitation; we kept it up and stopped the Chinese coming over." She did so, she said, because "the Union Pacific had been bringing them over in hordes and using them to break the labor movement."[2] During a protest at that time, she was hosed by the police, leading to her trenchant criticisms of authorities who trampled on the constitutional protection of free speech. Organized labor convinced Congress to pass the first Chinese Exclusion Act, though the reality of the active role of Mary Jones in its passage is uncertain at best.

What seems to be clear is her deepening ideological commitment to the labor movement. After the Chicago fire, Mother Jones would write in her autobiography, "I became more and more engrossed in the labor struggle and I decided to take an active part in the efforts of the working people to better the conditions under which they worked and lived." Mary Jones spent the quarter-century following the Chicago fire of 1871 observing workers' protests and organizations from the outside, a period about which she would later create many myths in order to place Mother Jones at the center of workers' agitation. Her active role in the labor movement began in the 1890s, but she claimed implausibly to have played a leading role in strikes during the years 1877 and 1886.

Mother Jones asserted that her first direct experience with labor organizing came in Chicago in 1870. As with so much of her early engagement with unions, Mother Jones exaggerated the extent of her participation. She told miners she helped organize Chicago streetcar workers in that year, when she "used to . . . go away over on the West Side and meet with those boys in the night alone" to proselytize about the benefits of unionism.[3] She said she then encountered members of a local lodge of the Knights of Labor, a national union for workers and some business owners, after the 1871 conflagration. She wrote in her autobiography about finding the Knights "in an old, tumbled down, fire scorched building" and "spend[ing] my evenings at their meetings, listening to splendid speakers."[4] The historical record contradicts her assertions. The Knights of Labor did not open its first "Local Assembly" in Chicago until 1877, and it did not admit women before 1880, and it is unlikely an inexperienced widow could organize streetcar workers.

Patterned after fraternal orders like the Oddfellows and the Elks, the Knights of Labor possessed a strong ritual-based culture and a commitment to collective self-help. Founded as a secret society in Philadelphia in 1869, the early Knights operated clandestinely to protect members from victimization, but this approach limited its growth. By 1878 secrecy had been dropped, and the organization expanded rapidly, admitting anyone regardless of gender, occupation, or (after 1883) race. Members paid a small subscription in return for the fraternal benefits of solidarity, sociability, and insurance against loss of income during times of sickness or injury. The Knights proposed creating a cooperative commonwealth in which all people would gain from the growth of industry, not just those who owned and managed the corporations.

Advocating an ideology rooted in the notion of the "just producer," the Knights welcomed business owners who treated workers decently, which in practice meant the masters of small workshops who allowed their employees to dictate the pace of production. The Knights preferred cooperation to conflict and sought to encourage harmonious relations between capital and labor. The order sponsored candidates in local elections and opposed corporations, recalling a time of republican simplicity, of equality and opportunity amid the small workshops representative of the American economy before the Civil War. Membership peaked in 1886 at around one million people, including small masters, shopkeepers, and artisans, and the organization sanctioned strikes against monopolistic employers. But a new wave of industrial violence in that year, followed by government repression of labor organizations, caused members to abandon the Knights. Membership fell by about 90 percent to less than 100,000 by 1890.

Leaders of the Knights of Labor (1886), courtesy Library of Congress Prints and Photographs Division

For Mother Jones the Knights retrospectively symbolized her entry into the labor movement, and she held the organization in high esteem. She claimed to have been active in 1877, a year of violent conflict between wageworkers and the owners of industry. In sworn testimony before an investigative commission in 1915 she said, "I was in New York [in 1877]. I came down [to Pittsburgh]. I was a member of the Knights of Labor at that time, and some of the boys met me and asked me to stay over with them, and I did. . . . I know most of the strikers; all had done everything they could to keep order."[5] She also wrote, "One of the first strikes that I remember occurred in the Seventies. The Baltimore and Ohio Railroad employees went on strike and they sent for me to come help them. I went. . . . I knew the strikers personally."[6] She said she rallied the striking railroad workers and marshaled community support for them.

Even stories repeated consistently are not necessarily true, and her testimony is a case in point. Mother Jones could not have been in Pittsburgh in 1877 because the strike happened almost overnight, with little advance preparation. When it started she was in Chicago, a full day's journey by fast train. Moreover, there is no record of her presence in the region at a time of intensive newspaper coverage. The facts are, in this case, beside the point: what is significant is that Mother Jones identified herself with 1877, a turning point in American history.

The railroad strikes Mother Jones claimed to have helped organize resulted from an economic downturn. In 1876, during the nation's centennial celebrations, optimism was rampant among business people and political leaders who believed that the economy would pull out of a cyclical slump. They predicted a rosy future for all, but unemployment remained stubbornly high and uncertainty was widespread. Sales fell, and employers responded by lowering wages and requiring more work from those who kept their jobs. In some cases new machinery increased output, and employers could cut costs by replacing expensive skilled workers. Politicians remained faithful to laissez-faire doctrines dictating that government should not intervene in the economy but let the free market allocate wealth. Most people believed poverty was the result of personal misfortune or divine punishment for unethical behavior, and the U.S. government did little to alleviate the hardships facing working families.

By 1877 the railroads, the country's largest industry, were in trouble. Some bankrupt railroad companies reduced the prices they charged customers to ship freight, forcing other railroads serving the same customers to follow suit to avoid ruin. The resultant rate wars depleted earnings and reduced the value of their stock. Employees took matters into their own hands when railroads lowered wages. On 29 December

1876, engineers on the Grand Trunk Railroad, the Canadian line whose contractor Mary Harris had supposedly confronted as a girl in Toronto, went on strike. The strikers forced the company to restore wage levels and adhere to employment contracts, establishing a pattern of militancy other railroad workers followed.

Strikes began in the United States in July 1877, led by trainmen. These engineers, firemen, conductors, and brakemen were responsible for running the trains and could not be easily replaced. They possessed strong labor unions, prominent among them the Brotherhood of Locomotive Engineers and the more militant but short-lived Trainmen's Union. The first strike occurred in Martinsburg, West Virginia, on 17 July. Here, at a small but important railroad junction about fifty miles west of Washington, D.C., trainmen on the Baltimore and Ohio Railroad responded to a 10 percent wage cut by refusing to allow freight trains to move through the town. The local militia arrived but took no action to clear the lines because the strikers were their friends and relatives. The governor of West Virginia then asked for and received federal troops, whose appearance ended the strike and enabled the Baltimore and Ohio to resume running the trains through Martinsburg.

The Martinsburg strike, though brief and ineffectual, encouraged other disaffected railroaders to take action. Baltimore and Ohio trainmen followed the Martinsburg example elsewhere on that line, including Cumberland and Baltimore, Maryland, where the trains halted. The most dramatic action occurred in Pittsburgh, Pennsylvania, the city to which Mother Jones claimed she had traveled in 1877. The Pennsylvania Railroad cut wages in June; then, in July, it announced that it would introduce a new way of running trains called doubleheading. Freight trains would have two engines, to pull twice as many cars, throwing half of the brakemen and conductors out of work. On the first day of doubleheaded running, 19 July 1877, trainmen refused to work. They closed Pittsburgh to all rail traffic by blocking key switches. As in Martinsburg, the militia sided with the workers. Business leaders and politicians in Pittsburgh, angry at the Pennsylvania Railroad for charging what they considered unreasonably high rates to transport their goods, supported the strikers. After local soldiers refused to disperse them, the governor sent a National Guard regiment from Philadelphia at the request of company officials. These troops shot into a large crowd of protesters and killed twenty-six people, causing fury in the city. Confronted by a larger group of local people—only some of whom were railroaders—the National Guard troops retreated onto railroad property. They took shelter in a roundhouse, which the crowd set on fire, forcing the troops to leave the city. The fire burned itself out, and the Pennsylvania Railroad lost some $5 million worth of buildings and rolling stock. Relations between labor and capital had taken on a new antagonistic tone, and strikes could become national contests involving government as an ally of big business.

The shootings in Pittsburgh intensified the strike, which spread to other industrial areas in Pennsylvania and then to Ohio, Missouri, Illinois, and even California. In Chicago, where Mary Jones may have witnessed labor protests, marching workers demanded higher wages and better working conditions. The strikers forced factories to close. The mayor, in an effort to regain control of the streets, ordered the police to fire on protestors, of whom thirty were killed. Demonstrators forcibly closed the Chicago rail yards of the Illinois Central Railroad and fired shots into the caboose of a train attempting to leave the Windy City in the dead of night on 25 July. Striking railroaders and sympathizers blocked the Illinois Central downstate by simply stopping their trains. Similar actions elsewhere brought the national rail network to a halt. The situation grew so bad that the government recalled federal troops from the Indian wars on the Great Plains to patrol the streets of Chicago, Baltimore, St. Louis, and other cities. When peace was finally restored at the end of the year, the "Great Uprising" had marked a turning point in relations among working people, business owners, and politicians. Most dramatic and unexpected had been the use of troops to protect business property. Also surprising was the number of shootings on both sides. It is no wonder Mother Jones claimed to have been at the center of the action: it was logical for the "mother" of the modern American labor movement to be present at the birth of its new militant phase. Where else could she be?

The strikes, like the formation of the Knights, were a response to changes in American industry. Many working people and small business owners advocated retaining the older ways of manufacturing products for local or regional markets, but others wanted to adopt a factory-based, mass-production industrial system to create nationwide markets for manufacturing and distributing goods. In strikes from 1877 on, shopkeepers, newspaper editors, and local politicians sympathized with striking workers and perceived their actions as a form of resistance to powerful outsiders, particularly anonymous capitalists residing in New York and working on Wall Street. Community support often enabled strikers to keep out the "scabs"—unemployed workers—companies brought in to take their jobs. Frustrated when their efforts to replace strikers were blocked, employers appealed to state governors, and occasionally to the federal government, for assistance, particularly for military support to defend strikebreakers from attack. That often led to violence.

Mother Jones worried about the "armies of unemployed" she saw, criticizing business owners who replaced skilled workers with machines and seeking to reverse the shift to an impersonal, bureaucratic society of insecurity and inequality. She recognized that people had been "inventing machinery, building railroads, telephones, telegraphs, and everything else" for decades but felt that "we are reaching a stage where these inventions are taking the place of labor."[7] Fighting back to take control of industry was the only viable option for working people.

Having learned firsthand in Memphis about the strength of labor unions, she set out to teach working people about the power they could wield when they worked together. She sought to fuse workplace unions with community solidarity, which is why she believed the strikes of 1877 were so important: local communities had stood behind working people to confront government and large corporations. For Mother Jones, as for many other labor leaders and union members, memories of 1877 fueled her desire for change and provided strategies for effecting it. Organizing community support for strikers was one of her favorite tactics during her career in the labor movement, raising morale and garnering supplies.

By 1883 unemployment had risen again, leading to increased militancy as working people took to the streets and demanded government assistance for those who were out of work. Another wave of violent strikes occurred in 1886 when employers rejected labor union demands for an eight-hour day. The government ignored the unions, and employers reduced wages.

Chicago became a center of unrest, and Mother Jones would again claim that she got involved in the struggle and even invented dialogue to explain how this happened.[8] In her autobiography she wrote about trying to organize union locals in fields beyond the city limits until "the boys came to me one night and they said, 'Mother the weather is getting cold and we have got a place to meet inside.' I said, 'Where? We have no money.' They said, 'No, we haven't, but a saloonkeeper told us he would give us a room back of his saloon. Would you mind coming?'" At this point in the exchange Mother Jones demonstrated to her audience her permissive attitude toward workers' culture, saying, "'No, I would not [mind]. I will go back of a saloon any time to help you boys. Where is the saloon?' He told me. I said, 'Let's go,' and we met there every Thursday night."[9] The significance of this exchange is twofold: first, it illustrates the tenuous basis on which union organizing rested, and, second, it shows Mother Jones identifying with and entering into the dominant masculine culture, gaining the trust of the workingmen she sought to recruit for the unions.

Among the leading agitators in Chicago in 1886 were anarchists, whom Mother Jones disliked because she found their program unrealistic.

Anarchists expected that overthrowing the government would enable people to reach their full potential unimpeded by laws or rigid ethical systems. Mother Jones argued later that anarchists distracted public attention from the needs of workers, who "asked only for bread and a shortening of the long hours of toil." After they called for an eight-hour day, "the people of Chicago seemed incapable of discussing a purely economic question without getting excited about anarchism," she noted.[10] Mother Jones recalled, "Although I never endorsed the philosophy of anarchism, I often attended the meetings on the lake shore, listening to what these teachers of a new order had to say to the workers."[11] She remained unimpressed, remembering how "the agitators gave them visions. The police gave them clubs."[12]

Not everyone was so clearheaded. The Knights of Labor and other unions inspired by anarchists set 1 May 1886 as the date for a national strike to demonstrate workers' commitment to an eight-hour working day. On that day, 300,000 workers—of whom forty thousand were in Chicago—refused to work. Though the police had anticipated trouble the day passed peacefully, but the protest did not end. A strike at the McCormick reaper works in Chicago attracted the attention of local unions. On 3 May, sympathetic workers gathered outside the McCormick factory to block arriving strikebreakers. The police responded by attacking the demonstrators, killing two and wounding several others. Chicago anarchists called for a rally the following day in Haymarket Square. On 4 May a small crowd gathered and listened to speeches denouncing the McCormick company and demanding political revolution. As the speechmaking was coming to a close and the crowd was preparing to leave, a group of policemen sent to break up the meeting by the police chief, against the orders of the mayor, charged into the crowd. Someone threw a bomb, which killed seven officers and an unknown number of civilians. The result was a nationwide crackdown on labor organizations, weakening the union movement and signaling the end for the Knights of Labor.

Haymarket became a watchword for fear and a rationale for arresting any radical leader who seemed to encourage violence. Labor unionism shifted from trying to create large industrial unions of all workers regardless of skill or occupation to forming organizations consisting of skilled workers in a single industry. This seems to have been another decisive moment in the making of Mother Jones. The violence against protesters in 1886, as much as in 1877, apparently contributed to her decision to help encourage coal miners to unionize. In her organizing she sometimes appeared to call for violent confrontation with the operators, but she coded her language carefully and rarely made overt appeals for bloodshed.

Her labor organizing came later. There is no historical documentation linking Mother Jones directly with the events of 1877 or 1886, and indeed she may have been traveling around the United States trying to overcome her grief after Memphis and Chicago. Sometime between 1871 and 1897 she might have worked as a prostitute, a common fate for destitute women in a patriarchal society. The evidence for this is unclear and derives mainly from the files of a detective agency hired by coal companies seeking to discredit her. The story was publicized during a particularly bitter strike in Colorado by a Denver-based magazine called *Polly Pry*, known for campaigning against organized labor. In 1904 *Polly Pry* printed an article about how Mary Jones ran a brothel in Denver until her companion absconded with her savings and one of her "girls." There is probably no substance to these stories, but old friends did not completely exonerate her when given the opportunity to do so, and dressmaking was a trade closely associated with prostitution at the time. Oddly, the phrase "the miner's angel," which was applied to Mother Jones because of her organizing efforts in coal country, could also refer to a prostitute living in a mining community. Mother Jones made several informed references to prostitution in her speeches, connecting low wages in Milwaukee to girls prostituting themselves. She also warned that arresting striking steelworkers might lead girls to sell "that which is most sacred to woman" in order to support their families.[13] Though possession of such knowledge, widespread in the nineteenth century, is not sufficient to prove that Mary Jones once worked as a prostitute, combined with the *Polly Pry* story and the absence of unambiguous refutations it does lend some credence to this rumor. Counterbalancing this story is the historical record, which reveals that Irishwomen deviated from social norms by drinking to excess and fighting but rarely by working as prostitutes.

After 1893 it is possible to see the cumulative effect of the influences on Mother Jones. The Haymarket meeting and its aftermath may actually have provided the pivotal moment in the making of Mother Jones that she claimed for the strike of 1877. In her autobiography she condemned the actions and teachings of the anarchists. Of a proposed Christmas Day march she wrote, "It had no educational value whatever and only served to increase the employers' fear, to make the police more savage, and the public less sympathetic to the real distress of the workers."[14] For Mary Jones, it is safe to say, the excesses of Haymarket and the resultant attacks on the labor movement demonstrated the futility of trying to smash the system violently. Capitalism needed to be overthrown, but moral suasion exerted by an organized working class would be the means to achieving that end. Though her rhetoric would contain many references to the need to demolish capitalism, it is telling that most of the actions of Mother Jones—forming union branches, giving speeches, coordinating strikes, organizing protest marches—remained within the confines of the law. Even when she broke the law by disobeying injunctions against speaking on private property she claimed she had an overriding constitutional right to exercise free speech against unjust and rapacious mine operators. Her notion of class war emphasized collective action not violent confrontation.

Though she could not have joined them as early as she claimed, Mary Jones probably learned much from observing the Knights of Labor. She may have attended their meetings and rallies and had her first experiences with public speaking as a member of the Knights. It is possible she made important contacts among the leaders of the labor movement; she certainly called Terence Powderly, its grand master in the 1870s and a fellow Catholic, her "faithfull friend" and wrote of the time they were "rocking the cradle of the movement."[15] Through the Knights she almost certainly encountered the United Mine Workers of America, the union that hired her as a paid organizer around 1900 and with which she would be closely associated for the rest of her life. In 1885, when she may have been a member of its Chicago lodge, the Knights of Labor created National Trades Assembly Number 135 (NTA) specifically for coal miners. For a number of reasons this initiative failed to fulfill its potential, and in 1890 the NTA merged with the National Progressive Union to form the United Mine Workers of America.

The myths she wrapped herself in allowed Mary Jones to present herself as Mother Jones, a character she created to educate and agitate among working people. Contemporary gender expectations combined with the roles of secular grandmother and the Virgin Mary influenced the making of Mother Jones. She was not, however, consciously setting a precedent or serving as an exemplar for other women to follow. The role of mother implies a limited supply, usually one per family, and Mother Jones aspired to be the sole mother of the labor movement. She would prove to be an inconsistent supporter of woman suffrage, and she organized industries in which the majority of the workers were male, concentrating her efforts on the hypermasculine occupation of coal mining. But, for the rest of her life, she remained true to her desire to teach working people how to confront privilege by organizing together to fight for justice. Class war and the rights of working people to economic and social justice dominated her last three decades.

4

Sampling the Labor Scene

WITH THE HORRORS OF MEMPHIS AND CHICAGO, the events of 1877 and 1886, and perhaps experience in the brothels of the West behind her, Mary Jones looked for opportunities to demonstrate her commitment to the cause of labor. In the 1890s she made connections to different types of protest movements and to various groups of reformers. Acquaintances and friends from this decade taught her about the working-class movement and cemented her place in labor lore. After observing the labor scene and then drifting for ten years or more, Mary Jones helped organize a march on Washington, D.C., and a strike in Alabama; worked in southern textile mills and visited a utopian community; attended a political convention and the launch of a radical newspaper; and began her career as a paid organizer for the mine workers' union. She brought her dressmaker's diligence to her appearance: with her white hair, flowing dresses, and round spectacles she cut a small but energetic and unique figure among labor organizers. Entering her seventh decade she would at last find her calling. In this phase of her life she became widely recognized as "Mother" Jones.

In spring 1894, "Mary Jones of Chicago" appeared in the press for the first time when she participated in "Coxey's Industrial Army." This event consisted of processions by unemployed people converging on the nation's capital seeking relief. Jacob Coxey, an Ohio businessman, decided the time had arrived to galvanize public opinion behind a campaign to assist those without work. In 1893 he met Carl Browne, an entrepreneurial reformer, at a convention in Chicago. This fortuitous encounter eventually brought Browne to Coxey's hometown of Massillon, Ohio, where they established an organization called the Commonweal of Christ to effect their "petition in boots." They hoped a massive show of strength would convince the federal government to borrow money for a national road-building program employing men without work. In the event the total number who arrived fell short of the organizer's goal of 100,000, in part because logistical and financial obstacles blocked several contingents en route. This march succeeded only in raising curiosity among the public and fear within the political elite, who had Coxey imprisoned for trying to speak from the Capitol steps. In the long run, however, Coxey's Army proved to be the first example of what would become a popular tactic of holding mass protests in Washington, D.C. It also brought Mother Jones into the labor movement.

Mother Jones volunteered to help organize Coxey's Army in Kansas City, though the historical record is silent as to how she encountered the movement or why she joined it there. Her group did not reach Washington because one of the leaders of her contingent stole its funds, an unfortunate but common occurrence. Mary Jones walked as far as St. Louis, giving speeches and raising money for the marchers. Though Coxey's Army failed to achieve its stated aims and she later dismissed the whole affair as "a great joke" leading only to "good roads," the experience contributed significantly to the making of Mother Jones.[1] Indeed, many of the motifs of her later speeches were evident in a ballad the marchers learned:

> For might was right when Caesar bled upon the stones of Rome,
>
> And might was right when Joshua led his men o'er Jordan's foam,
>
> And might was right when German troops poured down into Paris gay,
>
> 'Twas the logic of the ancient world, 'tis the gospel of today.
>
> You must prove your right by deeds of might, of splendor and renown,
>
> If you would march through flames of hell to dash opponents down,
>
> If need be, die on scaffold high, in morning's mist of gray.
>
> For liberty or death is still the logic of today.[2]

Mother Jones regularly repeated Patrick Henry's slogan "Give me liberty or give me death" in her speeches, and her anger at the oppression of the poor infused her oratory and contributed to her appeal for many listeners. For Mother Jones the collective might of the working people could and should combat the injustices she saw around her.

As she often would do with fellow labor leaders, Mother Jones became lifelong friends with Jacob Coxey. When Coxey marched again in 1914 he invited her to participate, commissioning her "colonel of the army of the Commonweal of the West." Writing from the "Commonweal Army Headquarters" in Massillon, "General Coxey" promised Mother Jones that "captains and companies will meet you in Colorado and accept your command 'on to Washington.'"[3] The invitation was issued in vain, but its existence shows Mother Jones earning the loyalty and respect of those who worked with her.

Mother Jones may have ridiculed Coxey's Army in 1894, but it helped her hone some of her most important organizational skills and tactics. She mobilized women to aid the marchers by providing food and moral support, as she would many times in coal strikes. The so-called mop and broom brigades she created in West Virginia became famous and contributed to her reputation as an innovative organizer. She also condemned efforts to restrict freedom of speech, as did Coxey after being refused the right to speak at the Capitol. Later, during numerous strikes, she berated private detectives who tried to arrest her for trespassing on coal company property, standing her ground time and again to deliver withering criticisms of the "pirates" and their minions who dared deny her First Amendment rights.

Her style of speaking took shape in the years after her experiences in Coxey's Army. Her rhetorical armory revolved around projecting the persona of a militant mother offering the comforts of prophecy and emotional appeals to men in need. Mother Jones was a storyteller sharing her optimism about what she considered the essential truth of the world: justice will return as soon as working people unite behind labor organizations. The future was bright because workers were organizing into unions. To further this process, she used personal stories and invented dialogues to connect with her audiences, blurring the distinction between herself and them in order to generate collective action. Thus, for example, she remembered how "I am one of those who believe as the immortal Victor Hugo did. I read Hugo's works when I was young. Hugo was my idol, he was inspiring. He said so many grand things. I felt that he had the agony of the race on his body." From her reading of Hugo she extrapolated the lesson that "we are in the early dawn of the world's greatest century, when crime, brutality and wrong will disappear, and man will rise in grander height, and every woman shall sit in her own front yard and sing a lullaby to the happy days of happy childhood, noble manhood of a great nation that is coming."4 She told "my boys" in no uncertain terms that the time for action had arrived and a brighter future awaited them if they organized.

Promises of a better life were a stock-in-trade of Mother Jones's speeches. Thus she told audiences in millennial tones, "This is the last great fight of man against man. We are fighting for the time when there will be no master and no slave. When the fight of the workers to own the tools with which they toil is won, for the first time in human history man will be free."5 She praised and criticized her listeners with equal fervor, often in the same breath. Mother Jones moved rapidly from exhorting immediate action to condemning audience members for their apathy, telling them, "You are as much to blame [for your poverty] as the mine owners because you didn't stick to your organization."6 She mobilized working people divided by the ruling ideology of personal responsibility, convincing individuals that "the American oligarchy of wealth" caused their misery and only collective action could improve their condition.7 For newly arrived immigrants the union would end their powerlessness and isolation in the face of aggressively oppressive capitalists.

At a time of intensifying racial segregation after the false dawn of Reconstruction, Mother Jones spoke to Americans regardless of race or ethnicity. Even as many unions banned nonwhites from joining, the United Mine Workers opened its membership to all miners. This was part strategic—it helped counter the use of African American strikebreakers by the companies—and part humanitarian impulse. Mother Jones told her colleagues at a 1902 convention:

> One of the best elements [in West Virginia], I am here to tell you, are the colored men. One of the best fellows we have is the black man. He knows what liberty is; he knows that in days gone by the bloodhounds went after his father over the mountains and tore him to pieces, and he knows that his own Mammy wept and prayed for liberty. For these reasons he prizes his liberty and is ready to fight for it. My friends, the most of us have been told that we have liberty, and we believed the people who told us that! Now, my friends, we should all work together in harmony to secure our rights. Don't find fault with each other; rather clasp hands and fight the battle together.8

She recognized that skin color was, as she put it, "an accident."9 Character and action spoke more eloquently to Mother Jones than a person's race. Though she never renounced her earlier support for Chinese exclusion, she proclaimed loudly and regularly the need to embrace all working people in the fight for positive social change.

Generating action required convincing the mind and the heart to join a cause in which potential failure coexisted with danger. Mother Jones used examples from her own life and from history—particularly the American Revolution and the recent past of the labor movement—to do just that. Her forays into history and autobiography relied on emotional effect; actual dates, events, or people were of secondary importance behind the need for action. A Cincinnati labor reporter called her a "quick-eyed, mobile-faced woman" who "held her audience by the charm of a well-used voice in words that reached deep into the hearts and minds of the friends present. Humor and pathos, fact and fancy, chased each other in quick succession and were never without their instant response."[10] A journalist from West Virginia who interviewed her wrote:

> She has good command of language and a powerful voice, which combine with her grey hair and commanding bearing & pleasant face [to] give her undoubtedly much influence. She understands her power & how to use it, and while in private conversation shows a surprisingly cultivated manner & correct speech. Her language, when addressing a crowd of miners, is much after their common style and is thickly interspersed with slang and homely wit.[11]

This would not be the last time a reporter noted the contrast between her personal bearing and her use of the vernacular. Like all good organizers, Mother Jones tailored her message to her audience by employing appropriate gestures and vocabularies.

Following her efforts in Coxey's Army, Mother Jones traveled to Birmingham, Alabama. Here, in April 1894, United Mine Workers members went on strike, soon to be joined by railroaders in the American Railway Union as it battled the powerful Pullman Company. She concentrated on organizing and inspiring the miners, but the combination of federal troops and public opposition doomed the effort. Her work had not been in vain, however, for she made two important and lasting connections during her time in Birmingham. She began her relationship with the miners' union, which would employ her as an organizer on and off for the next thirty years, and she met the charismatic union leader and socialist politician Eugene Debs, who would become a firm friend and adviser. Slightly overestimating their time as allies, she said of Debs in 1905, "We have been close comrades on the battle ground for 14 long years.

Mother Jones
Near the
Beginning of
Her Career as a
Union Organizer
(1902), courtesy
Library of Con-
gress Prints and
Photographs
Division

We can trust our lives in the *hands of each other*."[12] In 1920 she wrote to President Wilson seeking Debs's release from prison because "his life has been one of unceasing devotion and heavy sacrifice."[13] Debs returned the sentiment, calling her a "modern Joan of Arc" and defending her tactics, her outlook, and her character from attack.[14] She and Debs shared a vision of the ideal society in which people were free to reach their potential and workers earned wages commensurate with the wealth they created.

This vision began for Debs as a response to the concentration of wealth in the hands of railroad companies. He had been one of many railroad union leaders dissatisfied with the condition of railroad labor organizations because of their inability or unwillingness to challenge employers. The Brotherhoods remained weak and divided because they were craft unions, each one representing a specific group of skilled employees and therefore limited in its ability to influence the railroad companies. The bosses pursued a policy of divide and conquer, dealing with one union but not another and causing friction among the organizations. Debs, who served as an officer in the Brotherhood of Locomotive Firemen for a decade, left the Firemen in 1893 to lead a single union aimed at all railroad workers, skilled and unskilled.

This one big union, the American Railway Union (ARU), found an especially receptive audience among railroaders on the main western lines. Wageworkers on the Santa Fe, the Southern Pacific, and the Union Pacific quickly joined the new union because of the sorry financial state of their employers. The first test of the ARU came in February 1894 when the bankrupt Union Pacific cut wages and successfully secured a legal injunction forbidding its employees to strike. The union appealed the decision, and it was overturned. The standing of the new organization shot up in the eyes of railroaders. At the same time, the Great Northern Railway, headquartered in St. Paul, Minnesota, cut wages in an attempt to provoke a strike and destroy the ARU. That hope was dashed when Debs traveled to St. Paul to meet with the local chamber of commerce. He and James J. Hill, the president of the Great Northern, spoke to the leading industrialists of the city, many of whom relied on the railroad for shipping raw materials and finished products. Swayed by Debs and mindful of the effects of a strike on their own profits, they demanded an immediate settlement of the stoppage on terms favorable to the union. Hill had been unexpectedly defeated, and railroaders took notice: by the end of the year, the ARU claimed some 150,000 members, a third more than the total membership of the Brotherhoods.

This turned out to be its high point. In spring 1894 the Pullman Palace Car Company, which built and operated luxury passenger carriages at its eponymous company town near Chicago, cut the wages of its employees. The company required most of them to live in houses it owned and to purchase food and clothing in company stores. Wages went down, but rents and prices remained stable, cutting into the standard of living for Pullman employees. On 10 May 1894 a deputation of workers presented managers with a petition calling on the company to reinstitute the previous wage rates. Though they had secured a promise from the manager that there would be no retribution for doing so, the company fired the leaders of the delegation. Pullman employees immediately walked off the job.

They turned to the ARU for support, and on 12 June, the union called for a nationwide boycott of Pullman cars. Union members were to refuse to handle any train pulling Pullmans.

The companies had been planning for this eventuality. The General Managers Association, representing the twenty-four railroads terminating in Chicago, telegraphed President Grover Cleveland to request federal troops on the grounds that the union boycott interfered with U.S. mail shipments. The ARU called for patience and reminded companies that its employees continued to run mail trains and, in fact, uncoupled Pullman cars to do so. But a fight between strikers and strikebreakers at Blue Island, Illinois, gave the national government the pretext it needed to send in troops, who arrived on 4 July. In the wake of the escalating violence, Debs attempted to negotiate a truce, but the companies ignored him. Debs was arrested and imprisoned along with other union leaders, and the strike collapsed. The ARU shrank to a shell of its former self and stumbled along until, in 1897, Debs converted it into a political party called the Social Democracy of America, forerunner of the Socialist Party.

When the strike ended railroad workers in Birmingham returned to work, as did the miners Mother Jones had been organizing. Debs spent six months in prison for his role in the strike, emerging in November 1895 to popular acclaim. He embarked on a nationwide speaking tour in an effort to rebuild the ARU, help railroaders blacklisted after the Pullman strike, and stump for candidates in the upcoming election. His journey took him to Birmingham, where Mother Jones organized a reception in his honor and forced the mayor to allow him to speak in the opera house. Local miners meeting Debs's train "put him on their shoulders, and marched out of the station with the crowd in line" to the opera house, where he addressed the crowd. Remembering the occasion in later years Mother Jones sounded her anticlerical theme by writing, "The churches were empty that night, and that night the crowd heard a real sermon by a preacher whose message was one of human brotherhood."[15]

The Debs reception occurred in spring 1896, at a time when Mother Jones was traveling through the South. Later in life she wrote that she did this to see for herself the conditions under which children labored in the textile industry, though it may be that she was still searching for direction. In retrospect this would prove to be another formative experience in the making of Mother Jones, so much so that she told a reporter eight years later that "the [mill] children always called me 'Mother Jones,' and the name has stuck to me ever since that time."[16] In Cottondale, Alabama, she wrote that "I was given work in the factory, and there I saw the chil-

Eugene Debs Working on the Appeal to Reason, Girard, Kansas (1909), by kind permission of the Debs Collection, Cunningham Memorial Library, Indiana State University

dren, little children working, the most heart-rending spectacle in all life. Sometimes it seemed to me I could not look at those silent little figures; that I must go north, to the grim coal fields, to the Rocky Mountain camps, where the labor fight is at least fought by grown men."[17] She saw how "tiny babies of six years old with faces of sixty did an eight-hour shift for ten cents a day." She attacked the hypocrisy of the "pious" mill owners whose Sunday schools taught "the babies of the mills . . . how God had inspired the mill owner to come down and build the mill, so as to give His little ones work that they might develop into industrious, patriotic citizens and earn money to give to the missionaries to convert the poor unfortunate heathen Chinese."[18]

Mother Jones obtained work by telling the mill owner that her family would soon arrive, but he grew suspicious when no children or husband showed up. She moved on to Tuscaloosa and took a job in a rope factory where children worked twelve-hour shifts. From these experiences, and from working elsewhere in Alabama and South Carolina, she learned how a generation of children had been forced to forsake "childhood and childish things and become a man of six, a wage earner, a snuff sniffer, a personage upon whose young-old shoulders fortunes were built." The responsibility for this "appalling child slavery" rested with "everyone."[19]

Her travels through the South solidified Mother Jones's commitment to ending child labor, which served as one of the enduring foundations of her activism. This reached its apex in summer 1903, when she would lead "Mother Jones's Industrial Army" (sometimes called her "Children's Crusade"), a march of mill children from Philadelphia to New York demanding an end to child labor. Like many in the union movement Mother Jones wanted workingmen to earn a wage sufficient to ensure that their wives and children would not have to find remunerative employment. The "family wage" was part of the attempt to recapture the dignity of labor supposedly lost in the transition to factory work. It also, of course, maintained the economic subordination of women. To explain why the family wage was vital she would tell the story of a mother living in a mining district who lied about her children's ages to secure them work. The mother needed their earnings to buy a cow, for "in all the years her husband had put in the earth digging out wealth, he never got a glimpse of forty dollars until he had to take his infant boys, that ought to go to school, and sacrifice them." The moral of the story was a call to arms for "every man and woman to fight this damnable system of commercial pirates."[20]

While in the South, Mother Jones visited a utopian community called Ruskin in rural Tennessee. Many reformers tried to reject mainstream society by establishing communities, and a great wave of communitarian experiments had appeared throughout the United States in the first half of the nineteenth century. These utopians, so called because they sought to create the perfect society, failed on their own terms, but during the economic depression of the late nineteenth century reformers tried again by launching a second wave of utopian experiments. Mother Jones claimed that utopian communities could not succeed and asserted, "I have no patience with those idealists and visionaries who preach fine spun theories and cry down everybody but themselves. Let us keep our feet on the ground."[21] In her opinion, reform from within society would always prove more effective than withdrawing from the world.

Mother Jones visited Ruskin in 1895 during her travels following the Birmingham strikes. At Ruskin all property was owned in common, and no one person was more important than any other. Named in honor of the British reformer John Ruskin, it was established by Julius Wayland, who became one of Mother Jones's closest friends after he repudiated communitarianism. Wayland edited "the best paper in this country," and he would "set up at night" with her discussing the works of Voltaire, Victor

Hugo, and Thomas Paine.[22] Like Jacob Coxey, Wayland was a successful Midwestern businessman who had grown concerned over the direction he saw society taking in the Gilded Age. Like Mary Jones, he had experienced devastating loss, in Wayland's case the death of his father and four siblings during a cholera epidemic. Wayland grew wealthy as a publisher and land speculator but after witnessing the appalling working and living conditions in Pueblo, Colorado, became disheartened by poverty. He turned against capitalism and against conventional party politics. He published a newspaper advocating socialism, the *Coming Nation*, which appeared at a time of growing interest in socialistic means of creating a better society.

Wayland proposed building a utopian community, and in August 1894 Ruskin Commonwealth opened its doors near Tennessee City, Tennessee. Like the Puritans of seventeenth-century Massachusetts Bay, he hoped his experiment would serve as an example for others to follow. The community sputtered along on unsuitable land for two years and then moved some five miles to a new location. It enjoyed modest success, for by 1898 Ruskin housed three hundred residents and its members harvested thirty-two different vegetables, many of which they processed and canned for sale in local towns. The members built their own modest living quarters and collectively erected several impressive public buildings. Long before then, however, Julius Wayland had become disenchanted with the communal ideal and severed his ties with Ruskin. He moved to Kansas City, Missouri, where he would eventually begin a new publication, the *Appeal to Reason*.

Mother Jones would later claim that she knew Ruskin was doomed to failure, but then she was biased against the principles on which it rested. She did not think people could put aside their selfish interests to reject conventional society and work for the betterment of the whole. When she visited the community it had opened in a wave of enthusiasm and optimism, and she was one of many curious Americans who stopped in. Supporters traveled from around the country to visit and help, and money arrived from numerous sources. Among those who made the pilgrimage was Jacob Coxey, who may have sparked her interest in the community. But Mary Jones in the mid-1890s was in the process of becoming Mother Jones. It is unlikely that she would have found an experiment in communal living attractive at the very time she was creating a highly individualized and potentially powerful role for herself.

She remained friends with Julius Wayland, encouraging his efforts to publish the *Appeal to Reason* and staying with his family in Missouri and, later, Kansas. The first issue of the *Appeal* appeared on 31 August 1895. Mother Jones claimed she helped distribute the new periodical by traveling around Omaha, Nebraska: "In a short time I had gathered several hundred subscriptions and the paper was launched."[23] There is no corroborating evidence for this statement, but her friendship with Wayland solidified the homespun socialism of natural justice and an equitable distribution of opportunity she shared with Eugene Debs. She and Wayland were committed to educating ordinary Americans about their rights and their duty to transform the country. She was a regular reader of the *Appeal*; her correspondence is littered with references to its content and requests for specific issues. She found much to enjoy and absorb within its pages and would have responded positively to statements such as this, from an 1895 issue: "Under a bad social structure the worst elements will survive. Under a just social structure the just will survive. . . . Under the present system the cunning, the crafty, the avaricious, the thief, the briber and the perjurer survive, and their opposites perish. Reverse the system, substitute private monopoly by public monopoly and you will have just the opposite effects. Which prefer you?"[24] Mother Jones knew: she spent the rest of her life explaining why she supported public ownership of industries in the interest of all people over a private system benefiting the wealthy few.

The "private monopoly" attacked by the *Appeal to Reason* threatened the livelihoods of small business owners, farmers, and labor union members. In the 1890s these groups formed the People's Party, a political party inspired by the Populist movement, to dismantle monopolistic industries. It attracted Mother Jones because of its commitment to mass participation and to the destruction of trusts. She attended the 1896 People's Party convention in St. Louis with a group of Debs supporters led by William Demarest Lloyd. They wanted to secure the party's presidential nomination for Debs, but he refused to allow them to do so. The convention nominated William Jennings Bryan instead, destroying the People's Party as a national force because Bryan had already secured the Democratic Party nomination. Moderate Populists joined the Democrats in a failed attempt to win the presidency for Bryan, while socialists searched for other alternatives. The factionalism she witnessed contributed to Mother Jones's dislike of internal bureaucratic struggles and reinforced her desire to operate without institutional constraints.

After the disappointment of the 1896 People's Party convention Mother Jones turned her attentions fully to labor organizing. She began her careerat the age of sixty at a time of deteriorating relations between workers and bosses. Large corporations extinguished competition by cooperating in monopolies. Even industries characterized by many small units had to lower costs in an effort to meet the demands of the monopolies they relied on for sales. Coal miners therefore suffered as the competition to reduce costs created poor working conditions and limited their power at work. The strikes of 1877 had marked a turning point in workplace relations, and those of 1886 demonstrated beyond doubt that antagonism and conflict had become the basis for labor relations in the United States. This situation led Mother Jones and many others to view the United States as a society divided into two big social classes, the owners and the workers. These classes represented opposing sides in the class war, which would lead, as she put it, to a time when "there will be no robber class and no working class."[25]

The growth of monopoly capitalism raised the question of who should benefit from the profits of industry. Two competing answers emerged: the owners claimed that they should reap the rewards of their skill at investing capital in a risk-filled marketplace, while working people countered that those who actually produced the wealth by making the goods or services from which capitalists profited should enjoy a fair share of the spoils. Mother Jones consistently advocated the labor theory of value. By this, she, and many other thinkers on the Left, argued that wealth belonged by right to the working people who built, dug, carried, or made materials and services. The labor theory of value infused her agitation and remained the basis for her desire to wage class war.

The depressions of the Gilded Age bankrupted numerous businesses, but the survivors emerged reorganized and highly capitalized. Wealth and power were being concentrated in the hands of fewer and fewer individuals, most notably bankers like J. P. Morgan and industrialists such as John D. Rockefeller Sr. and Andrew Carnegie. Mother Jones would battle "Morgan, Belmont, Harriman and old Oily John" in coalfields, courthouses, and congressional hearings across America, challenging their claim to have earned their wealth and condemning their anti-union activities.[26] Big business, she argued, prospered on the backs of working people, for monopolists such as Rockefeller "crush them, rob them, persecute them until he has made his millions out of their precious blood."[27] She asked, "Where did the Carnegie millions come from?" answering with a reference to the famous steel town near Pittsburgh, "Go to the graveyard at Homestead. . . . Ask the tombstones there, and they will rise in the ghostly light and say that it was the murder of the poor innocent mothers and children of Homestead that heaped up his millions."[28] She thought capitalists wanted to subvert democracy and accused Morgan of conspiring with dictators, for he "goes to Russia and shakes hands with the czar," whom she called one of "these foreign vultures of oppression" trying to destroy liberty.[29]

The rich legitimated their wealth as the natural order of things, arguing that concentration was the inevitable outcome of the struggle for survival. They used the philosophy of Social Darwinism to justify the accumulation of wealth. According to this way of viewing the world, wealth was the reward for evolutionary superiority and moral goodness while poverty was the price paid for backwardness and sin. Employers also asserted that individuals, not groups of classes, possessed the power to shape their destinies. Workers were free to rise or fall according to their abilities under this Liberal interpretation of labor relations. Central to the argument was the idea that working people could legitimately act only as individuals because they were legally equal to the owners. Thus employers declared labor unions unacceptable because they were combinations in violation of economic "laws." Social Darwinism and Liberal ideology provided business owners a scientific justification for breaking unions and crushing strikes: this is why Mother Jones argued that working people had a right and an imperative to promote and defend their own interests collectively. Her activism and her organizing were part of a struggle by labor unions to create collective organizations in the face of stubborn and often violent resistance by employers and even by workers who had accepted the individualistic interpretation of society.

In June 1897 Mother Jones traveled to Chicago with A. S. Edwards, one of the leaders of the Ruskin community, for the annual convention of the American Railway Union. Though essentially destroyed by the Pullman strike, the ARU had struggled on until, at this meeting, its leaders converted it into a political party called Social Democracy of America (SDA). Debs wanted SDA to create a utopian community—he called it a "co-operative commonwealth"—for unemployed railroaders and to serve as an example for others to follow. Other socialists, like prominent Milwaukee leader Victor Berger, focused on power at the municipal level and argued that SDA should run political campaigns to unseat the two main parties. Mother Jones remained unconvinced by either approach and, distressed by the infighting, returned to union organizing.

Just as Birmingham had brought Mother Jones into contact with Debs, so it would bring her into the United Mine Workers of America (UMWA). She would spend the majority of her active years in the labor movement as an organizer for this coal miners' union. The UMWA grew by sending dedicated representatives into the field to explain how and why the union would help miners. Traveling and speaking at great personal risk, these paid organizers tried to convince workers to join the organization. To accomplish this difficult and time-consuming task they had to avoid company officials and meet with miners in their saloons, as they left work, and occasionally in their homes. Mother Jones described organizing in terms of educating the miners, stating, "I went into the mines to put literature into the hands of those [wage] slaves."[30] On another occasion she described her work in the field as "putting Literature into their hand and making them read and think for themselves."[31] That was the essence of educating and agitating. Though slow and dangerous, organizing had its rewards, for as she wrote after a gathering of miners in West Virginia, "I would not exchange that meeting for all the palaces or millions earth has. The affection that came from their weary hearts beamed out of their eyes dim[m]ed by the darkness of earth caverns meant volumes for the future generation."[32] This was the type of reception Mother Jones warmed to, and it kept her going through danger and despair.

As Mother Jones repeatedly discovered, organizing could be a risky business. Over the course of her career she would be threatened at gunpoint, kidnapped and deported, imprisoned for making or threatening to make speeches, and tried by court-martial. Coal companies resisted unionization by controlling their employees. Like the Pullman Company, though on a larger and more diffused basis, the companies owned the houses and stores their employees needed. Often working in isolated valleys and on virtually inaccessible mountainsides, the miners were at the mercy of the companies. Miners who complained about working conditions or fought for higher wages risked losing their livelihoods and their homes. Part of the mystique of Mother Jones, and of her success as an organizer, was her ability to withstand terrible weather and treacherous roads to find these obscure places and show the miners how to defeat the bosses. She also knew her work would bear fruit only gradually, telling her fellow organizers at a union convention:

> We are building for long years to come, and the foundation which you lay with aching backs and your bleeding hands and your sore hearts will not perish with the years. It will grow and grow and live, and when the enemies of this organization shall lie moldering in the grave and the world will have forgotten that they ever lived, your organization and your work will live.[33]

Patience, in this version of her message, was a virtue and indeed a necessity, a far cry from her promise of rapid change for those she recruited to the union.

In July 1897 the UMWA received an unexpected boost when mine owners instituted a 20 percent pay cut. Though fewer than ten thousand miners had joined the union by then, double that figure struck work in the Pittsburgh area alone. Into this ferment walked Mother Jones, some thirty years after she claimed to have helped striking railroad workers there. Whether she was sent by the union or traveled of her own volition is unclear, but, drawing on her experiences with Coxey's Army, she bolstered the miners' morale. She convinced them to join the union and gave a living demonstration of the power of militant motherhood. She brought women into the strike by mobilizing farmers' wives to help feed the strikers and involved miners' families in processions and demonstrations to keep morale high. When the strike ended successfully in 1898, miners in an area called the Central Competitive Field, embracing large parts of Illinois, Ohio, Indiana, and western Pennsylvania, received a pay increase, a shorter working day, and the right to watch their coal being weighed. The UMWA gained the power to deduct members' dues from their pay packets, and its membership increased to over 100,000. Mother Jones, like the union, had made her mark.

The conclusion of the strike did not end the conflict, however. While most mine owners in the Central Competitive Field accepted the new contract and recognized the UMWA as a legitimate organization, the Chicago-Virden Coal Company, located south of Springfield, Illinois, refused to abide by the agreement. Its operators claimed that paying higher wages would render it unable to compete in the Chicago market, some two hundred miles to the north. The company therefore prepared to fire its entire mining work force and import African Americans from Alabama, paying them below the union rate. It employed mine guards and built a wooden stockade next to the railroad near Virden, Illinois, to protect the new miners. On 12 October 1898 a train loaded with replacement workers prepared to stop near the stockade. Local miners opened fire and exchanged shots with the guards; the train sped on to St. Louis, but only after seven miners and four guards had been killed. The "Virden Massacre" served as a sad coda to three decades of violence and a warning to those who hoped for a new tenor to labor relations.

After the miners' strike Mother Jones traveled around the United States gathering support for an appeal for clemency on behalf of S. D. Worden, an ARU member active during the 1894 Pullman strike. Worden had been convicted of causing a train wreck by tampering with a trestle and had been sentenced to death. Mother Jones traveled to Washington, D.C., to seek a pardon from President McKinley. On her way there, "'Mother' Mary Jones of Kansas City" stopped off in Chicago to address the Social Democracy of America, though perhaps here she only reopened old wounds. The Worden appeal had already cost the union significant sums of money, and it is unknown whether she obtained further support from the ARU's successor. Her actions set a precedent, for this would be the first of many appeals by Mother Jones on behalf of imprisoned labor leaders in the years ahead.

By the end of the nineteenth century, Mother Jones had emerged. Her own explanation for the origins of her new persona came in a 1911 affidavit, where she swore

> she entered the Labor movement during the strikes of 1877; that she became a member of the Knights of Labor, and in 1895 she became a member of the Kansas City Local of the Socialist Labor Party and is now a member at large of the socialist Party, that since 1894 she has been an active speaker and participant in the strikes of the miners, and since 1900 has been officially engaged by the miners union in the work of organization and strike service.[34]

Though she characteristically misremembered the details, her summary shows how deeply Mother Jones identified with the labor movement. After a decade of travel she settled on two causes to which she could devote the rest of her active life: the miners' union and socialist politics.

5

Organizing Coal Country

THE FIRST DECADE of the twentieth century found Mother Jones working as a paid organizer for the miners' union. Her early experiences in this capacity included being arrested, intimidated, and forced to leave town. From these she learned "there are no limits to which powers of privilege will not go to keep the workers in slavery."[1] Emancipating the "wage slaves" became her mission, and she urged union organizers to "do your duty . . . as citizens of the United States [and] protest against . . . injustice to the American people" and to "link hands in the mighty battle for the emancipation of the working class from the robbing class."[2]

Mother Jones used her ability to instill pride and a passion for change in critical strikes in Pennsylvania and West Virginia in 1900 and 1902. In these, as in so many states, rich seams of coal fueled economic growth. Coal burned more efficiently than wood; this quality combined with its availability facilitated the expansion of steam-powered engines on iron rails and in factories. Investors could locate machines away from the unreliable streams and rivers necessary for powering waterwheels. They moved into towns and cities where ready supplies of workers and customers could be found. Coal gave rise to urban mass production and the development of a national communications and transportation network in the form of the railroads.

Mother Jones saw mining as a vital industry and miners as crucial to movements for social change. The United Mine Workers of America hired her as a paid organizer to travel around the country bringing miners into the union and organizing strikes where necessary. Mother Jones had her own agenda, which she summarized in 1902 as, "I wanted the powers that be to understand who the miners were; to understand that when they laid down their picks they tied up all other industries." By demonstrating the power of the miners, she hoped "the operators would learn what an important factor the miner is to his support," and she urged miners to recognize that "these fights must be won if it costs the whole country to win them. These fights against the oppressor and the capitalists, the ruling classes, must be won if it takes us all to do it."[3] For organizers like Mother Jones the difficulty was to convince the miners themselves of their importance and of the great potential of their combined strength. Organizing put Mother Jones on the front line of the class war, and she used her position to convince miners they would only advance through collective action.

Coal in the eastern United States came in two basic types, anthracite and bituminous. Anthracite—or hard coal—is solid and rich in carbon. It burns hot, making it ideal for smelting iron and for driving machinery. It also burns relatively smoke free, a desirable quality when heating homes. The anthracite region Mother Jones helped organize was largely in eastern Pennsylvania, where railway companies owned many of the mines. Approximately 95 percent of the anthracite coal used in the United States between the Civil War and the beginning of the twentieth century came from this region. Bituminous coal, by contrast, is soft, and relatively easy to dig out of the ground, but burns with less intensity and more smoke than anthracite. Nonetheless, it was in great demand. The bituminous region included the Central Competitive Field (western Pennsylvania, Ohio, Indiana, and Illinois) organized by the UMWA during the strike of 1897. The other main bituminous coal–producing state was West Virginia, which would remain stubbornly non-union and therefore a thorn in the side of the UMWA until the New Deal of the 1930s.

The mining regions Mother Jones helped the union organize were changing from a predominantly British work force to a multiethnic labor force composed primarily of recent immigrants from eastern and central Europe. This complicated organizing. The "walking delegates" had to communicate with miners in many different languages, whether through written works, speeches, or gestures. Mother Jones used all of these and added touches of drama, including phonographs to play music, bands when instruments were available, and occasionally photographs. To overcome social divisions, however, she consistently framed her rhetoric around the notion of a single working class in which ethnic and national differences were secondary to class unity. She also understood that her work would be slow and arduous, recalling how "the fight can be won, and will be won, but the struggle will be long and education, agitation and class solidarity all must play a part in it."[4] Mother Jones certainly wanted to play her part, telling a reporter for the *New York Times* that "I am always happiest when I am in the midst of the gang that is hurting the other fellow."[5]

Miners led a hard life. Many of the mines were owned by corporations that had been buying up coalfields, but small operators continued to control numerous mines. The day was long—often twelve hours or more; the pay, low; and the work, dangerous. Operators often ignored state regulations designed to protect miners, a problem captured by Mother Jones when she said, "The state law says the men must be paid every two weeks in legal tender money. They are paid when the bosses get good and ready and in soup tickets." She explained that the companies defied the law, for it "requires the coal to be weighed fairly. It is misweighed by the operators as they see fit. The law requires 1500 cubic feet of air for each miner. This is not done. Baby boys are compelled to breathe the poisonous air that brings them to disease and early graves."[6] By "soup tickets" she meant scrip redeemable only at company stores. Sometimes called "pluck-me" stores because of their high prices, workers hated them. In Charleston, West Virginia, Mother Jones told a story to show how operators used company stores to exploit the powerlessness of miners:

> [You] want to get something to eat for your wife, and you are off that day, and the child comes back and says, "Papa, I can't get anything." "Why," he says, "There is four dollars coming to me," and the child goes back crying, without a mouthful of anything to eat. The father goes to the "Pluck-me" store and says to the manager, "There is four dollars coming to me," and the manager says, "Oh, no, we have kept that for rent!" "You charge six dollars a month, and there are only three days gone." "Well," he says, "it is a rule that two-thirds of the rent is to be kept if there is only a day."[7]

Vignettes like this captured the anger and grievances of miners in West Virginia. Though such practices were illegal, they persisted because the state did not enforce its labor laws. Implementing existing legislation became a rallying cry for the union. Another recurring union demand was for miners or their representatives to watch the weighing of coal; miners felt that the operators cheated them by underrecording their daily production.

Appointing trusted men to the position of "checkweighmen" became a key demand. Cramped conditions and child labor both permeated coal mines and formed further bases for miners' grievances.

Deadly conflicts such as that in Virden, Illinois, were not isolated incidents but high points in an ongoing struggle for control over working conditions in the mines. As the dispute in the bituminous Central Competitive Field wound to its conclusion, a new conflict erupted in the anthracite district of eastern Pennsylvania. It began with a wildcat strike (one not authorized by a union) near the mining town of Hazelton. Three hundred miners fed up with low wages and dangerous working conditions marched from Hazelton to the town of Lattimer on 10 September 1897, intent on closing the mines there. When armed deputies blocked their progress and ordered the men to turn round, the miners refused. The policemen shot into the procession and killed nineteen miners. The "Lattimer Massacre" demolished the operators' portrayal of harmony in the coalfields. Mother Jones seized the moment and called the nineteen who died the "murdered victims of a murderous mine owners association!"[8]

Lattimer was a turning point for the union, highlighting how, as Mother Jones remembered, the miners were "slaves whose lifeblood is coined into profits that the few may riot in luxury."[9] The outrage that followed the killing of unarmed men presented the UMWA with an opening to switch from organizing the bituminous mines to recruiting members in the anthracite region. After three years of organizing, two large strikes and numerous small ones broke out. The two biggest, in 1900 and 1902, lasted for six weeks and six months respectively. In both cases over 100,000 miners went on strike; in both years the union won in Pennsylvania but lost in West Virginia.

Mother Jones later claimed that United Mine Workers president John Mitchell sent her to the anthracite region during a wildcat strike in Arnot, Pennsylvania, in August 1899. Whether dispatched by the union or not, she arrived in September just as the miners were preparing to return to work, their demands unmet and their morale sapped. Mother Jones recalled of Arnot how "the men were going to work next morning. I addressed a meeting that afternoon. Nobody went to work next morning, but I was thrown out of the hotel at eleven o'clock at night—I was an undesirable citizen." She then decided to find lodging on her own and "went up the mountain. I saw a light and kept crawling up until I got there. When I got to the house a man there said, 'Did they put you out of the hotel?' I said, 'Yes, but I will put them out before I get through with them.'"[10] She stayed with the man and his family, who were unceremoniously evicted by the company for showing hospitality to a union organizer. Mother Jones

John Mitchell Arriving in Shenandoah, Pennsylvania (1902), courtesy Library of Congress Prints and Photographs Division

brought the family, with their possessions in a horse-drawn cart, to a rally the next day.

Mother Jones staged great street theater in the strike zone and helped turn the tide in favor of the union. Tactical errors by the mine operators contributed to this shift. They hired strikebreakers who were easily turned away by the mop and broom brigade Mother Jones organized to keep watch over mine entrances. Then, when company officials appealed to local farmers to refuse food to the miners, Mother Jones rode out into the countryside on an old wagon pulled by a mine mule. Explaining the strike's significance for the country as a whole and pleading with farmers for help, she returned to Arnot with her wagon overflowing with produce. Through deprivation and the chill of winter she helped keep the miners' morale high. In February 1900 the Arnot contest ended when local mine operators offered small wage concessions and the miners returned to work.

By now the UMWA had officially appointed Mother Jones one of its "walking delegates." She earned $500 annually, though she frequently had to pay expenses out of her salary. For three years she spent the bulk of her time traveling through Pennsylvania and West Virginia. In August 1900 she returned to eastern Pennsylvania for a union convention in Hazelton.

Miners' representatives met to formulate a response to operators' refusal to adopt the Arnot agreement across the anthracite region. At the convention Mother Jones "urged on the miners the necessity of thorough organization [as] the only hope for improving existing conditions."[11] The delegates voted in favor of a strike, and the union promised to enforce a boycott on coal sales in the anthracite region to calm the fears of operators in the Central Competitive Field that the strike would hurt them. The union drafted a document asking mine operators to create a uniform system of weights, reduce the price of the blasting powder miners had to buy, abolish company stores, increase wages, and eliminate a sliding scale linking wages to the price of coal. The owners ignored the union's overtures, and the anthracite strike began on 17 September 1900. Within two weeks over 90 percent of the regions' mines had closed.

Mother Jones was becoming a figure of some renown. The press consistently depicted her as an orator who could stir mining families to action. One journalist labeled her "a Chicago virago . . . urging disorder in language that made the women hysterical and got the men to marching."[12] She would doubtless have appreciated this unintentional allusion to the Cailleach, the mythical old Irishwoman who was stronger than a man and outlived her husbands.

She certainly did not appreciate the disinformation campaign operators waged against her. They used a Greek Orthodox priest to tell reporters "that he had been told by a parishioner that 'Mother Jones' was coming to Shenandoah with $80,000 to distribute as a relief fund."[13] The union did offer assistance to striking miners, but Mother Jones did not distribute its money. The operators consistently claimed that their happy miners only went on strike because of the blandishments of outside agitators like Mother Jones. The pro-business press repeated this line, holding Mother Jones personally responsible for unsettling the miners and for causing the strike.

The miners' grievances were real enough, and she was undoubtedly guilty of helping to spread the strike, but she did not create it. When miners in Mocanaque ignored the strike call, however, the newspapers speculated that Mother Jones "will probably be sent to the village to persuade the women that it is their duty to urge the men to join the strikers."[14] She was, and she did. On 22 September she led a "long line of miners' wives and daughters, armed with brooms and sticks," accompanied by 250 miners and a band, in a march to the mines at Beaver Meadow and Coleraine.[15] She and her fellow organizers understood that the strike could only succeed if all eastern Pennsylvania miners refused to work. As at Lattimer in 1897, deputy sheriffs again blocked their route. Stymied, the procession marched through the streets of Beaver Meadows before returning to Hazelton. The miners had advertised both the strike and their strength, planting seeds they hoped would grow later. Four days after the Beaver Meadows march Mother Jones led a mop and broom brigade to Panther Creek as part of a procession of over two thousand miners. Once again the marchers failed to reach their objective, dispersed this time by a detachment of National Guard troops. The pattern of conflict initiated in 1877 was being repeated: the government sided with businesses against workers.

By the end of September the strike had taken full hold, and the press continued to fulminate against "outside agitators" and "foreigners from Illinois" causing disturbances and interrupting the supply of coal to cities along the East Coast. Mother Jones was ridiculed for suggesting "in get-up, voice and language a page of French history of a century back."[16] Given her love of the writings of Victor Hugo, she may well have reveled in being compared to the women of the French Revolution. For some newspaper readers, however, the analogy would have had very different resonances: the French Revolution created terror, and its advocates murdered the wealthy. Mother Jones was therefore a force that needed to be stopped before she ignited a full-scale rebellion.

Slowing Mother Jones proved an impossible task. On 6 October she led eight hundred miners and six hundred women across twelve miles of treacherous mountain footpaths from McAdoo to Lattimer. The Lattimer mines continued to operate, a symbolic sore spot for the union. Mother Jones and her McAdoo contingent marched repeatedly through the streets of Lattimer, distracting the sheriff from the presence of two other groups, from Jeddo and Coleraine, hiding in the hills. When the working miners began to assemble for their day below ground these other strikers, numbering at least one thousand men, charged down the hill and chased them off. The sheriff, remembering the Lattimer Massacre, refused to shoot at the charging miners, who disarmed one of his deputies and sent him rolling down a slate pile after he had fired a shot. The working miners fled, and the strikers put guards outside the homes of the Lattimer miners. The company then agreed not to reopen the mine until the strike had been settled.

This would be one of the final marches of the strike. Warned by local sheriffs that they would fire into the next public procession of miners, UMWA president John Mitchell told his organizers to hold rallies but not to march. Mother Jones cancelled another planned action against the Beaver Meadow mines but tried one more time and organized a procession to Tamaque and Coaldale on 16 October. This attracted some twenty-five hundred miners intent on closing those few mines still working, but they abandoned the action when confronted by National Guard soldiers. An attempt to arrest Mother Jones failed, and strikers who broke away from the main group succeeded in closing down the mines at Nesequehoning. In Tamaque guards bayoneted strikers who tried to stop miners from going to work. Mother Jones wrote of the encounter that, after Colonel O'Neill had ordered the procession to halt and threatened force if they did not, she engaged the officer in conversation. In her autobiography she recalled the dialogue thus:

> "I'll charge [with] bayonets," said he.
>
> "On whom?"
>
> "On your people."
>
> "We are not enemies," said I. "We are just a band of working women whose brothers and husbands are in a battle for bread. We want our brothers in Coaldale to join us in our fight. We are here on the mountain road for our children's sake, for the nation's sake. We are not going to hurt anyone and surely you would not hurt us."

She remembered how, after this exchange, the National Guard soldiers "kept us there till daybreak and when they saw the army of women in kitchen aprons, with dishpans and mops, they laughed and let us pass. An army of strong mining women makes a wonderfully spectacular picture."[17] This retelling is not entirely faithful to contemporary newspaper reports, but it does capture the sense of joy Mother Jones felt in the drama she directed. As the day closed, "we marched over the mountains home, beating on our pans and singing patriotic songs."[18]

The 1900 anthracite strike ended successfully for the miners despite the presence of National Guard troops and intimidation by local law enforcement officials. External actors reacting to political imperatives made sure of that. President McKinley's chief political adviser, Ohio senator Marcus Alonzo Hanna, urged the operators to settle with their men because of the forthcoming election. Hanna reasoned that if the strike continued, the Republicans could lose the presidency. He warned operators that an electoral victory by the supposedly anti-business Democratic Party candidate, William Jennings Bryan, would favor the union and damage profits. The operators therefore agreed to a 10 percent pay raise but refused to recognize the union. When she heard of the offer, Mother Jones "urged the men to accept a little now and prepare for a time when they could demand and secure more." She told the anthracite miners to "take this advance now and save the [blasting] powder question for another time."[19]

The men accepted and returned to work, but Mother Jones would not be so accommodating after the 1902 strike.

Before that next major stoppage in the anthracite fields, the UMWA shifted its focus to the bituminous coal state of West Virginia. Unlike any other state Mother Jones would encounter, West Virginia exhibited a daunting unity of political and industrial purpose and arrayed it against the union. Coal company officials became political leaders—from sheriffs and district attorneys to senators and successive governors—with alarming regularity. Such connections made organizers wary and their lives dangerous because the corporations and politicians colluded against them. Mother Jones would encounter many of these officials in her battles in that state.

Railroad companies such as the Baltimore and Ohio and the Chesapeake and Ohio, with head offices in New York or Philadelphia and a focus on the bottom line, owned much of the land in West Virginia. The price of West Virginia coal had been falling steadily as the railroads opened coalfields in isolated valleys, making access dangerous and difficult. The state's mining industry had the highest numbers of miners killed and injured at work in the United States, and the companies exerted a control over mine workers' lives unparalleled in other mining regions. Miners endured low wages frequently paid in scrip, which was illegal but was used because it reinforced the miners' dependence on employers. Protesting would have resulted in miners losing their jobs and their homes, for in these out-of-the-way mining towns (often called "camps") the companies owned the housing. Sustained organizing was complicated by the operators' intransigence and the isolation of the mining camps. All of this added up to what Mother Jones called "medieval West Virginia" or, occasionally, "this God Cursed Monopolistic State."[20]

The state's resistance to unionism threatened the UMWA because cheap coal from an unorganized West Virginia could undermine the agreements reached in the Central Competitive Field. The UMWA organized an unsuccessful strike in 1894, and on 27 July 1897 called a mass rally in Charleston to publicize the plight of the miners of West Virginia. Eugene Debs, Samuel Gompers, and other labor leaders representing dozens of unions spoke at the rally, pledging to help the union recruit members in the state. Around seventeen thousand people attended, and thousands more came to subsequent meetings held in the coal districts the union wanted to organize first. Nothing seemed to work: some West Virginia miners did join the nationwide strike of July 1897, but the union made few lasting inroads.

The 1902 campaign began on 31 October 1901 when the union held a statewide convention in Huntington. Here miners' delegates aired their grievances, and the convention concluded by drafting an agreement to present to the companies. Mother Jones, correctly anticipating that operators would reject the union's overture, "advised the miners to go home and resort to arms if necessary."[21] John Mitchell had a different perspective: hopeful that owners would respond favorably to the union proposal and temperamentally averse to conflict, he thought the operators would recognize the union and accept its demands. He was to be disappointed. After being repeatedly ignored by the mine operators, he finally issued a strike call on 24 May 1902. The strike would begin on 7 June.

In 1902, Mother Jones joined with other organizers (some of whom had already been working in the state for a year) to recruit miners and plant union locals. She began by leading the recruitment drive in the southern half of the state, and she did so with some success in the face of overwhelming odds. Her presence was well known and widely reported, with the press alerting readers to the fact that by June 1902, "'Mother' Jones, the noted female agitator of Pennsylvania, has been here [in West Virginia] for some time, and leads a swarm of organizers. They have succeeded in inducing the miners to hold a number of meetings, and the strike feeling is now very high."[22]

In the northern fields, however, the Fairmont Coal Company proved particularly resistant to the union's efforts. It launched a public relations campaign claiming that the union organizers were upsetting its contented miners. The company hired private detectives to follow and harass union representatives, making life difficult for them by exerting its power over meeting halls and hotels to deny them places to speak and stay. The union pushed ahead, but dissent within its leadership weakened the campaign. One powerful vice-president, Thomas L. Lewis of Ohio, opposed the action from the very beginning and hampered efforts to send more organizers and money to West Virginia, preferring to concentrate resources on the simultaneous anthracite-field strike instead. This, he felt, was winnable; he also wanted to run against UMWA president John Mitchell at the next union election and sought to build a coalition of union locals willing to support his candidacy. This type of internal political battle would anger Mother Jones and cause her to abandon the union for a decade; such power struggles soured her on institutions of all forms.

Mitchell decided to follow Lewis's lead because trouble was brewing in the anthracite district. A strike had begun in eastern Pennsylvania on 12 May 1902, after the operators refused to meet with the union. Mother Jones took time out from her work in the southern coalfields of West Virginia and traveled to her old stomping ground of Hazelton in July. Here the union was in good shape, with organizers meeting a positive response. Over 150,000 miners were out on strike, and efforts were under way to close the mines still operating. She would visit Pennsylvania several times more during the year, but in 1902 Mother Jones focused on West Virginia. She began the year headquartered at Montgomery, in West Virginia's southern fields, from where she and her team of organizers enjoyed some success in creating union locals. In February she felt sure she would have the extensive Kanawha River mines, with their seven thousand miners, unionized within three months.

The West Virginia strike began well for the union because of the intensive organizing campaign beforehand. There were sporadic outbreaks of violence on both sides, including one occasion on which Mother Jones rescued a union leader being attacked by a gang of mine guards. In this instance she encountered a fellow organizer, who led Mother Jones to an isolated spot where the guards were beating another organizer. At that moment an interurban railcar appeared, and Mother Jones tricked the guards into thinking it was full of miners coming to rescue their colleague. The guards fled, and the injured organizer could be taken to hospital.

The operators did not rely on physical intimidation alone. In the 1902 strike they added a powerful new weapon to their anti-union arsenal in the form of legal injunctions. Assuming the miners would not remain on strike if union leaders and organizers were imprisoned or out of the state, the operators petitioned several friendly circuit court judges to stop the union from interfering, as the owners saw it, with their employees. Compliant judges then issued injunctions restraining union organizers from meeting with miners on the grounds that the union was engaged in an illegal conspiracy to hurt the companies by forcing them to accept only unionized miners. Aware that if they tried to hold rallies on company property they would be arrested for trespassing, the organizers rented fields for their public meetings. But the injunction took the operators' power one step beyond simple trespassing: when Thomas Haggerty, Mother Jones, and other union officials spoke on a piece of rented land near Clarksburg, they violated the injunction by attempting to convince the miners to stop working.

The first set of injunctions, acquired through circuit courts, only covered single counties and could be evaded by crossing county lines. Soon after the strike began, however, a Baltimore financier who had invested in debt owned by the Fairmont Company obtained a statewide federal injunction against the union. At the company's request he argued that the conspiracy into which the union had entered would deprive him of payments against the outstanding debt that were rightfully his. Federal

Mother Jones Eyes
the Camera (1902),
courtesy Library of
Congress Prints
and Photographs
Division

judge John J. Jackson of Parkersburg, West Virginia, a Lincoln appointee and ally of the coal companies, agreed with the claim that the strike would hurt the financier and issued a statewide injunction in mid-June. A federal marshal presented it to Mother Jones on 15 June. Before then the union had been confident of victory, John Mitchell writing to Mother Jones on 13 June, "I am overjoyed at the success of the strike movement in West Virginia," and encouraging her to "hire bands, or anything that is necessary."[23]

With success seemingly assured in the southern field, Mitchell had moved Mother Jones to the north, where things were going badly. She boosted morale, but the 15 June injunction disrupted the strike. Five days later the UMWA rented a field for a rally outside the Pinnickkinnick mine near Clarksburg. As miners gathered to listen, a marshal arrested male organizers. Then, when Mother Jones began to speak, the marshal asked one of the arrested organizers to inform her that she was in violation of the injunction and was under arrest. She refused to stop speaking and, according to a newspaper report, denounced "the mine operators as robbers, and defied Judge Jackson, placing him in the same class, and asserting that he, as well as the newspapers, and even the preachers, are in league with the interests of the mine owners against the mine workers." At the end of her oration she implored her "boys" to "keep up this fight! Don't surrender!"[24]

The organizers were taken to Parkersburg and imprisoned. Informed that she was to be incarcerated in a local hotel, Mother Jones said, "I would rather go board with Uncle Sam, I have better company than at the hotel. . . . My colleagues and I have fought this battle for years, and when they are jailed, I will be jailed, and when they are hung, I will be hung."[25] Though Mother Jones demanded to be put in a cell with the others, the jailer and his wife refused, placing her in their own living quarters in consideration of her age. The prisoners' hopes for a quick release were dashed when lawyers for the Fairmont Company successfully petitioned to postpone the trial for three weeks. The owners hoped this would weaken the resolve of the striking miners, and in all likelihood the strike would have collapsed without immediate action by the UMWA.

The injunctions and arrests threw into sharp relief a split within the union between those who advocated extending the strike to other bituminous states and those who wanted to contain it to West Virginia. Union president John Mitchell was firmly of the latter opinion and had the power to realize his wishes. At the union headquarters in Indianapolis he delayed and equivocated. He hid from other leaders the fact that union locals had sent him the number of petitions required to call a special convention to consider the question of extending the strike. Mitchell quietly built up support for his position within the union leadership and then called the special convention for July. Though many locals and districts in other states wanted to strike in sympathy with West Virginia, Mitchell and his allies carried the day. After their speeches to the special convention, union delegates voted to send financial support to the West Virginia miners but did not call on miners in other districts to strike. Mitchell worried about angering mine operators in states covered by the employment contracts that had done so much to strengthen the union.

By the time of the special convention Mother Jones had been bailed. She traveled to Indianapolis and spoke in support of Mitchell's nonexpansionist position, having been swayed by him from her original desire for a national miners' strike. As would so often be the case, she framed the strike as an era-changing event of world-historical importance. In her speech she compared the current political climate to the American Revolution, warning delegates that "this generation may sleep its slumber quietly, not feeling its mighty duty and responsibility, and may quietly surrender their liberties. And it looks very much as though they were doing so." Taking a page from history she reminded her audience, "These liberties are the liberties for which our forefathers fought and bled. Things are happening today that would have aroused our Revolutionary fathers in their graves. People sleep quietly, but it is the sleep of the slave chained closely to his master." She feared the freedoms secured in the Revolution would be surrendered by an apathetic generation unless the miners won and stirred up the people. She did see hope on the horizon when "the people will wake up and say to their feudal lords 'We protest,' and they will inaugurate one of those revolutions that sometimes come when the slave feels there is no hope, and then proceed to tear society to pieces."[26] Optimism regarding the future was one of her recurring themes and one of the sources of her popularity.

She was winning no popularity contests with the mine owners of West Virginia, however. Mother Jones returned to the Mountain State on 24 July to face Judge Jackson. In Parkersburg, Jackson unabashedly expressed his animosity toward unions. He disliked them on the grounds that they violated people's right to work. He followed the Liberal doctrine holding that employees had a right to, as he put it, "quit work at any time they desire to do so." But, he explained,

> I do not recognize the right of laborers to conspire together to compel employees who are not dissatisfied to lay down their picks merely to gratify a professional set of agitators, organizers, and walking delegates who roam all over the country as agents for some combination; who are vampires that live and fatten on the honest

labor of coal miners, and who are busybodies, creating dissatisfaction among a class of people who are quiet and do not want to be disturbed.[27]

He considered union organizers traitors to the United States whose agitation upset otherwise happy coal miners. He rejected arguments that the organizers' speech was protected under the First Amendment and saw them as participating in a conspiracy to overturn the law of supply and demand.

Judge Jackson also held strong opinions on the role of women and spared no effort to share them with Mother Jones. He told her to follow "the lines and paths which the Allwise Being intended her sex should pursue."[28] No woman could possibly be as assertive as Mother Jones without being goaded by men. He harbored the suspicion that she was a dupe who had allowed "herself to be used as an instrument by designing and reckless agitators." She should work for "charities" or follow conventional "avocations and pursuits" open to women.[29] When Judge Jackson told her she "ought to join some Charity Organization," she retorted, "If I had my way I would tear down every Charity Institution in the country today [and] build on their ruins the Temple of Justice."[30] Others voiced their opposition to Jackson's statement: the *Chicago Tribune* editorialized against his stand on the proper role of women, noting that the women's "'sphere' has so expanded that it takes in more than it did when the judge was a young man." The editorial pointedly noted, "Presumably Judge Jackson has a poor opinion of Joan of Arc, Anna Dickinson, Mrs. Lease, and other women who have wandered outside the 'true sphere' of domestic duties, nursing and sewing for the heathen."[31] Not to be outdone, Mother Jones called the judge a scab because she heard he had convinced President Lincoln to appoint him in place of the rightful appointee, a charge she later recanted.

Others in the courtroom were not so convinced of Mother Jones's innocence. In his summing up, Reese Blizzard, the prosecuting attorney, alleged that she had the power and charisma to convince contented miners to strike, famously labeling her "the most dangerous woman in America," a tag she proudly wore for the rest of her life. He argued that she should be found guilty and jailed. Judge Jackson did not follow Blizzard quite that far, sentencing the male defendants to a minimum jail term of sixty days but setting Mother Jones free, suspending her sentence on the grounds that she was "posing as a martyr." He told her to leave the state, which she obligingly did for a short time. She ignored his suggestion never to return. She repeatedly insisted he send her to prison, but Jackson refused, saying, "I will not send her to jail or allow her to force her way into jail."[32]

He sought to avoid creating a martyr whose imprisonment would cause further unrest among the miners of West Virginia and gain more publicity for their cause.

The injunctions deepened the division between miners and state authorities. Fearful of retribution against Judge Jackson, armed guards stood in the courtroom when he passed sentence, while the operators paid for others to be posted outside his home. Jackson had become a lightning rod for the miners' anger, and his decision caused consternation at union headquarters. Mitchell promised that the union would appeal Jackson's decision, calling it an "outrageous violation of all American principle. If the constitution of the United States can be set aside by injunctions the courts are greater than the constitution. They are a law themselves and there is little use for legislatures."[33]

The press widely reported Jackson's speech. While some newspapers supported the injunctions and his verdicts in the case, most condemned his wording. Reeling from the bad publicity and desperately entreating Fairmont Company lawyers to convince New York papers to support his opinion, Jackson struck a face-saving deal with the new UMWA leader in the state, Thomas L. Lewis. Lewis, who had opposed the strike in the first place, agreed to tone down the union's rhetoric and end mass meetings. In return the prisoners were released and the remainder of their sentences suspended. Jackson's hopes for positive publicity were realized when the *New York Times* praised his decision as "good law" rendered by "so able a jurist" but regretted his "somewhat intemperate language."[34]

The anthracite and bituminous strikes continued. Mother Jones told reporters at the end of September that "suffering is now the lot of the striking miners in the coalfields of Pennsylvania and West Virginia. Thousands of families are living on the highways, dependent for their subsistence on the good will of sympathizers. Conditions are appalling beyond words." She noted that "over 2000 families have been forced from their wretched shacks to live in the open air. I have seen children dying for the lack of proper medicine and care." She tried to minimize reports of escalating violence, claiming that the operators exaggerated its frequency and extent, saying, "If two dogs meet, growl, and fight, the operators call that a riot and have the troops brought to the scene." Her optimism shone through, though, and she concluded, "Yet the men will win. . . . The future glows with brightness."[35]

As in 1900, national political concerns worked in the miners' favor in 1902. Even before the strike began, Marcus Hanna, working with John Mitchell, tried unsuccessfully to broker a deal. They cooperated through the auspices of the National Civic Federation, an organization promoting the mutual interest of workers and owners. The federation brought operators and union leaders together in New York City, but they could not avert the strike because operators refused to recognize the union as a legitimate bargaining agent for the miners. Henry Cabot Lodge, a senior Republican and close friend President Theodore Roosevelt, warned him of the potentially disastrous consequences for the party if the anthracite strike dragged on into November, when elections were to be held. The operators did not want to repeat the wage increase of 1900 and rejected out of hand the idea that they should recognize the union. Heeding Lodge's advice, Roosevelt worked behind the scenes, first to gather information and then to propose ways to settle the strike. By the end of September, with no end in sight and coal supplies dwindling, he decided to act and called for a conference between the owners and the union to be held in Washington on 3 October 1902. The presidents of the railroads owning mines in the anthracite fields convened along with John Mitchell and other UMWA leaders. At that meeting Mitchell quietly and effectively outlined the union's case for the president, while the railroad bosses denigrated the union and asserted the impossibility of compromise. The conference disbanded without resolving the crisis, and Roosevelt formed a commission to investigate the strike. He also drew up a contingency plan under which the army would reopen the mines on behalf of the government, bypassing the owners. Roosevelt fretted that the mine owners were missing the point of what he was proposing, writing to a friend on 19 October, "I wish that capitalists would see that what I am advocating . . . is really in the interests of property, for it will save it from the danger of revolution." At the same time he made it clear he understood that "demagogues and agitators will not be pleased with the plan."[36] He may well have had Mother Jones in mind when he penned those words.

As Roosevelt worried, Secretary of War Elihu Root met with J. P. Morgan, whose banks held much of the debt of the railroads. Using his influence over the railroad presidents, Morgan cooperated with Root in drafting a statement for the mine owners to sign. In this statement they agreed in principle to abide by the findings of a presidentially appointed commission. Mitchell accepted the idea of empowering a commission, and on 20 October, the union voted to end the strike in the anthracite field. The men returned to work, the commission began its deliberations, and the Republicans retained their hold on Congress.

Mother Jones returned to West Virginia. Here, in winter 1902, she traveled with a friend from Illinois, UMWA organizer John H. Walker. They created union locals along the New River, Mother Jones often paying the required fees out of her salary. She recalled that it was a bloody business, noting in her autobiography how

> the work was not easy or safe and I was lucky to have so fearless
> a co-worker. Men who joined the union were blacklisted throughout
> the entire section. Their families were thrown out on the highways.
> Men were shot. They were beaten. Numbers disappeared and no trace
> of them [was] found. Store keepers were ordered not to sell to union
> men or their families. Meetings had to be held in the woods at night,
> in abandoned mines, in barns.[37]

This appears to have been no exaggeration: frontier justice reigned in the mining valleys of the state. In February 1903, at Stanaford Mountain, a deputy sheriff tried to arrest miners enjoined from meeting or marching near the mines. They chased him away, and the next night a posse of sheriff's deputies exacted their revenge by killing seven miners and wounding twenty others. Mother Jones later claimed to have been in the area and wrote how, alerted to the violence by a railroad station agent, she climbed up to the camp. She remembered entering one of the miner's cabins and finding a mother and son weeping "over the father's corpse." The coroner reported that the men had been murdered by gunmen in the employ of the coal company, but "nothing was ever done to punish the men who had taken their lives."[38] Memories of this injustice infused her rhetoric on numerous future occasions.

The 1902 West Virginia strike, unlike the simultaneous action in Pennsylvania, ended in defeat for the UMWA. The union did win one small but significant victory when operators of the Kanawha Valley recognized it, bringing some seven thousand miners into the union. Elsewhere, though, threats, promises of modest pay raises, "yellow-dog" contracts banning unions, and strikebreakers had the effect the operators desired. Beginning in early October, miners returned to work on terms offered before the strike began. Locals across the state recognized the impossibility of victory, and the fight for union recognition ended. Most West Virginia miners drifted away from the UMWA, and it would be another decade before West Virginia experienced a major coal strike, with Mother Jones at its center once more.

Long before then the anthracite coal commission had issued its report. This came in March 1903, and it recommended a 10 percent pay increase for miners (one-half of their demand), reducing the working day from ten to nine hours, allowing the miners to elect the checkweighmen who recorded their coal production, building uniform coal cars, and empowering a board to arbitrate future disputes. The commission ignored union demands for a universal ton, a written contract, and recognition. Despite its shortcomings the commission represented a historical sea change in labor relations. It had consisted of a military officer, a mining engineer, a mine owner, a federal judge, the Catholic bishop of Peoria, Illinois, and Edgar E. Clark, the grand chief of the Order of Railway Conductors. The last two had been appointed at Mitchell's insistence: labor had made its way to the national political table. Where in 1894 President Grover Cleveland had ordered federal troops to shoot workers during the Pullman strike, President Roosevelt had invited organized labor to become a partner in negotiations ending the conflict.

Mother Jones did not hide her disappointment, however. Unlike in 1900, when she had counseled compromise, she saw the 1902 strike as a missed opportunity for the union to make real, lasting gains. She felt that the union held all the cards, but Mitchell, awed by a presidential invitation and swayed by Roosevelt's considerable charm, had thrown them away. The union had the funds to win a protracted fight, and the operators were nervous about public opinion, particularly as winter approached. Mother Jones believed Mitchell had made a tactical error. She later wrote that "Mr. Mitchell was not dishonest but he had a weak point, and that was his love of flattery; and the [coal] interests used this weak point in further-ance of their designs."[39] The Mitchell–Roosevelt partnership angered her. She claimed that "the operators could have been made to deal with the unions if Mr. Mitchell had stood firm. A moral victory would have been won for the principle of unionism."[40] Though they remained on friendly terms for a while afterward, Mother Jones wrote in her autobiography that "Mr. Mitchell died a rich man, distrusted by the working people whom he once served."[41] On his part, President Roosevelt would confirm her low opinion of him in 1903 when he refused to meet her at the conclusion of the greatest piece of street theater of her career, the march of the mill children from Philadelphia to New York City.

6

Calling on President Roosevelt

THE COAL STRIKES OF 1902 took their toll on Mother Jones's faith in labor unions. Though she continued to correspond politely with John Mitchell, she grew disillusioned with him. In an October appearance in New York City she compared him to Abraham Lincoln, but privately she warned him to be wary of "what has come in the past to those who have been applauded by the public."[1] The 1902 anthracite strike had presented Mitchell with an extraordinary opportunity to win formal recognition for the United Mine Workers, but, swayed by President Theodore Roosevelt, he had chosen to compromise with the mine owners. Mother Jones felt he had allowed the president's charisma to trump his undoubted strategic abilities. That at least was how she framed matters in her autobiography. The reality was, as usual, more complex. Though at the time she clearly felt Mitchell had fallen short, her anger did not materialize until later. She continued to respect his leadership and to work for the UMWA while making overtures to the Socialist Party about becoming a lecturer.

Her active engagement with socialist politics dated from at least her friendship with J. A. Wayland, editor of the *Appeal to Reason*. Mother Jones advocated government ownership of industry and rewarding workers with the wealth they produced. She addressed a party rally at the Cooper Union in New York City in October 1902 on the subject of the mining strikes, making a favorable impression on journalists. One reporter noted that she "was attired in a black gown, her grey hair was neatly dressed, and she looked more like a dignified matron of Colonial days than the woman who has roughed it in the mines with what she terms in a slight Irish brogue 'me bhoys.'" Her rhetoric remained undiluted. She informed her listeners, "If you people know what an idiotic gang that crowd of capitalists are you'd have everything you want," and went on to condemn the legal system, the churches, and the police for upholding an unjust order.[2]

In March 1903 Mother Jones participated in a socialist rally in the Chicago Auditorium. She described the appalling living and working conditions in the mining districts of West Virginia and Pennsylvania, claiming that the miners "were beginning to realize that in socialism lay the only remedy, and they were eagerly adopting its teachings and methods." She then connected political action with the cause that would become her all-consuming passion during the summer of 1903: ending child labor. With dramatic exaggeration and employing pathos to good effect, she told her audience, "I see little children dragging themselves home from their work long after the sun has set, and throwing themselves down on the floor of their wretched homes utterly exhausted. They go to work at 4 o'clock in the morning and some of them work fourteen hours a day for two weeks, receiving at the end of that time 50 cents for their labor." She followed with an emotional appeal for pity, noting how "when they go to work in the morning they never know that they may not have to sacrifice an arm, or a leg, or a life during the day. Many of them are crippled or killed outright, but the news is skillfully kept from the newspapers. I do not say it is a shame that these children should be compelled to work fourteen hours a day. I say it is an outrage they should be allowed to work one hour a day." She demanded to know "whether you are going to continue weakly to vote for the parties which are upholding the masters of these children, or whether you will strike like men for socialism at the ballot box."[3] Though destined to be disappointed in the electoral prospects of the socialist politics she supported, Mother Jones would remain convinced that voting socialist was the only justifiable action for those who possessed the franchise and desired social justice. The Democrats and the Republicans, she complained, were controlled by capitalists and offered nothing to working people.

Her March appearance for the Socialist Party and a subsequent letter to its secretary, William Mailly, led to an opportunity to work for the party. While she eventually declined, it is clear that Mailly's proposal came at her initiative. Her letter to Mailly has not survived, but his reply made her "an official offer to become a lecturer." Mailly hoped she would do so because "I can see by your letter that you are tired of your present work."

Breaker Boys in Kohinor Mine, Shenandoah City, Pennsylvania (1891), courtesy Library of Congress Prints and Photographs Division

He anticipated being able to pay her "$3.00 a day and your hotel and traveling expenses," which would have represented a significant increase on her United Mine Workers' salary of $500 a year less expenses. He would schedule her for four or five lectures weekly, mostly to local branches of the institution. Mailly told her, "It would be a big thing for the party and for me if I could get you," and promised, "You need not become tangled up in any of the party affairs if you did not wish to," an admission that internal wrangling was a fact of life in the organization. He tried to set her mind at rest about being perpetually exhausted, writing, "From a personal standpoint I believe you would be better off and you would not be over-worked as you are now." He also appealed to her vanity, noting, "You are a favorite with all the comrades [and] you would have none of the worries that beset you now." Mailly tempted her further with the news that this was an auspicious time for the socialists, who looked forward optimistically to the election of 1904.[4]

The idea would percolate for a year or so, but for now Mother Jones expressed disgust at how working people voted. In Toledo, Ohio, in 1903 she condemned union members who "get down on your knees like a lot of Yahoos when you want something" and beg for it. By supporting the two main parties, she told the large audience, "you haven't sense enough to take peaceably what belongs to you through the ballot."[5] Because of corruption and laziness, the Democrats and the Republicans were only interested in helping those who already had power and could not be trusted to do what was best for the country. She particularly excoriated "that school of reformers who say capital and labor must join hands." In her eyes, "a contented workman is no good. All progress stops in the contented man. I'm for agitation. It's the greatest factor for progress."[6] Despite Mailly's offer and her telling an audience of labor union members in Cincinnati, "Let us have a class conscious proletariat party," her turn to political activism lay in the future.[7]

Before she engaged in party politics with the socialists Mother Jones agitated for the abolition of child labor. The 1900 census had revealed that one in every six children under the age of sixteen worked in remunerative employment in the United States. Worse, most observers agreed this was an underestimate because parents lied about their children's ages to get them employed. Children's earnings constituted one-third of total family income in many urban neighborhoods, and their meager wages often meant the difference between starvation and survival. Progressive Era reformers lamented the psychic and social costs of child labor, and ending it became one of their key demands. Mother Jones, long dedicated to stopping the practice, became a leading exponent of legally banning child labor in 1903, though her refusal to consider cooperating with Progressives such as Jane Addams or Florence Kelley limited her influence. Shunning middle-class reformers derived from her belief that they were not interested in radical change, merely ameliorating conditions as they existed. Her analysis of the situation was, overall, accurate.

Condemning child labor had been one of the recurring topics in Mother Jones's speeches. She wove it in with seemingly unrelated subjects, such as her presentations to UMWA conventions about recruiting members and organizing strikes. In 1901, for example, she asked the union to take a stand against child labor, telling delegates, "You have done your work magnificently and well; but we have before us the grandest and greatest work of civilization. We have before us yet the emancipation of the children of this nation."[8] She told miners that they were responsible for the fact that children continued to work because they participated in a system by which "the capitalistic class has met you face to face today to take the girls as well as the boys out of the cradle."[9] But the main beneficiaries were the owners, who, she contended, "have built their mines and breakers to take your boys out of the cradle; they have built their factories to take your girls; they have built on the bleeding, quivering hearts of yourselves and your children their palaces."[10] Child labor undermined the nation, and banning it would be a giant step toward the family wage, revealing her conventional view of gender relations. Mother Jones believed that instituting a family wage would allow women and children to remain in the sanctity of the home while male breadwinners entered the rough world of work.

In her Toledo address she raised the subject of child labor at the conclusion of her oration. She told the well-dressed upper-class women who came to hear her speak, "While this commercial cannibalism is reaching into the cradle; pulling girls into the factory to be ruined; pulling children into the factory to be destroyed; you are doing all in the name of Christianity, you, who are at home nursing your poodle dogs. It's high time you got out and worked for humanity. Christianity will take care of itself."[11] The guilt she heaped onto her upper-class listeners also drove Mother Jones: guilt about surviving the Irish famine, the yellow fever, and the Chicago fire; guilt at participating in an economy built on the work of children; and guilt at rumors of her checkered past. In an effort to assuage this guilt her refrain during summer 1903 was, "I work for the children unborn. No children in the mines and mills of the future is my cry."[12]

An unexpected opportunity to put this cry into action arrived in 1903. On 1 June, Philadelphia silk weavers struck when manufacturers tried to weaken local unions, especially the Textile Workers' Union. The workers, some of whom had walked out in late May, demanded a fifty-five-hour maximum workweek and the prohibition of night work for women and children. By the time Mother Jones traveled to the area in June, six hundred or more mills had closed and 100,000 workers, including sixteen thousand children, were out of work. In this, the largest strike in Philadelphia's history, the employers hoped to outlast the workers in order to crush their unions and regain complete control over the workplace.

Mother Jones failed initially in her efforts to garner publicity for the strike. She held a series of well-attended rallies near Independence Hall, but the local newspapers ignored them. She took a group of children to city hall, but the mill owners paid no attention. Reporters told her they could not cover her meetings because capitalist shareholders controlled the newspapers. To this she replied, "Well, I've got stock in those little children."[13] She found inspiration in the Liberty Bell's concurrent tour of the country, seeing in it a precedent for taking Philadelphia-area factory children to New York City. She also drew on her experiences with Coxey's Army and, more recently, a planned trip that never took place. In August 1902 the anthracite miners' wives had announced their intention to "emulate the example of Coxey's army and march on foot to Washington to appeal to congress for help." Mother Jones explained at the time that "the wives of the miners will march on Washington if the strike is not settled by next winter. We will shake them up down there. We will have a popular congress there when the other congress is in session."[14] The strike ended before the march could take place, but clearly the idea remained with Mother Jones. She proposed the 1903 textile workers' march to publicize the strike and shine a national spotlight on the practice of child labor.

In retrospect the march appeared more organized and coherent than it was at the time. Mother Jones wrote in her autobiography:

> I decided to go with the children to see President Roosevelt to ask him to have Congress pass a law prohibiting the exploitation of childhood. I thought that President Roosevelt might see these mill children and compare them with his own little ones who were spending the summer on the seashore at Oyster Bay. I thought, too, out of politeness, we might call on [J. P.] Morgan in Wall Street who owned the mines where many of these children's fathers worked.[15]

In reality, the march began after she had contacted New York socialists and proposed walking to the city "to collect funds for the 75,000 or more striking textile workers at the mills of Philadelphia."[16] The executive committee of the Socialist Party planned to meet her and help organize events to bring the plight of the textile workers before the public, promising financial support and publicity for the strikers.

The march was plagued by bad weather, disgruntled participants, and adverse publicity. The textile employees who formed "Mother Jones's Industrial Army"—the name invoked Coxey's Army—worked in the silk mills of Kensington, Pennsylvania. Numbering between 340 and 400 people, they paraded out of Philadelphia behind a band of six fifes and five drums. Bearing banners announcing "Fifty-Five Hours or Nothing," "Give Us More Schools," "Prosperity! Where is Our Share?" and "We Ask Only for Justice," the children carried with them "an assortment of glass jewelry, fancy dresses, masks, megaphones, and other articles for use in getting up tableaus. 'Mr. Capital' and 'Mrs. Millowner' will be shown gorgeously attired."[17] Mother Jones styled the marchers "Mother Jones's Crusaders" and only later used the phrase "Children's Crusade," but the majority of the marchers were adults. Diversion at a time of stress and hardship seems to have been one of her goals, for Mother Jones wrote that "they were on strike and I thought they might as well have a little recreation."[18] Each marcher carried utensils, with eight wagonloads of bread and canned food. A portable oven accompanied the procession.

Leaving Philadelphia on 7 July 1903, they marched to Easton and then to Morrisville, on the banks of the Delaware River. Mother Jones visited Trenton, the state capital, on 9 July, where she spoke to the Plumbers' Union of her desire to hold "a mass meeting in Madison Square Garden."[19] Here she mentioned President Roosevelt for the first time, telling a crowd of some five thousand people that "Roosevelt is right on race suicide, but he is only partly right on its cause. Women have learned that their children are taken away from them and put to work when they should be in school. What is the use of bringing a lot of children into the world to make more money for plutocrats, while their little lives are being ground out in the mill and workshop?"[20] Asked about rumors that she was leading her army to see Morgan and Roosevelt, she told a reporter, "Oh, that's only a joke. Sometimes it takes extraordinary means to attract ordinary interest."[21] The president had become a strategic device, but his summer residence was not yet the planned end point of her march.

By Trenton the army was down to about 280 people, including twelve boys aged thirteen or younger. The next day the weather turned against the marchers, a storm thwarting their plan to enter Princeton. On the outskirts of the town they found shelter in an old barn on an estate owned by former president Grover Cleveland. His unintentional magnanimity (Cleveland and his family were away at the time) won him Mother Jones's endorsement "if he should happen to be the next nominee for President of the United States."[22] She was either forgetting or ignoring Cleveland's role in the Pullman strike, providing another example of a pattern of behavior evident throughout her career: Mother Jones praised prominent men who showed her kindness regardless of their previous action toward workers. This capacity for forgiveness would confound and occasionally enrage her colleagues in the labor movement.

After the storm abated the procession made its way into Princeton, where Mother Jones took advantage of her proximity to one of the nation's oldest institutions of higher education to deliver a lecture. On open ground adjacent to Princeton University, on 11 July, she pointed to the young marchers standing next to her and told the professors and students gathered to hear her "that the rich robbed these little children of any education of the lowest order that they might send their sons and daughters to places of higher education. That they used the hands and feet of little children that they might buy automobiles for their wives and police dogs for their daughters to talk French to." Offering her auditors "a text book on economics," she showed them a ten-year-old boy who earned a weekly wage of $3 for six ten-hour days and "who was stooped over like an old man from carrying bundles of yarn that weighed seventy-five pounds."[23] This sort of practical demonstration had the desired effect of earning publicity and shocking audiences by forcing them to see the evils of child labor firsthand. That she occasionally exaggerated did not concern Mother Jones; the higher truth and the greater good were more important than a strict accounting of her case. She wanted action, not investigation.

Just five days into the march her "industrial army" numbered only about forty people as incessant rain and continued discomfort discouraged some of the marchers. It is not clear whether the reduction was planned, with a grand beginning and a core of marchers reaching New York City, but nonetheless some of the participants criticized Mother Jones herself. She had not been walking but traveling by train and streetcar, joining the marchers on the edge of towns to lead them into the centers, for "Mother Jones is sixty years old and over, and is not much on rigors herself, so she has kept up with the army on railroad and trolley cars."[24] The members of the army had been mostly sleeping in tents, while their sixty-five-year-old leader stayed in hotels. Her advanced years did not excuse her behavior in the eyes of one defector, who told a reporter as he abandoned the march, "We seem to be a sort of sideshow to help her get some notoriety about the country."[25] Another, more pragmatic marcher blamed the attrition on an inadequate supply of beer.

The tone and content of her speeches did not always meet with approval, either. The president of the New Brunswick Labor Federation distanced his group from one of her remarks by noting that "while organized labor is in full sympathy with 'Mother' Jones's views on child labor, she did not express the sentiment of organized labor toward the Church." This union leader saw "no reason why the Church and labor should not be considered as allies, working together for the uplifting of humanity."[26]

Relief came in Rahway, New Jersey, where the owner of the Rahway Inn housed the marchers free of charge. Their first act upon entering the city "consisted of taking a bath in the public fountain," after which the men received a complimentary shave.[27] The marchers enjoyed similar acts of generosity in other towns. In Elizabeth, for example, the local branch of the Socialist Party fed the dwindling army, now down to thirty marchers. After two days in Elizabeth, where "most of the saloons in the districts where working people live or work are holding open house, and everything is free to the members of the army," the marchers seemed quite happy to stay put. Though Mother Jones asked them to desist from consuming alcohol, one participant told reporters they had "been better received here than at any place along the road."[28]

By 13 July, six days after leaving Philadelphia, Mother Jones changed her objective from collecting funds in New York City to traveling "to Oyster

Bay to ask the President what is the meaning of prosperity, and incidentally to arouse public sympathy for the textile workers who are out on strike at Philadelphia."[29] Roosevelt, enjoying his customary summer hiatus at Sagamore Hill, began to plan his escape from the approaching army. The *New York Times* asserted that Mother Jones would need to make formal arrangements to meet with Roosevelt and speculated, "It is reasonably certain the President would not receive the 'army' as a body."[30] The next day the newspaper reported that "plans have been perfected quietly to prevent 'Mother' Jones and her so-called army of textile workers from visiting Oyster Bay. The matter is in the hands of the Secret Service and the New York Police Department."[31] Undeterred, Mother Jones told an audience at a Socialist Party picnic in Paterson, New Jersey, "I am going to complete the journey to Oyster Bay with my army to see the President. The newspapers say he will not see me. I am going there to find out if he is the President of the capitalists only, or whether he is the President of the workingmen too. If he is the President of the capitalists only, he will be wiped out at the next election."[32]

Two days later she was in a conciliatory mood, informing reporters:

> I have sent President Roosevelt a respectful letter explaining to him what my errand is and asking for an appointment. I have received no answer. I wish to state it is my public belief that the president has not seen my letter. He is too much of a gentleman to have treated with contempt any message simple and respectful, to his high office and to himself, as this letter was. We deserve President Roosevelt's commendation and congratulations rather than the discourtesy of subordinate persons who misrepresent him.

Taking a swipe at John Mitchell, she continued, "The president has had conferences with other labor leaders, as his clerks ought to know, who, by no fault of their own, could not show any such record as ours."[33] She referred to her letter published in New York–area newspapers on 16 July in which she challenged Roosevelt, "as father of us all," to take an interest in the textile strike and to pressure Congress into passing an eight-hour bill. Recounting the horrors of child labor, she requested "that the children be taken from the industrial prisons of this nation, and given their right of attending schools, so that in years to come better citizens will be given to this republic."[34]

On 22 July, two weeks into the march, the small army camped out at Jersey City Heights, within striking distance of New York. Representatives from the Socialist Party and the Central Federated Union of New York tried to obtain a parade permit from the acting police commissioner, Major Ebstein, but were rebuffed. Undeterred, Mother Jones took her case to city hall. Meeting with the mayor, Progressive Seth Low, she requested the much-needed permit and told him "that her army was a peaceful organization of working people en route to Oyster Bay to see President Roosevelt, and that none of them had the least idea of violating any law and she requested that he give her permission to parade the streets."[35] Low saw the light after Mother Jones complained about the hypocrisy of hosting German royalty and Chinese politicians at taxpayers' expense while refusing the same right to American citizens. Parade permit secured, "the army band, consisting of two fifes and two drums, was assembled, and the army formed in line of battle. In front of the warriors walked a number of local Socialists, while the army itself was led by 'Mother' Jones."[36]

Mother Jones remained optimistically convinced that Roosevelt would meet with her. She told reporters, "Oh yes, I shall certainly go to Oyster Bay, but I will take only these three little boys with me, to see the President. If he refuses to see the boys, why, I will not see him, that's certain." She continued, "I think he will see us. Why shouldn't he? We are law-abiding American citizens."[37] Referring to the lavish reception provided during the recent visit of Prince Henry of Germany, she said,

> We are quietly marching toward the president's home. I believe he can do something for these children, although the press declares he cannot. Congress last year passed a bill giving $45,000 to fill the stomach of an old prince, and [Roosevelt] indorsed that, and if he could do that he surely could tell congress to pass a bill that would take the children out of the God-accursed mills and put them in the schools.[38]

Her faith in the president's power would be sorely tested before the march ended, as would her belief that he was a "gentleman."

Prior to leaving for Oyster Bay the army had a date at Coney Island. Visiting as guests of the owner of Bostock's Animal Show, the marchers enjoyed watching leopards, monkeys, and a baby elephant perform before turning the tables on the beasts and putting on their own show. In front of a painted backdrop featuring two Roman emperors and a large crowd in the Coliseum, the children stood in cages normally reserved for the animals as Mother Jones told an enthusiastic audience,

> After a long and weary march, with more miles to travel, we are on our way to see President Roosevelt at Oyster Bay. We will ask him

to recommend the passage of a bill by Congress to protect children against the greed of the manufacturer. We want him to hear the wail of the children who never have a chance to go to school, but work from ten to eleven hours a day in the textile mills of Philadelphia, weaving the carpets that he and you walk on.[39]

She warmed to her theme, speaking on the evils of child labor and the fact that, though "you are told that every American-born male citizen has a chance of being president," children who work in mills and mines were robbed of that dream.[40] The crowd cheered her on, and this and other positive receptions gave her renewed hope and strengthened her belief that she would reach her objective. The newspapers reported on 27 July, two days before Mother Jones planned to travel to Oyster Bay, "The coming of 'Mother' Jones and her army is awaited with much interest. Despite stories that they would be kept out of Oyster Bay nothing of the kind is anticipated, and no such step was ever considered." But the story continued, "About their going to Sagamore Hill is another matter."[41] An optimist who expected to get what she wanted, Mother Jones ignored this last statement.

Before setting off for Sagamore Hill, however, the army attempted to meet with Republican New York senator Thomas C. Platt, who was then seeking reelection. Borrowing the baby elephant from Bostock's Animal Show, Mother Jones led her parade to Manhattan Beach. Making their way along the Atlantic shore and into the grounds of the Oriental Hotel, the marchers waited while Mother Jones tracked down Platt. The venerable senator, having been warned of her approach, fled through a rear entrance and escaped by train to New York City. Having missed her quarry, the doughty reformer consulted with the hotel manager, who agreed to feed her army and charge the bill to the senator. But Platt's escape was a sign of things to come.

Despite the publicity newspapers gave her letter, Mother Jones received no reply from President Roosevelt. Undaunted, she traveled on 29 July by train from New York City to Oyster Bay with two of the adult leaders of her march and three of the boys. They stayed in the village for less than an hour, time enough to be turned away from Sagamore Hill when Roosevelt's acting secretary, B. F. Barnes, told her that she needed to make an application in writing for an appointment. Unbeknownst to Mother Jones, the president had taken two of his sons and three of their cousins for an overnight campout at a nearby bay. When she discovered this, she accused him of cowardice and added it to her supply of barbs to throw at "Teddy." Worried about the consequences if Roosevelt continued to evade the labor leader, the *New York Times* editorialized, "If he refuses to see her she will become a martyr of a sort—a woman with a grievance against him not altogether imaginary."[42]

Exasperated but stubborn, Mother Jones wrote to the president on 30 July as Barnes had advised her. She informed him that she knew of the existence of state laws banning child labor and of the constitutional limits on his power. But she requested his intervention because factory and mine owners regularly flouted the laws and he had, after all, intervened on the side of working people in the 1902 anthracite strike. Playing on his fears about race suicide (the contemporary belief that white Americans were being "outbred" by other races), she proposed that he champion federal legislation banning child labor:

> I ask, Mr. President, what kind of citizen will be the child who toils twelve hours a day in an unsanitary atmosphere, stunted mentally and physically, and surrounded with often immoral influences[?] Denied education, he cannot assume the duties of true citizenship, and enfeebled physically he falls a ready victim to the perverting influences which our present economic conditions have created.[43]

Mother Jones had a straightforward agenda in mind. Her plan, as she had told reporters on 23 July, was "to ask him to consider the advisability of putting into his next message to congress some recommendation for national laws" banning the employment of children.[44] In her letter of 30 July she asked Roosevelt "if our commercial greatness has not cost us too much by being built upon the quivering hearts of helpless children? We who know of these sufferings have taken up their cause and are now marching toward you in the hope that your tender heart will counsel with us to abolish this crime."[45] She requested a meeting with him, alerting him to the fact that "our destination is New York City, and after that Oyster Bay. As your children, may we hope to have the pleasure of an audience? We only ask that you advise us as to the best course."[46] Barnes brushed her off two days later with a letter reminding her how "under the constitution it is not at present seen how Congress has power to act in such a matter. It would seem that the States alone at present have the power to deal with the subject."[47]

The parade of the mill children was over. It had provided publicity, not all of it positive, for the aging labor organizer and shone a national spotlight on the issue of child labor. As the remaining marchers made their way back to Philadelphia, the press rallied around Roosevelt and ridiculed Mother Jones. Contradicting its earlier statement that she would become a martyr, the *New York Times* condemned "such absurd humbugs as the leaders of industrial armies like Coxey's or Mother Jones's." Recalling her visit to Bostock's Animal Show, the newspaper asserted, "We are probably justified in assuming that the voice of the Coney Island lions in response to Mother Jones's harangue signified that they found it very cheap and sawdusty in the detail of stuffing, and that from most and probably all points of observation she was a tedious and oppressive incubus to be coughed down out of hand."[48] The *Chicago Daily Tribune*, which until the very end had shown some sympathy for her actions, chided her for "going to the wrong place and the wrong person." It suggested that she should have taken her "small army of operatives" to ask the senior senator from the Quaker State to "persuade the Pennsylvania legislature to enact stringent child labor laws." The newspaper conceded that the fact "that such laws are needed is undeniable" but worried that President Roosevelt should not "take in hand . . . the regulation of the child labor laws."[49] Finally, not two weeks after the march had ended in defeat, the *Times* claimed to have uncovered the real motive for Mother Jones's action: she and the male marchers had been in the pay of the socialists, and "her pilgrimage through New Jersey has been a shrewd move in the interests of the Socialist Party."[50]

It is certainly true that the events of 1903, and her growing distance from the United Mine Workers of America, found Mother Jones becoming increasingly involved with the Socialist Party. But it is also true that labor unions assisted the march at least as frequently as socialist groups, and she actively sought their help. Indeed, she convinced the UMWA to donate $9,000 to aid the striking Philadelphia textile workers. Mother Jones did begin to move more firmly toward political activism, but not before she traveled to Colorado and Utah to assist striking miners. As her correspondence of 1902 demonstrated, she had not ignored socialist politics. She long held that the workers of America produced the wealth of America; by 1903 she was beginning to articulate clearly and forcefully the labor theory of value holding that all wealth beyond the original costs of raw materials derived from the application of human effort. Those who altered raw materials to make commodities sold in the marketplace—that is, workers—should receive the bulk of the value so created. This was no doubt reinforced by her reading of the *Appeal to Reason*, especially after it hired Ernest Untermann, American translator of Marx and Engels, to give the paper a firmer grounding in socialist theory. Her ideas may have been slightly eccentric—at one point she called J. P. Morgan a socialist because he had consolidated New England railroads into a single trust—but they were uncompromisingly and, once reached, consistently held. She saw and deplored the injustice evident in the unequal distribution of wealth and railed against capitalists who lived like kings while their workers starved in slums.

Her encounter at Sagamore Hill generated an intense hatred of Theodore Roosevelt. After 1903 Mother Jones would treat him with a contempt born of disillusionment. He had shown himself to be a friend of labor in the 1902 anthracite strike, demonstrating respect for John Mitchell and bringing labor unions into negotiations brokered by the executive branch. But Mother Jones was uninterested in precedent; she wanted results, and she wanted them immediately. For her it followed that if Roosevelt could intervene to end a strike, he could intervene to end child labor, a practice she perceived as an unambiguous evil. That he not only failed to act but had willfully ignored her she found unforgivable. Mother Jones would continue to court powerful men, including John D. Rockefeller Jr., and would exonerate them from charges that they hurt working people if they met with her and treated her courteously. Roosevelt had signally failed to do either.

Her invective against Theodore Roosevelt never let up. In 1905 she called him "the Capitalist Henchman Rosefelt," and by 1912, when he ran for the presidency as the Progressive Party candidate, she sarcastically invoked his postpresidential African safari by calling him "Teddy the monkey chaser."[51] She would call him a coward, telling audiences how he sent "secret service men from his palace down at Oyster Bay, all the way to New York, to watch an old gray-headed woman."[52] She continued to advise working people to vote socialist, when she suggested they bother to vote at all. Her dealings with Roosevelt left her ambivalent about the ballot: she preferred direct action with the aim of seizing control of the factories, mines, and railroads to voting. She nonetheless became increasingly involved in socialist agitation and even became a lecturer for the Socialist Party. Before that, however, she would travel to Colorado for her first taste of labor conflict in the West.

7

Defending Undesirables, Promoting Socialism

MOTHER JONES HAD BECOME a national figure at the time of the march of the mill children, attacked and praised with equal vigor. From October 1903 to June 1912—a period devoid of strikes on a par with the precedent-making 1902 anthracite dispute—she traveled incessantly. Widely known as the "miner's angel" for her work in the coalfields, she spent her time fighting injustice, organizing unions, and promoting socialism. This nine-year period began with an unsuccessful coal strike in Colorado, after which Mother Jones resigned from the United Mine Workers and joined the Socialist Party as a lecturer, and ended with her leaving the party to be reemployed by the union. Defending American and foreign activists arrested by the U.S. government absorbed much of her time. Two cases in particular occupied her energies, one involving leaders of the Western Federation of Miners and a second embracing leaders of the Liberal Party of Mexico. Mother Jones became dissatisfied with the Socialist Party after a dispute over money in 1911 and her perception of its leaders as more interested in living well than in waging class war. By 1912 she had rejoined the UMWA and, in June of that year, fought once more against West Virginia mine operators.

Because socialist thought was used to create and justify totalitarian regimes after 1917, it is easy today to equate communitarian ideologies with tyranny. For Mother Jones and many other Americans in the first decade of the twentieth century, however, the equation was reversed: the capitalist United States threatened freedom, while socialist ideas promised liberty and equality. Socialists attacked the U.S. government for pursuing a virulently anti-labor policy at home and a quiet but no less aggressive expansionist economic program abroad. Socialism, they argued, held out the prospect for creating a society in which the producers of wealth—that is to say, the working class—could expect a decent standard of living assisted by the government. For its advocates socialism implied seriousness of purpose, and they enjoyed a wide-ranging library of books, pamphlets, and newspapers expounding and explaining socialism. To the dismay of Mother Jones and others, socialists argued regularly and bitterly among themselves about the correct path to the future and the finer points of their doctrines. The two main socialist parties, the Socialist Party of America (led by Eugene Debs) and the Socialist Labor Party (a smaller group revolving around Daniel DeLeon) seemed to Mother Jones more inclined to battle each other than to fight for working people. To its enemies, socialism threatened to destroy democracy, and its adherents were labeled dangerous fanatics whose words and actions unsettled contented working people.

Mother Jones sat simultaneously on the fringes and at the center of this ferment. Her commitment to institutions, whether labor unions or political parties, was lukewarm at best, and her philosophy was an idiosyncratic synthesis of three sincerely held and doggedly pursued beliefs: labor produced all wealth and should therefore share in it equally; justice was being systematically destroyed by capitalist control of the legal system; and only by engendering class conflict could reform occur. Inciting class war to create a just society under the banner of the labor theory of value linked her United Mine Workers organizing with her Socialist Party activism.

Her effectiveness as an organizer and speaker was tempered by scandals at the beginning and end of her decade of socialist agitation. The first instance occurred in early 1904, when a Denver tabloid called *Polly Pry* published rumors of her career as a prostitute and madam. The second case began in 1909 after she had demanded repayment of a personal loan from a leading socialist, John Mahlon Barnes, who countered that he had repaid her. When an investigative committee of the Socialist Party found him innocent she rejoined the United Mine Workers. The two episodes left her feeling alone and served as bookends to a period during which she fought against injustice, promoted socialism, and suffered bouts of ill-health.

In October 1903 UMWA president John Mitchell sent Mother Jones to Colorado to prepare the ground for an impending strike by coal miners there. Colorado had become a state as recently as 1876 and was being rapidly opened by mining companies because of its wealth of natural resources.

The most important, iron ore and coal, attracted the attention of investors from across the globe. They bought shares in the four corporations that, by 1903, had gained control of the Colorado mining industry. The Northern Coal and Coke Company owned most of the mineral deposits in the upper half of the state, while in the southern field the Victor Coal Company and the American Fuel Company (both owned by Denver businessman John C. Osgood) vied for hegemony with the Colorado Fuel and Iron Corporation (CFI), operated by East Coast capitalist John D. Rockefeller Jr. from his office at 26 Broadway in New York City. One of the most powerful and feared business magnates of early-twentieth-century America, Rockefeller would provide Mother Jones with a brutal but charming adversary.

Rockefeller had purchased CFI in 1902 and hoped to make a quick killing. Unfortunately for his hopes of an instant profit, the property had been overvalued and proved a bad investment because of corruption and incompetent management. Rockefeller and his father, John D. Rockefeller Sr., flush with cash after selling their interest in Minnesota's Mesabi iron ore deposits to U.S. Steel, had been taken for a ride by a business partner, George Gould. Gould, son of deceased railroad baron and incorrigible swindler Jay Gould, knew of the problems at CFI but recommended the investment to Rockefeller anyway. The inability of CFI to provide Rockefeller with the windfall profits he expected stiffened his already firm opposition to unions, making life difficult for Mother Jones and her fellow United Mine Workers organizers.

When Mother Jones arrived in Colorado it was another mining union, the Western Federation of Miners (WFM), that was earning headlines. From its 1893 origins in Butte, Montana, the WFM had grown quickly in the western states, earning a not entirely undeserved reputation for radicalism and violence. It had been on strike against the metalliferous mine owners since February. The 1903–4 strike began in Colorado City with demands for higher wages quickly followed by the firing of local union leaders working in the mines. The strike then spread to other mines in the area, took a violent turn, and culminated in the deaths of thirty-three people in the bombing of a copper smelter at Cripple Creek. Mother Jones met WFM leaders William "Big Bill" Haywood and Charles Moyer, with whom she remained in contact after the strike. She abhorred conflict between unions, always trying to find common ground for the sake of class unity and avoiding expensive and divisive arguments. She did not care which union a worker joined provided he or she did so. All labor unions fought the same battle against capitalists in her eyes. As Mother Jones put it in a speech to the UMWA, "Whenever you can organize a man bring him into the United Mine Workers, bring him into the Western

Federation, bring him into the Carpenters' Union—bring him into any union." Convincing working people to join unions meant "you have taken one away from the common enemy and joined him with you to fight the common enemy."[1] This was no less true in Colorado. Though the two mining unions competed for some of the same workers, Mother Jones wrote to her friend William B. Wilson, secretary-treasurer of the UMWA, that the Federation leaders "strongly and honestly agreed with me that there should be no lines dividing labor. We are to meet some time in the future and outline Plans for the amalga[mation.] These are fine fellows, and if I bring no other result my visit here will not have been lost."[2]

These hopes were dashed by fundamental differences between the two unions. Where the UMWA leadership was cautious and willing to compromise with mine operators, the WFM leaders were socialists inclined to pursue militant means in the cause of revolution. The UMWA leaders sought to improve living and working conditions for members; those who guided the Federation saw strikes as a path to radical social change. The UMWA bargained with owners in search of mutually agreeable compromises, while Federation leaders fought for "a complete revolution of the present system of industrial slavery." Mother Jones found virtue, if not common ground, in both approaches. Like the UMWA she saw the value of compromise, but with the WFM she wanted to overthrow the capitalist system. She agreed with Federation leader Charles Moyer that "as labor produces all the wealth, such wealth belongs to the producer thereof."[3]

Always an optimist at the beginning of a strike, Mother Jones felt sure of victory in Colorado despite overwhelming odds. The UMWA could claim only a few hundred members in a state with thousands of coal miners, but they had many grievances. The biggest complaints were low pay and deductions for food and rent. The owners falsely claimed that their miners were well paid, reporting that they earned between $80 and $100 monthly, but an investigation around the turn of the century by the Colorado Bureau of Labor Statistics discovered an average annual income of $370, around $31 per month. This was approximately a third of the earnings of bricklayers in Colorado, a group with whom miners were often compared with respect to their skill levels.

As in West Virginia, conditions in the mining camps restricted union organizing. Colorado miners lived in company housing and bought food and supplies at company stores. The operators paid the men by the ton, raising the specter of being underpaid, and miners knew they risked being fired and evicted for showing an interest in unions. Ethnic differences limited the potential for cooperation between the two fields. In the north, miners of British extraction predominated; Italians, Slavs, and other more recent immigrant groups held sway in the south. Business owners controlled politics in the state, a fact driven home the year before Mother Jones arrived when the legislature, responding to pressure from large employers, refused to act on a referendum mandating an eight-hour day. Though it was passed by voters in 1902, politicians allowed the measure to die quietly.

Despite these forbidding odds the UMWA requested a conference with the four big coal companies to discuss miners' grievances. The owners categorically refused to meet the union. Miners' delegates therefore gathered in Pueblo, where they authorized a strike and endorsed socialist politics, demonstrating that state-level leaders had a greater taste for militant action than their national counterparts in Indianapolis. Despite the union's weakness in Colorado, 90 percent of the coal miners in the state joined the strike when it began on 9 November 1903, indicating the depth of their unhappiness. Newspapers reported that "the men today walked out in such numbers that even the officers of the union are astonished" and warned that "every indication points to the most disastrous labor struggle the state has ever known."[4] Mother Jones saw things in similarly apocalyptic terms, writing to the Colorado State Federation of Labor, "You are the bulwark of the nation. The day dawneth when you shall get your own."[5] The companies moved quickly to evict striking miners, who immediately relocated to tent colonies established by the union. Citing Roosevelt's mediation in the anthracite strike of the previous year and fearing the effects of a prolonged strike on the economy, state business owners appealed to the president to intervene. Coal reserves were negligible, a situation businessmen blamed on the coal companies, telling reporters that "even for the last three months, while the present strike has been under discussion, the industries were misled by the operators, who told them they would be cared for in any contingency."[6] Such was the unexpected strength of the strike that coal-powered streetcars stopped running in Boulder, where the mines were located three short miles outside the city.

John Mitchell initially threw the weight of the union behind the Colorado strikers. At a convention of the American Federation of Labor (AFL) on 14 November 1903 he opposed Samuel Gompers, the powerful president of that federation, by calling for a levy on AFL funds of $1,000 to assist the striking miners. But when the Northern Coal and Coke Company offered to settle the strike in its mines by increasing pay and instituting the eight-hour day, Mitchell reverted to type by calling for a compromise. He recommended that the miners of the northern field accept the offer and return to work. On 21 November, miners' delegates met in Louisville, near Denver, where the week before they had rejected an inferior offer by just six votes. This time, following speeches from union leaders urging acceptance, settlement seemed assured. But near the end of the meeting Mother Jones arrived with UMWA district president William Howells. Howells spoke against accepting the offer, and the miners then called for Mother Jones to address them. She obliged and, in one of the shortest speeches of her career, reminded them of their duty to coal miners in the southern field. She convinced them to remain on strike, telling them:

> Brothers, you English speaking miners of the northern fields promised your southern brothers, seventy percent of whom do not speak English, that you would support them to the end. Now you are asked to betray them, to make a separate settlement. You have a common enemy and it is your duty to fight to a finish. . . . The enemy seeks to conquer by dividing your ranks, by making distinctions between North and South, between American and foreign. You are all miners, fighting a common cause, a common master.[7]

She placed class solidarity above other sources of identity, telling miners, "I know of no East or West, North or South when it comes to my class fighting the battle for justice." Victory in the class war could only be attained by remaining unified: "I would say we will all go to glory together or we will die and go down together."[8] After her speech the delegates rejected the company offer by a vote of 228 to 165, and the men remained on strike, but the Mother Jones effect turned out to be short-lived. Two days later, after Mitchell had told UMWA leaders in the region to impress upon the men the importance of settling the strike, delegates voted 483 to 130 to return to work on terms offered by mine operators. Mother Jones was livid: this, along with his sellout at the conclusion of the 1902 anthracite strike, led her to brand John Mitchell a class traitor.

The vote of the miners in the northern field highlighted one of the limitations of Mother Jones's approach to organizing: when she was not physically present, her work risked collapsing. Her success rested on her personality and charisma as much as on her organizing skills. As a speaker her power derived from the contrast between her dowdy appearance and the rhetoric she delivered in the vernacular of the miners. By refusing to become embroiled in union politics, or indeed in the inner workings of any organization, she placed a self-imposed limit on her power. Her reasons for doing this are clear: convinced of the righteousness of her cause and of her duty to lead it, she would not make the types of compromises—ideological and personal—necessary to forge sometimes unsavory alliances in order to exert internal institutional influence. But Mother Jones worked in an increasingly bureaucratic age when the efficient and sustained mobilization of resources occurred through the very type of institutional maneuvering she denigrated.

As winter dragged on the conflict grew more violent. State authorities claimed to have uncovered Western Federation of Miners' plots to dynamite the mines at Cripple Creek, to derail a train carrying strikebreakers, and to blow up the governor. The National Guard, present from the beginning of the metalliferous strike, increasingly favored the mine operators. The arrival of guns and ammunition from the federal arsenal at Rock Island, Illinois, prompted the local commander, General Sherman M. Bell, to warn that "we will fight it out in Colorado if it takes every ablebodied man in the state, and some who are disabled, to the end that order is maintained and socialism, anarchy, and moyerism are wiped off the earth and there is not a grease spot left to assassinate, dynamite, molest, disturb, or in any manner interfere with the commercial conditions and the peace of illustrious Colorado."[9] The militia made no bones about spying on the miners, with newspapers revealing how "military representatives" attended every meeting conducted by union officials "and what passes is promptly reported to the commanding officer."[10]

Businessmen helped authorities by forming Citizens Alliance groups to intimidate strikers. Members of these alliances stole the records of union locals in Victor Company mines to provide evidence for prosecuting union leaders. But the unions and their allies fought back. After touring the southern fields, state labor commissioner W. H. Montgomery blamed the strike on John D. Rockefeller Jr., who, he claimed, "deceived John Mitchell and Mother Jones into fomenting the disturbance."[11] Mother Jones reported that the military treated union leaders "inhumanely" and forced them "to drink out of the place where horses did." Organizers were put on trains, taken out of the strike district, "and unloaded after a long ride miles from any place of shelter."[12]

Early in January 1904 the mine operators stepped up their campaign to discredit the union. In a series of articles supposedly documenting the misdeeds of union leaders, *Polly Pry* published allegations that Mary Jones had worked as a prostitute and operated a brothel. Based on files compiled by the anti-labor Pinkerton detective agency, *Polly Pry* claimed that Mary Jones had worked as a prostitute in Chicago, Denver, Kansas City, Omaha, and San Francisco and had opened a brothel in Denver. Though she neither convincingly nor unequivocally refuted these accusations, her grandmotherly persona as Mother Jones stood in stark contrast to the charges. Other pro-business newspapers reprinted the story, claiming to present the truth about "the mottled record of 'Mother Jones.'"[13] At about the same time Mother Jones contracted pneumonia. Bertha Howell Mailly, wife of the Socialist Party secretary, traveled to Trinidad, Colorado, to nurse her, taking her to Omaha, Nebraska, to convalesce. No doubt this kindness, and some gentle persuasion on Mailly's part, helped to convince Mother Jones that her future lay with the Socialist Party.

In March, as miners' delegates met to discuss ending the strike, Governor James H. Peabody declared martial law in the strike regions of the state. Undeterred, and no doubt relishing the challenge, Mother Jones returned after recovering from her illness. She spoke to striking miners in Trinidad on 24 March, urging them to continue the fight and bolstering their morale. Two days later, she and four other leaders were arrested and placed on a train bound for La Junta, some sixty-five miles to the northeast, and told to stay away from the strike zone. The crackdown continued. Moyer was arrested on charges of desecrating the American flag after the WFM had produced posters with slogans such as "Free Speech Denied in Colorado" printed on the thirteen bars of the Stars and Stripes, and an Italian-language newspaper was closed down for allegedly inciting miners to violence. These actions occurred with neither warrants nor writs of habeas corpus because martial law did not require them, leading Mother Jones to charge the governor with creating a dictatorship.

Predictably Mother Jones refused to stay away from the strike zone. She traveled from La Junta to Denver, taunting Governor Peabody about her presence in the state capital and broadcasting her intention to return to the southern mining region. She traveled to Trinidad in April, only to be deported almost immediately. This time she went to Utah, where she was quarantined for supposedly being exposed to smallpox, a claim she charged was spurious and used as a pretext to detain her. She escaped and undertook a speaking tour of the East Coast to raise funds for and awareness of the Colorado strike. By the middle of June, however, the stoppage collapsed in the face of the intransigence of operators in Colorado's southern field. The strike in Colorado had cost the UMWA $500,000, mainly for food and shelter. Weakened by the settlement in the north as Mother Jones foretold, the strike proved unsustainable, and the union called it off. The miners accepted an offer to return to work with a small pay raise but no recognition of the union. The strike officially ended on 15 June 1904, an unmitigated disaster. Mother Jones blamed the "ring of fools that had charge of that strike in Colorado," calling them "dirty ignoramuses," though at this stage of her career she excluded Mitchell from that group.[14]

Following the end of the strike Mother Jones allied herself more closely with the Socialist Party. Like many other socialists, Mother Jones did not draw a sharp line between political activism and organizing workers into labor unions, continuing to engage in both. Eugene Debs reinforced this tendency when he published a short book entitled *Unionism and Socialism* in 1904. In August of that year, while still officially employed by the United Mine Workers, Mother Jones addressed the Central Federated Union in New York City on what seems to have been a promotional tour to sell Debs's book. After talking about the Colorado strike, her "real mission" (as a newspaper report put it) was revealed, and the organization agreed to buy 250 copies.[15] The pamphlet, published in a series of "Ten-Cent Books," argued that "the trades-union expresses the economic power and the socialist party expresses the political power of the Labor movement."[16] Debs argued that craft unions had become a dangerous irrelevance, dividing workers when common action against the increasingly unified capitalist class was needed. Unions and party should reinforce each other and sound the death knell of capitalism by ending competition for jobs just as the capitalists created trusts to control the marketplace. This, for Debs, would herald the dawn of a socialist society. For Mother Jones, *Unionism and Socialism* reinforced her belief that labor unions and political parties were two sides of the same coin and that strikes offered "the Class War in its reality."[17]

Disillusioned with union infighting and exhausted by the Colorado strike, Mother Jones resigned her commission as a UMWA walking delegate in January 1905 and joined the socialists as a paid lecturer shortly afterward. She did so because she felt isolated from union leaders and feared that some of them betrayed her behind her back. She believed that the time for change had arrived, writing to John H. Walker, "I am going out for the cause to wake the people up, and I can be more independent as I am."[18] This decision highlights the strengths and weaknesses of her approach to agitation. She knew best, would not listen to advice from others, and would share neither the limelight nor the credit.

Despite her aversion to the internal workings of institutions, a new one temporarily seized her imagination at the beginning of 1905. In January of that year she attended a secret meeting in Chicago where representatives of the radical wing of the labor movement joined with socialist leaders to discuss creating a new union for all workers. This body was needed, they felt, because of the failings of the conservative American Federation of Labor. The AFL, led by Samuel Gompers, served as an umbrella group primarily for craft unions consisting of skilled workers. These organizations fought for higher wages and better working conditions on behalf of their mainly white, male members. Seeking only what its leaders believed they could realistically attain, the AFL usually ignored or condemned calls for social change and refused to endorse policies that might promote workers' control of industry.

According to those who met in Chicago in January 1905, the AFL split the working-class movement by creating a privileged segment who could negotiate with capital while ignoring the needs of the majority of unskilled workers. Part of the attraction of the proposed union for Mother Jones was its pledge to fight for all American workers. Also at that meeting were Moyer and Haywood, Ernest Untermann (whose writings she knew from the *Appeal to Reason*), and other organizers and politicians whose work would have appealed to her. These included leaders from the American Labor Union (connected with the Western Federation of Miners) and Daniel DeLeon's Socialist Labor Party. The secret meeting ended with plans for a convention in June to discuss a manifesto forming a new union. Condemning the contemporary labor movement as "worn-out and corrupt" and for ignoring "the irrepressible conflict between the capitalist class and the working class," the manifesto urged formation of an "economic organization of the working class, without affiliation with any political party."[19]

The June convention resulted in formation of the Industrial Workers of the World (IWW), a rare moment of unity among radical working-class activists. William "Big Bill" Haywood opened the proceedings with the ringing pronouncement, "Fellow workers, . . . this is the Continental Congress of the working class." The purpose of the gathering, he continued, was no less than "the emancipation of the working class from the slave bondage of capitalism."[20] Revolutionary change comparable to that of 1776 was in the air. The IWW proposed to build a single union for all workers regardless of industry, skill level, ethnicity, race, or gender. It proposed continual agitation culminating in a general strike, after which those who produced wealth would gain control of the economy, society, and politics. Capitalism would expire when workers ignored the government and seized factories and mines.

Mother Jones found such a sentiment congenial, but she played almost no role in either creating or promoting the IWW beyond attending those first two meetings. At the June convention she voted in favor of adopting the proposed constitution, remarking that "I was not here when the report of the constitution was read, but I have sufficient confidence in the makeup of the Constitution Committee to commit my destinies to them."[21] Failing to attend the reading of the new organization's first constitution suggests at the very least a reluctance to become embroiled in the minutiae of organizational life. Mother Jones withdrew rapidly from active involvement in the IWW, but she shared certain ideological traits with the new union. Like the "Wobblies," as its members became known, Mother Jones was committed to class conflict as a means to putting the labor theory of value into practice. She consistently envisioned society as consisting of two classes; as she put it in 1907, "I have learned that there is an irrepressible conflict that will never end between the working-class and the capitalist-class, until these two classes disappear and the worker alone remains the producer and owner of the capital produced."[22] In this endemic, persistent, and ultimately winnable conflict, workers had a duty to fight for their rightful share of the wealth they produced. Their achievements were remarkable, but their gains, negligible. As she told miners in Pittsburg, Kansas:

> Now, in these years, in the last fifty years in the history of this nation, look and see what the miners, and the miners alone, have done. Look at the thousands and hundreds of thousands of miles of railroads that you have built. Look at the liners that are plying the oceans, connecting nation with nation. Look at the telegraph lines, look at the streets, the subways, the elevated ways—who has built them—the miners. You move the nation.[23]

Despite this, she reminded working people, "you never got a good square meal in your life, and you know you never did. But you furnish the square meals for the others who rob and oppress you."[24] In 1909, at a meeting to support striking New York City shirtwaist workers, she promised, "This is the last great fight of man against man."[25] Winning the class war would give working people control of the economy and with it "the ownership of those means [of production] so the boys will only work four hours a day."[26]

Like the IWW, Mother Jones had no interest in cooperating with the owning class. She particularly excoriated mutualists who claimed that labor and capital had a shared interest in the profitable operation of the capitalist economy. The National Civic Federation (NCF) came in for particular vituperation. Founded in 1900 by journalist Ralph Easley to provide a neutral meeting ground for the discussion of labor problems, the NCF attracted John Mitchell, Samuel Gompers, and Marcus Hanna to its conferences. Mitchell had tried to use the NCF as a vehicle for negotiations with mine operators, and he remained close to Easley. Hanna, the former coal mine owner who had advised McKinley to settle the 1900 Pennsylvania strike, urged employers and employees to find common ground. Mother Jones argued that such territory did not exist. She labeled capitalists in the NCF "that gang of commercial pirates" and lambasted labor leaders like Mitchell and Gompers as "parasites and bloodsuckers" for cooperating with it.[27] She also asserted, erroneously, that Hanna had created the NCF and, putting words into his mouth, claimed he had said, "These workers are men and women, we have got to do something, we have got to blind them, we have got to hoodwink them some way."[28]

Mother Jones's rhetoric echoed that of the IWW, which called the NCF an enemy of the working-class movement and dubbed labor leaders who joined it traitors. The 1905 IWW *Manifesto* claimed that capitalists "conceal their daggers beneath the Civic Federation and hoodwink and betray those whom they would rule and exploit."[29] Worse, the NCF cultivated amicable relations with the craft unions of the AFL to "hinder the growth of class consciousness of the workers [and] foster the idea of harmony of interests between employing exploiter and employed slave."[30]

By diverting labor unions and socialists from class struggle Mother Jones feared that the NCF would block progress for working people. She labeled the Civic Federation "a menace to the working movement" and blamed it for the loss of strikes in Colorado and Pennsylvania.[31] She claimed that the wealth and prestige of capitalists funding the NCF seduced labor

Business Unionism Personified: John Mitchell and Samuel Gompers, courtesy Library of Congress Prints and Photographs Division

leaders, who fell for flattering statements about their power and importance. Mother Jones saw them as deserters from the cause who attended NCF meetings to enjoy expensive cigars and potent liquors. She snidely claimed, "Most of them have paunches as big as William Howard Taft from sitting down at Civic Federation banquets." The real problem, she complained, was that "they have been settling the labor problem to the satisfaction of the master class. They are not fighting the class struggle!"[32] She urged unions to "tell those who represent labor in the Civic Federation to get out of it or get out of the labor movement."[33]

While Mother Jones and the IWW agreed on the evils of mutuality and the NCF, they clashed on two crucial issues: the need to maintain harmony within organizations and how to destroy capitalism. Despite the hopeful tone and apparent unanimity of the opening convention, internal divisions soon ripped the IWW apart. Union leaders fought over whether to capture AFL affiliates or to create rival unions, while the socialists brought their ideological factionalism with them into the new organization. Supporters quickly seceded, culminating in the departure of Debs, its most famous leader, and the Western Federation of Miners, its largest affiliate, in 1907. By 1908 only a few radicals remained, united by their opposition to the AFL, political parties, and any compromise with capitalism.

Mother Jones despised such doctrinal disputes. She was also ambivalent about the IWW's use of violence to promote change. The IWW called for the revolutionary overthrow of capitalism by any means possible. Its 1908 constitution declared, "There can be no peace" between worker and boss, for "between these two classes a struggle must go on until the workers of the world organize as a class, take possession of the earth and the machinery of production, and abolish the wage system."[34] Commendable as she would find these sentiments, Mother Jones opposed the IWW's advocacy of aggressive physical confrontation with the forces of capital. Indeed, when it reemerged in the second decade of the twentieth century the IWW became synonymous with violence, though more often its victim than its perpetrator.

Mother Jones took a different tack. Commonly perceived as a firebrand, she rarely encouraged violence. She had witnessed too much death in her life, from the Irish famine to the yellow fever to the murder of fellow organizers in West Virginia and Colorado, to countenance bloodshed. For her, guns in the hands of workers were to be used as a last resort. She did occasionally hint that violence might be an appropriate weapon, though. During the bitter West Virginia strike of 1912 she told miners, "Talk about a few guards who got a bullet in their skulls! The whole lot of them ought to have got bullets in their skulls!"[35] In 1905, shortly before the IWW convention, a Utah newspaper claimed that she advised "the shooting of all officers of the law, including President Roosevelt, if they stood in the way of the principles which she advocates," though given her outlook this seems unlikely.[36]

Most of the time Mother Jones counseled strikers to use "not guns . . . but brains" to defeat their enemies.[37] She was proud of having taught miners to think for themselves. Speaking a month after the assassination of President McKinley in 1901 she had warned, "Violence was not to be thought of. The law gave the workers their redress at the ballot box," and told her listeners that the assassin attacked the entire body politic and was therefore an enemy of "all working people."[38] She advised striking miners to avoid confrontation by going "up in the mountains and bury your guns."[39] Her reasoning was moral: capitalists hired armed thugs to intimidate and kill strikers, but unarmed working people controlled the higher moral ground and were therefore more likely to win public sympathy. In an interview with a New York Times reporter, published under a subheading proclaiming her the "Incendiary Labor Leader Who Terrorized West Virginia," she famously said, "I hate violence; I favor drama."[40] Her career was filled with street theater designed, as she put it in the same interview, to "provide the shock" needed to open the eyes of the oppressed.[41] She certainly used revolutionary rhetoric to inspire collective action, but, as she wrote to a wealthy Chicago woman, such language was necessary to combat injustice. This would continue "till the working-class send their representatives into the legislative halls of this nation and by law take away the power of this capitalist class to rob and oppress the workers."[42] The IWW showed no such interest in democratic politics, and while Mother Jones wavered over the efficacy of the ballot, she rarely advocated the type of violent confrontation IWW leaders claimed they wanted to incite.

Mother Jones dissociated herself from the IWW and played no active role in the union after 1905, but she did participate in the defense of two of its leaders accused wrongly of murder. On 17 February 1906, "Big Bill" Haywood and Charles Moyer, along with George Pettibone, were illegally extradited from Colorado and secretly shipped to Boise to stand trial for the murder of former Idaho governor Frank Steunenberg. In the wake of the killing of Steunenberg by a bomb planted at the front gate of his house on 30 December 1905, police arrested Harry Orchard, who had publicly threatened the former governor. Orchard confessed to the killing and implicated WFM leaders Haywood, Moyer, and Pettibone as his accomplices in planning the assassination. The prosecuting attorneys, including Senator-elect William Borah, hired an anti-labor Pinkerton detective named James McParland to coach Orchard. McParland spent a

George Pettibone, Bill Haywood, and Charles Moyer, courtesy Library of Congress Prints and Photographs Division

year preparing Orchard to testify that the accused wanted Steunenberg dead in retaliation for his efforts to destroy the WFM in Idaho during the 1899 Coeur D'Alene strike.

As Haywood, Moyer, and Pettibone languished in jail their case made national headlines. Prominent Americans spoke out on both sides, with President Theodore Roosevelt declaring the three defendants, along with Eugene Debs, "undesirable citizens." To this Mother Jones retorted, "How the spectacular performer in Washington has put his foot in it. The word[s] 'undesirable citizen' will go down in history. He and his crew of pirates would no doubt give a great deal to undo that."[43] The defendants hired Clarence Darrow, the most famous defense attorney of his day, to argue their case. Darrow told Mother Jones, "It will be a long drawn out trial, and it will need a great deal of finance to carry it on, and we must have it."[44] She subsequently undertook a speaking tour to raise funds for the defense and wrote about the case to generate further publicity. In New York City she adopted millennial rhetoric to declare, "We stand in the dawn of the world's greatest war. . . . It will be the war between the robbed and the robbers, and the robbers will go down." Referring to the unpunished shootings at Stanaford mountain and the hideous practice of child labor, she wondered, "When they talk of hanging Moyer and Haywood, now why didn't they talk of hanging the men who shot down innocent working men in Virginia? Why don't they talk of hanging the commercial pirates who are murdering the little children in the mills of the South?"[45] Writing in the *Appeal to Reason* she blamed "the murderous march of King Capital" for the arrests and called Idaho governor Frank Gooding a dupe of "the capitalist system."[46] Of Haywood, Moyer, and Pettibone she wrote, "No one who knows them believes in his heart that they had anything to do with the crime for which they are now in jail. They are as innocent as any of us, and the mine owners know this as well as anybody."[47] In this instance her faith was well placed. In his attempts to show McParland how well he had learned his lessons, Harry Orchard confessed to murdering Steunenberg along with numerous other people he could not possibly have killed. His unreliability as a witness destroyed the prosecution case. The jury found Haywood, tried first as the most notorious of the three, innocent in July 1907. Pettibone was acquitted six months later, and the case against Moyer was dismissed.

The fight to save Haywood, Moyer, and Pettibone was another episode in Mother Jones's long-running campaign for social justice. Just as she had appealed for clemency in the case of S. D. Worden of the American Railway Union in 1897, so she would continue to defend those she perceived as victims of capitalist injustice. Another case occupied her in the years 1907 to 1909, this one with international ramifications. In June 1907, shortly before Haywood was exonerated, a Mexican revolutionary by the name of Manuel Sarabia was arrested in Douglas, Arizona. A leader in the Liberal Party of Mexico, which advocated civil liberties, a market economy, and separation of church and state, Sarabia had vocally opposed the rule of Mexican president Porfirio Díaz. Known for systematically destroying his opponents, Díaz had worked hard to attract investment from the United States to Mexico, and his success at quashing unions and silencing dissidents pleased large American corporations. With its rich deposits of raw materials, cheap labor, and friendly regime, Mexico attracted nearly half of all foreign investment from the United States in the first decade of the twentieth century.

To escape death, many of the so-called *revoltosos* fled to the United States, but Sarabia's deportation to Mexico signaled the beginning of a campaign by the federal government to assist Díaz. Freed after the intercession of the labor movement Sarabia returned north of the border, but in January 1908, he and three other leaders of the Liberal Party of Mexico were arrested. The federal government charged Sarabia, Antonio Villarreal, Librado Rivera, and Ricardo Flores Magón with conspiring to cross into Mexico from Arizona and incite rebellion to overthrow the Díaz regime. The four *revoltosos* were detained in Florence, Arizona, in a prison

Mother Jones called "the bastile of capitalism," a reference to the famous castle destroyed at the beginning of the French Revolution.[48]

Mother Jones became a leader of the campaign to free the *revoltosos*. By sheer coincidence she had been speaking to striking miners in Douglas on the same day as the first arrest of Sarabia. She had worked with other labor leaders to secure his return from Mexico, but the second wave of incarcerations proved more difficult to overturn. Mother Jones saw this as evidence that the U.S. government was controlled by capitalists who wanted to expand their influence internationally. She also assisted a movement to save two Russian dissidents from extradition, detecting a pattern of cooperation with foreign dictators by Washington. As she told the 1909 United Mine Workers convention in an appeal for assistance on behalf of the *revoltosos*:

> Today, after a century or more of history in this nation, we find two diabolically tyrannous governments reaching their hands into this country and asking us to deliver men who have taken refuge here and surrender our rights to the czar of Russia and the military despot of Mexico. You will realize, my friends, that international economic interests are back of all this; you must realize that for this change in our nation's history there is a cause. Economic interests, both in Mexico and Russia, are dictating the policy of our government today.[49]

She reprimanded American corporations for caring only about "cheap labor" and condemned the federal government for becoming a "general scavenger for the most ferocious murderer on the face of God's earth."[50] She claimed that Washington was "allied with the masters of the big corporations in trying to enforce international absolutism and to make slaves of the workers who shall be unable to escape their chains."[51]

Despite raising over $4,000 for the defense of the four *revoltosos*, her efforts could not secure their freedom. For two years they remained in jail awaiting trial. Mother Jones traveled in June 1909 on their behalf to the nation's capital to meet with President William Howard Taft. Though he promised to review their case, earning her lasting gratitude in the process, nothing happened to alter their plight. Finally, in November, the four Mexican dissidents were found guilty of violating the Neutrality Acts and sentenced to eighteen months in prison. Writing from their cells Magón, Villarreal, and Rivera thanked Mother Jones for "your splendid work" and praised the "noble example" by which she "will live forever in the hearts of all liberty loving Mexicans."[52]

Detaining the *revoltosos* delayed but could not prevent the collapse of the Díaz regime. In 1911 a violent uprising brought Francisco Madero to the presidency and, a few months later, an invitation to Mother Jones to visit. She did just that. Along with leaders of the Western Federation of Miners, she met officials in the government of Mexico to discuss stemming the flow of Mexican miners to the United States. She found President Madero "a very broadminded man . . . [who] would carry out the laws of justice as far as he was able to."[53] His rule lasted barely a year before rebellion brought about his demise and death. Civil war temporarily engulfed Mexico, though Mother Jones later returned to another warm welcome.

The Colorado strike, the formation of the IWW, and legal wrangles dominated her life between 1903 and 1912, but woven around them was work for the Socialist Party. Mother Jones traveled regularly to speak with socialist groups and campaigned for socialist political candidates. She cooperated with novelist Jack London, whose muckraking journalism provided evidence for socialists to support calls for reform. In June 1906 she sat on stage in New York City as London lectured on "the revolution which is at hand."[54] She campaigned hard in 1908, when Eugene Debs ran for the presidency and garnered over 400,000 votes, about 3 percent of the total. In the same year she traveled to Denver to address the Western Federation of Miners' annual convention as delegates contemplated amalgamating with the UMWA. When she rose to speak she met "a great ovation" and called for "a closer union among all members of organized labor."[55] The proposal failed, but Mother Jones's popularity and her position on organized labor were manifest.

Mother Jones always appeared happiest organizing striking workers and severed her ties with the Socialist Party in August 1911. Her anger at the party reached boiling point when it cleared John Mahlon Barnes, the party's national secretary, of failing to repay loans she had made him. In May 1910 she asked him for the $250 she had lent to help him with personal expenses associated with his move from New York to Chicago. Mother Jones wanted the money "to defend my comrades who were in the bastile in Los Angeles."[56] Unmoved by her appeal on behalf of the *revoltosos*, Barnes angrily sent her $50 and made no effort to repay the remainder. Mother Jones lodged a complaint against him with the Socialist Party and swore an affidavit accusing him of financial and personal misconduct, including having an affair with an employee at party headquarters. Shamed, Barnes left the party but continued to serve as Debs's campaign manager. Bitter, Mother Jones abandoned socialist politics and returned to the union movement.

The Barnes case confirmed her suspicion of institutions. She felt that the party had lost sight of the class struggle because its leaders, insulated from the battles in the streets and the mountains, wasted their time taking luxury trips to Europe to meet with socialists there. Of one such junket she complained, "Instead of giving that money wrung from the blood of the working class back again to the commercial class, would it not have been better for us to have sent it to our comrades to fight them with?"[57] Between foreign travel and the excess she saw in party offices, Mother Jones worried that "the class struggle is lost sight of entirely" and party leaders would soon be "banqueting with [the] Civic Federation."[58] She exonerated Debs but lampooned others in the Socialist Party in an ungrammatical letter to her lawyer, Thomas Morgan. Here she claimed that the leadership was trying to discredit her by telling people, "To Hell with old Mother Jones Shes getting old We will make her shut up She must go off and die."[59]

At first she thought she should fight to reform the party, but, as she wrote in August 1911 to Morgan, "I am up to my ears in work here and have not a moment to spare for anything only the Industrial battle."[60] And indeed, she was busy by then, planning her return to West Virginia. Always happiest on the road, she downplayed the significance of institutional resources for mobilizing working people. In an increasingly bureaucratic age, when people, ideas, and principles could be brought together through organizations like labor unions and political parties, Mother Jones denied herself the advantages of working in and through institutional structures. Instead she took to the road once more and helped revive the battle against mine operators in the Mountain State.

8

The Coal War Resumed

THE YEAR 1912 EXPLODED with drama. Remembered by historians for its pivotal four-way presidential election, it also witnessed the sinking of the *Titanic*, a New York City police corruption scandal, an extra game to decide baseball's World Series, increased unrest in Europe, and an epoch-making coal strike in West Virginia. By 1912 Mother Jones had proven her newsworthiness. Her exhilarating speeches, constant travel, and radical language contrasted with her sedate appearance attracted attention. Wherever she went the press reported her presence and repeated her phrases. Newspapers in towns and villages she had visited picked up stories from the Associated Press and other newswires. Dailies in Baltimore, Chicago, New York, and elsewhere employed correspondents to report on her activities during major disputes. Mother Jones, with her theatrical flair, carefully crafted image, fiery rhetoric, and openness to journalists, blazed a memorable trail wherever she went.

Mother Jones could have played a significant role in Eugene Debs's campaign for the presidency had she chosen to do so. Ironically her retreat from politics, signaled by her departure from the Socialist Party, coincided with the 1912 election in which Debs gained his highest proportion of the popular vote (6 percent). In that year the Wilsonian Democrats defeated Debs and a Republican Party divided between William Howard Taft's conservative Republicans and breakaway Progressives who lined up behind former president Theodore Roosevelt. Historians have called this an election in which all four candidates ran as Progressives, propounding platforms that Mother Jones would have found mildly positive. Timing was not her strong suit.

But at this point in her career Mother Jones considered electoral politics futile. The front lines of the class war, she felt, were found in the coal mines where the industrial battle was engaged at its most basic and brutal. In 1912 she immersed herself in a renewal of the West Virginia coal wars. This latest involvement with Mountain State miners would last for a year, culminating in her incarceration after a controversial court-martial. In her rhetoric during the strike Mother Jones demonstrated her ability to appeal to working-class audiences using their cosmology and earthy vocabulary. Lacing her orations with religious imagery, she employed the language of redemption, guilt, divine intervention, martyrdom, and salvation to earn the trust of devout miners.

Mother Jones rejoined the United Mine Workers in 1911 or 1912 after her old friend John P. White gained its presidency. White invited her to become a paid organizer once more, aware that she had never really stopped agitating for unions. During the preceding decade, while employed by the Socialist Party, she had helped to organize workers in dozens of industries all across the country. In 1910, foreshadowing her return to the union, she assisted the UMWA during a strike in eastern Pennsylvania. She wrote for the *New York Call*, a socialist daily, about her travels through the anthracite region in the wake of a similar tour by Theodore Roosevelt. Labor unions had never been far from her mind even at the height of her agitation for the socialists.

In 1910, Roosevelt visited the area around Wilkes-Barre and Scranton in the company of John Mitchell to examine what he called "the social conditions" in mining communities. Newspapers showed the former president chatting with mining families and encountering a "life-sized portrait" of himself in one of their houses. He met a friendly reception wherever he went, and "scores of times men and women toilers implored him to run again for the Presidency."[1] As Roosevelt rode through the area, journalists noted that "his chief delight was in meeting the wage earners who spend their working hours far underground. The miners were not embarrassed in his presence, and this pleased him most of all. They treated him as if he had worked side by side with them for years."[2] The region's miners seemed nostalgically grateful for his role in settling the 1902 anthracite strike and solidly supportive of his running again for the presidency. That Roosevelt traveled in the company of John Mitchell, who was received like a hero in eastern Pennsylvania, did not hurt either man's popularity.

Theodore Roosevelt, the Bishop of Scranton, and John Mitchell (1910), courtesy Library of Congress Prints and Photographs Division

Mother Jones assailed Roosevelt's brief foray into "her" territory as a publicity stunt. She noted that he spent as much time with dignitaries as he did with the ordinary people he had supposedly come to see. Of a dinner with the bishop of Scranton and "the $6000 Civic Federation beauty, pet of the mine owners," she wrote, "What would Christ have said if he could have looked down upon this trinity of sleek parasites as they sat at the bishop's table gorging themselves with the richest of food and the finest of wines, while thousands of their brothers down in the valley had no where to lay their heads?"[3] Then she excoriated Roosevelt and Mitchell—whom she sneeringly called "the ex-labor leader"—for seeing the area "mostly from the comfortable seats of a large touring car."[4] Had Roosevelt chosen to walk with her instead, she charged,

> he would have seen women old and young carrying sixteen gallons of water on their heads across the coal strippings for a distance of a mile. He would have seen the motherhood of the future dwarfed morally, mentally, physically and spiritually in the mills where they are required to work ten hours a day and walk three or four miles each way going and coming from their work for a . . . pittance. He

would have seen the victims of his [1902 coal] commission, whose award was so favorable to the coal barons that they have forced upon the miners ever since poverty and degradation.[5]

Mother Jones rarely forgot a personal slight, and Roosevelt's refusal to meet with her at Sagamore Hill still stung.

Peace in the coalfields remained tenuous despite Roosevelt's commission, and in 1910 Mother Jones once again entered the fray in Pennsylvania. Centered on the Irwin field, this strike revolved primarily around wages. Mother Jones assisted in the town of Hazelton and then, after a speaking tour of Ohio and Illinois to raise awareness of and funds for the strikers, organized in Greensburg. She occupied her time "holding big meetings here for the miners" and drifting away from the Socialist Party as she became embroiled "in an industrial battle against the powers that oppress my class." As a result, she told the socialist lawyer Thomas Morgan, "I have neither time nor strength to waste with that bunch of middle class dictators" in charge of the Socialist Party.[6] Her anger at party leaders who seemed to prefer luxury and foreign travel to fighting the class struggle led her back into the union.

The anthracite strike proved a prelude to her return to full-time union organizing and to the mine wars of West Virginia. The two principal sites of the 1912–13 strike, Cabin Creek and Paint Creek, occupied adjacent narrow valleys. They flowed north into the Kanawha River, which itself wound its way through Charleston and into the Ohio River. The steep, tree-filled cliffs of the mining valleys protected mine operators from outside interference and allowed them to control the camps. The two creeks, each no more than twenty-five miles in length, had a total population of around thirty-five thousand, of whom seventy-five hundred worked in the mines. Cabin Creek had fifty-five separate mines, and Paint Creek had forty-one more. Miners rented company houses, purchased goods in company stores, and traveled along company-owned roads. A railroad, a dirt track, and a streambed filled each valley floor. Organizers had to walk through water to avoid arrest because the roads and railroads were private property. They knew from hard experience how dangerous it was to try to enter the mining valleys of West Virginia and told each other stories of organizers who went in by train and came out in coffins.

When she walked around the area Mother Jones had to travel through creeks after being ordered off the roads. Legal niceties such as constitutional rights to freedom of speech, movement, or assembly had no place in the universe of West Virginia mine operators. Hired detectives followed any stranger who came into the mine camps, recording their movements and noting the names of people with whom they spoke. Sometimes organizers were detained and interrogated; occasionally they were beaten and expelled. Company thugs intimidated organizers to let the union know its presence was unwelcome, and miners who seemed receptive to unionism lost their jobs and their company-owned houses.

Paint Creek had been unionized after the 1902 strike, and it remained one of the few UMWA strongholds in the state. When the miners' contract expired in April 1912 the operators announced their intention of withdrawing recognition of the union by refusing to meet with its negotiators. The operators expected to rid the area of union influence, a calculation based in part on the growing ethnic diversity of their work force, which had changed from primarily British in origin to mainly eastern and southern European in less than a generation. Paint Creek operators sought to divide and conquer their workers by playing one group off against another and thereby weakening the hold of the union over all of them. But the operators underestimated class solidarity, which transcended ethnic divisions. Living as they did in close quarters and working underground in constant danger, miners were painfully aware of the social gulf between themselves and the operators. Class identity and class consciousness pervaded both sides. Attitudes toward union membership symbolized this growing divide: workers wanted to join the union, while the operators sought to crush it.

West Virginia mine operators produced coal for markets as far away as Chicago, sending the black diamonds by train across the coalfields of competitors who were physically closer. In order to compete West Virginia mines had to operate at lower costs than mines in the Midwest or Pennsylvania. They also relied on preferential rates from the railroad companies, which owned many of the mines in the state. As a result miners in the Mountain State earned about a third less than miners in the Central Competitive Field (Illinois, Indiana, Ohio, and western Pennsylvania) organized by the United Mine Workers in 1897. West Virginia operators had an economic incentive to keep unions out. Fearful of competition operators in the Central Competitive Field offered to finance UMWA efforts in that state. The union rejected the overture, but West Virginia operators suspected their rivals of financing the union's organizing drives in order to force up the price of West Virginia coal.

In March 1912, UMWA officials approached the Paint Creek operators to negotiate a small pay increase and the automatic deduction of dues from pay packets. Mobilized by Quinn Morton, manager of the largest mines on the creek, the operators threatened to withdraw recognition from the union. Drawing on its experiences with previous strikes the UMWA prepared for a walkout by establishing tent colonies on rented land, the largest at unincorporated Holly Grove. Mining families evicted from their company-owned houses moved here, though conditions were primitive and grew worse as the number of inhabitants increased and winter approached. Holly Grove would also become a target for the operators' attempts to end the strike through violent intimidation.

When the union contract expired on 1 April the companies refused to open negotiations for a new one, and on 18 April, West Virginia miners struck. Many Kanawha River Valley mine operators, fearing a lengthy holdout, quickly negotiated with the union and settled their disagreements. After a month only the mines on Paint Creek remained shut. But the conflict escalated when, on 10 May 1912, Paint Creek operators hired mine guards from the Baldwin-Felts agency of Bluefield, West Virginia, to break the strike. The agency promised the operators that its men would force the miners back to work by September and the mines would then be operating at full capacity.

Preparations for war began. Paint Creek operators built concrete walls with guard towers and gun emplacements around the mines and advertised for replacement workers. No one could have predicted how violent and enduring the conflict would be, but when it ended a year later at least fifty people—miners, family members, and mine guards—had died, over two hundred had been jailed, and forty-seven (all miners or union organizers) had been tried by court-martial. When strikers tried to close mines worked by "scabs," Baldwin-Felts guards shot into tent colonies and harassed anyone who seemed sympathetic to the strike. Governor William E. Glasscock declared martial law three times.

Mother Jones injected herself into this combustible situation. She traveled to Paint Creek, having read about developments in West Virginia while staying in Butte, Montana, preparing to assist striking railroad shopmen in the western states. Canceling a speaking tour of California, Mother Jones "tied up all my possessions in a black shawl—I like traveling light—and went immediately to West Virginia."[7] She remembered making a dramatic entrance to Paint Creek in June 1912, when "a little boy came running up to me and said, 'Mother Jones, did you come to stay?'" After she replied in the affirmative he announced, "They beat my mamma up, and they beat my little brothers and sisters, and beat me, and if I live to be a man I am going to kill twenty of them for that."[8] In reality, given the volatile conditions and the close watch guards kept on the creek, she probably snuck in under cover of darkness. Regardless of the truth, her story provides an accurate gauge of labor relations in a valley torn by belligerence and brutality.

Mother Jones's arrival coincided with an upsurge of violence. Staying in the house of a "sympathetic merchant" in the unincorporated town of Eksdale and traveling by "buggy," she mobilized the miners.[9] As happened so often when she was close to the center of hostile confrontation, her role in encouraging gun battles around the company town of Mucklow is unclear. In fiery speeches she called on miners to fire back at guards who attacked tent colonies, but she also counseled restraint. Fighting between strikers and guards near Mucklow in early June resulted in the death of an Italian miner, the first fatality of the confrontation. A month later, as the guerilla warfare continued, miners hidden behind trees in the woods above Mucklow fired into the town to intimidate replacement workers. After this battle the Kanawha Valley sheriff appealed to the governor to send in the National Guard. It was becoming clear that the local legal system, devised to enforce the law in rural settings, was inadequate for the needs of the concentrated populations and modern economy of the Kanawha region. Though in appearance rural, below the surface mining had created an industrial society. Two elected constables and two justices of the peace—the latter appointed primarily because of their standing as landowners—could neither police the area nor dispense justice under the conditions prevailing in 1912.

In response to the sheriff's plea, the governor sent a West Virginia National Guard company into Paint Creek, but when the violence continued he mobilized the entire guard. The situation stabilized, but when the National Guard left for training exercises in Pennsylvania on 24 July strikers besieged the mines at Mucklow. After cutting telephone lines to prevent mine guards from calling for reinforcements, marching miners attacked two Baldwin-Felts guards traveling unaccompanied along the railroad, killing one. Reaching their target they engaged in a battle with the guards there, killing two more and firing some three thousand bullets. The governor then issued a "Peace Proclamation" charging local authorities with empowering a grand jury to try offenders and pleading for a spirit of cooperation and harmony in the Kanawha Valley. Glasscock's call went unanswered, and the violence continued. Aware that sympathy in the valley lay with the strikers, and that any civil trial would almost certainly result in acquittals, local judges and county attorneys refused to call a grand jury.

Following a further clash between Baldwin-Felts guards and striking miners, the governor traveled to the region to assess the situation for himself on 30 August. Back in Charleston he declared martial law, on 2 September 1912. The National Guard returned, and this time the governor charged the nearly fifteen hundred soldiers with confiscating weapons and escorting the Baldwin-Felts guards—widely seen as inflaming the violence—out of the valley.

Then, confrontations between mine guards and striking miners spread beyond Paint Creek, in large measure due to Mother Jones. On 4 August, acting with neither the permission nor the knowledge of the UMWA office in Indianapolis, she had ridden a train into neighboring Cabin Creek to announce a meeting over which she would preside on unincorporated land two days later. Cabin Creek had long been a target of union organizers, but local operators ferociously and persistently resisted unionization. In 1902 it had remained one of the few non-union valleys in the Kanawha River region. Here, in 1912, Mother Jones enjoyed one of her finest triumphs when she convinced the miners of Cabin Creek to join the strike. After her speech and continued agitation, they published their demands. These fell into two groups, mining operations (the right to appoint checkweighmen, standardizing coal cars, and accurate scales at all mines) and civil rights, including protecting freedoms of speech and assembly, ending compulsory company stores, and, above all, gaining union recognition as their bargaining agent. The miners of Cabin Creek sent their demands to the operators and awaited a reply.

The action shocked the operators, especially Charles Cabell, the paternalistic manager who oversaw most of the mines in Cabin Creek. Cabell had lived among the miners for many years and felt he understood them. He knew many of them by name and assumed they respected him in return. He had built recreational facilities and churches for their use and believed he was acting in their best interests when he closed down the only saloon in the valley. Like many paternalists, he vehemently opposed unions and prided himself on keeping them out of his mines, using the same tactics of intimidation as his Paint Creek counterparts. That the miners had grievances did not surprise him; that they would organize in search of redress he found astonishing and horrifying. He dug in and refused to meet with their delegates. The strike had spread, and Mother Jones was largely responsible.

The Kanawha River Valley strikes consolidated the status of Mother Jones as a national figure. Miners, operators, journalists, national guardsmen, and even the mine guards came to know her well. In one incident she met, and made a favorable impression upon, one of the owners of the Baldwin-Felts agency. On 12 August she led a contingent of striking miners along the railroad tracks adjacent to Cabin Creek for a meeting at one of the mines. In the middle of the afternoon the two hundred or so marchers encountered a group of mine guards, led by A. C. Felts, sent to intercept them. Felts wrote that Mother Jones assured him the miners "meant no harm being there, that they were marching peacefully and quietly, and did not intend to do any one any harm." She then told Felts

> she believed we were all men and by that term she meant that we were really more than gentlemen, giving her own definition and opinion of the modern gentleman. We talked pleasantly for probably 30 minutes, she and I both asking and answering questions. In the course of this conversation she stated that she hoped to see the time when our guns (pointing to the machine gun) would be abandoned and mounted into plow shares.[10]

Her reasonable language and pleasant demeanor contrasted sharply with her reputation as a firebrand, a reputation the mine operators and their Baldwin-Felts guards disseminated.

Mother Jones certainly knew how to make an impression on those she met. She attracted widespread media attention, with reports of her West Virginia agitation appearing in newspapers as far away as Utah and California. *Baltimore Sun* journalist Harold West traveled with her for several days and reported on conditions in Paint Creek and Cabin Creek. He publicized the almost feudal power of the coal companies in the region, writing angrily of how the septuagenarian organizer was forced to "walk the creek" and risk contracting pneumonia because the companies owned the roads and footpaths. He took great pains to show how Mother Jones the person differed from coal company propaganda. Operators told him "that she was an old 'she devil' and that she would receive no 'courtesies' there, that she was responsible for all the trouble that had occurred, and that she would receive no consideration from the companies." West contrasted this image with a speech in which "she counseled moderation, told the men to keep strictly within the law and to protect the company's property instead of doing anything to injure it." Like many others, he reported on her use of the vernacular, her willingness to swear to emphasize a point, and the rapturous greetings she received from striking miners wherever she went. He recorded her background as a schoolteacher and wrote how he was surprised to find her using "language of the cultured woman" in interviews.[11]

As A. C. Felts and Harold West discovered, Mother Jones consistently advised against violence, though she made allowances in certain circumstances. For one thing, she reasoned, if the men destroyed the mines, they would only be hurting themselves because in the near future the workers would own them. As she told Glasscock, "I will tell you why we are not going to destroy your property, Mr. Governor. Because one of these days we are going to take over the mines."[12] The labor theory of value demanded that outcome, an end to which she devoted herself. She explained to a *Charleston Gazette* reporter, "I am simply a social revolutionist. . . . I believe in the collective ownership of the means of wealth."[13] For her, working people had a duty to take what was rightfully theirs, and "when force is used to hinder the worker in his efforts to obtain the things which are his, he has the right to meet force with force."[14]

Following a week of intensive preparations, Mother Jones led more than two hundred miners from Kanawha Valley to the state capital to present their grievances to the governor on 15 August 1912. Glasscock had left Charleston in advance of the invading army of miners, inspiring Mother Jones to claim that he had fled in fear. On the steps of the West Virginia capitol building she lambasted him as a coward and then told the crowd how she had helped close down a mine, commenting that "I will tell you the truth, we took a couple of guns, because we knew we were going to meet some thugs." Reaching back to her favorite eras in American history, she found precedents for resorting to violence, advising her listeners that "we will prepare for the job, just like Lincoln and Washington did. We took lessons from them, and we are here to prepare for the job."[15] At the conclusion of the meeting, she would later testify, she suggested that instead of purchasing liquor the miners should each "buy a gun."[16] All reports indicate that they followed her advice and emptied Charleston of firearms.

If history provided a justification for direct action, so did the potent mixture of theology and masculinity Mother Jones combined to explain retributive justice. In Charleston she warned, "We are law-abiding citizens, we will destroy no property, we will take no life, but if a fellow comes to my home and outrages my wife, by the Eternal he will pay the penalty. I will send him to his God in the repair shop. (Loud applause.) The man who doesn't do it hasn't got a drop of revolutionary blood in his veins."[17] She advised miners, "Boys, I want to say to you, obey the law," and assured the governor and the mine owners, "I will guarantee there will be no destruction of property."[18] She did come close to advocating violence, telling the miners, "I don't want a single officer of the militia molested in any way. I am not going to say to you don't molest the operators. It is they who hire the dogs to shoot you. . . . I am not asking you to do it, but if he is going to oppress you, deal with him."[19] She noted that the political climate encouraged open conflict, for, as she put it, "I want you, my boys, to buckle on your armor. This is the fighting age. This is not the age for cowards, put them out of the way."[20] Only a careful listener could hear the subtle distinctions she offered. In fact, Mother Jones seemed to encourage fighting, stating at a public meeting on 6 September, "I am going to say to the police, the militia, the Adjutant General, and to every one in this audience, that we will carry on this fight, we will make war in the State until the Baldwins are removed."[21] She may have been using the words "fight" and "war" metaphorically, but to miners in the midst of battle the message was clear: Don't compromise your manhood by shying away from bloodshed.

Despite her recommendation to obey the law, maintain the peace, and respect property, Mother Jones also understood the power of preparing for the worst. Her advice to miners to bury their guns when the militia sought to confiscate them and to buy guns when the opportunity arose was a recognition that class war in America was asymmetrical. Any advantage, however small, had to be retained; a few hunting rifles and a handful of pistols were preferable to no weapons at all.

Remaining armed was one of the topics Mother Jones mentioned when she addressed the need to preserve civil rights. Though she proclaimed herself personally against guns, she noted how "the Constitution permits the right to bear arms everywhere."[22] She demanded an end to martial law and the banning of mine guards. To striking miners in Montgomery, she said, "Now, boys, we are facing the day when human liberty will be yours. I don't care how much martial law the governor of West Virginia proclaims, I have had martial law proclaimed where I was more than once, but I didn't stop fighting."[23] Martial law, she argued, failed but was preferable to the rule of thugs, as she called the Baldwin-Felts guards, who "beat, abuse, maim and hold up citizens without [due] process of law, deny freedom of speech, a provision guaranteed by the Constitution, [and] deny the citizens to assemble in a peaceable manner for the purpose of discussing questions in which they are concerned."[24] She warned the coal operators that "the right of free speech will be carried on if they hire all the militia in the state to murder us. We won't surrender that right. We will hold meetings. We will hold peaceful, law-abiding meetings."[25] In Charleston she issued an ultimatum, warning, *"We will give the Governor until tomorrow night to take them guards out of Cabin Creek,"* and then declaring, "IF THE GOVERNOR WON'T MAKE THEM GO THEN WE WILL MAKE THEM GO."[26] She offered examples of how the mine operators used the guards to intimidate the men, as in the case of a miner who lost his leg in a mine accident and was evicted because he sought compensation from the company. The guards "went into his house . . . and threw out his whole earthly belongings, and he and his wife and six children slept on the roadside all night."[27] For Mother Jones the need to protect constitutionally guaranteed rights went hand in hand with the demand for removal of the mine guards.

The governor's first declaration of martial law in September 1912 occurred because of ongoing violence in the strike region. Of greatest concern to local authorities was the obvious planning and coordination behind raids on the mines. Cutting telephone lines and mounting military-style campaigns to launch hour-long fusillades into selected mines suggested a level of organization that unnerved the constables and justices charged with keeping the peace. Martial law suspended civil authority and established military courts, eliminating habeas corpus and granting the governor, as commander in chief of the state militia, the power to suspend civil rights. When the National Guard demilitarized Paint and Cabin creeks, it confiscated some fifteen hundred rifles, five hundred pistols, seven machine guns, and more than 200,000 rounds of ammunition. Later events would prove that the miners had buried some of their weapons, but initially they accepted disarmament because they won one important concession: the despised and feared Baldwin-Felts mine guards were expelled from the strike zone. Other restrictions under martial law were more vexing: intoxicating liquors were banned, freedoms of assembly and speech were denied, and the militia searched all parcels and people entering the area. Information was smuggled out, and food in, by West Virginia socialists, who reported regularly on events in the strike zone.

Martial law did succeed in calming the area, and on 14 October, the governor lifted the restrictions and withdrew the militia. The union tried unsuccessfully to arrange a conference with the operators to end the strike. The operators adamantly believed they could crush the UMWA and maintain the status quo. They rehired the guards, reequipped their arsenals, and prepared for the resumption of hostilities.

They got what they had bargained for. Sporadic violence, primarily in the form of sniper fire by the miners, gave way to an attack on a train carrying replacement workers into Cabin Creek. That train was carrying U.S. mail, a fact Governor Glasscock feared would give the federal government a reason to intervene and limit his authority in the state. As a result he declared martial law for a second time, on 15 November 1912. An uneasy truce developed, but the miners recognized some of the National Guard soldiers as former Baldwin-Felts employees who had enlisted and therefore refused to allow their weapons to be confiscated. Many took Mother Jones's advice to bury their guns until needed. Martial law remained in place for less than a month, but Glasscock did not publicly announce its lifting for fear of renewed violence.

During this second martial law period Mother Jones organized brigades of women to harass strikebreakers and, seeking to bolster morale, embarked on a speaking tour to raise funds for food and clothing for the inhabitants of the tent cities. She traveled to Cincinnati, New York, and Washington, D.C. At the Cooper Union in New York City she spoke at a fund-raising event of how "men are afraid of gattling guns. . . . They quake in their boots when they see one pointed at them. But what is the power of a gattling gun compared with the power of an old gray-haired woman. They won't shoot me. They said they would, but they didn't."[28] She also testified before a congressional investigative committee that employment agencies in Ohio were illegally sending strikebreakers to the region without informing them of their destination or telling them they were replacing strikers. Accompanying her were two teenage boys who had been sent to the Kanawha River mines unaware of either their destination or their purpose. They had tried to leave, but the employment agency told them there was no transportation. After being assisted by striking miners they traveled with Mother Jones and appeared alongside her before the committee.

The area remained relatively quiet until early in 1913. On 7 February a company physician tried to take a replacement worker injured in a mining accident to hospital but came under rifle fire near the strikers' tent colony at Holly Grove. The physician escaped, but the miner died of his wounds, and the doctor telephoned Mucklow to report the incident. A group of mine guards intent on revenge set off for Holly Grove but were turned back by gunfire and then found themselves pinned down by a further barrage in Mucklow itself. The mine guards telephoned Quinn Morton, the lead operator of the Mucklow mines, in Charleston. Morton purchased guns to augment the armory in Mucklow and traveled the twenty-five miles to Paint Creek.

Morton and a posse assembled by the sheriff contacted the Chesapeake and Ohio Railroad for permission to use an armored train stationed near Paint Creek. Nicknamed the "Bull Moose Special" by miners, it left Paint Creek junction at 10:30 in the evening with its lights off and slowly made its way toward Mucklow. As it passed near Holly Grove gunfire rang out. Witnesses differed widely on the cause of the exchange, disagreeing on whether the first shots came from the train or from the miners' tents. One miner was killed, and a woman was wounded, but the unprovoked attack—as the strikers saw it—generated anger. Three days later the striking miners attacked Mucklow in retaliation, and gunfights in the hills afterward left thirteen miners and three guards dead. On 10 February 1913 the governor renewed martial law for a third time after these incidents.

Newspapers sympathetic to the mine operators left no doubt about who caused the deaths. The *Charleston Mail* reported, "Bloodstains mark the road to Mucklow and Ronda. Just how many men have met death in the past 48 hours, following the preachings of Mary Jones, the 'Bloody Mary' of the United Mine Workers of America[,] is unknown."[29] This report claimed that, at the funeral of a miner killed in the Mucklow gun battle, "Mother Jones made an appeal to the men to get their guns and shoot them to hell, meaning the mine watchmen and others who will not join [the strikers'] ranks."[30] On another occasion a reporter quoted Mother Jones saying, "Arm yourselves, return home, and kill every goddamned mine guard on the creeks, blow up the mines, and drive the damned scabs out of the valley."[31]

It is unlikely Mother Jones employed such inflammatory rhetoric in public. For one thing, she was far too clever to make statements that could be used against her or to characterize the strike as lawless. For another, we know the content of some of her speeches because the mine operators hired a stenographer to take verbatim reports. These transcripts—from an unfriendly source—show her carefully skirting the line between provocation and conciliation. Overt demands for violent action appear only in excerpts of her speeches reported by journalists trying to discredit her. It is of course possible Mother Jones told the men to take their revenge violently, but if she did so, she chose her occasions well: in the surviving full speeches, she rarely exhorted miners to break the law. At a public meeting in the courthouse square in Charleston on 6 September 1912 she told strikers, "Don't meddle with the [railroad] track," but advised them, "If you catch sight of a Baldwin blood-hound put a bullet through his rotten carcass."[32] The Baldwin-Felts guards did use dogs to follow miners after gun battles, so it is feasible Mother Jones referred not to the humans but to their canine companions. If so, this remains an easily decoded command to kill the guards. More frequently, though, she asked the strikers to show respect for property and to protest legally, telling them in the same Charleston speech, "Now, my brothers, don't violate the law. Let them see that you are law-abiding."[33]

Mother Jones led a delegation of about five hundred miners to Charleston on 13 February to protest their treatment by the mine guards. When they arrived at the Charleston train station, she was arrested, transported to Pratt—location of the militia headquarters—and imprisoned. She was charged with conspiracy to murder in connection with the shooting of a mine guard at Mucklow. Held supposedly incommunicado in a boardinghouse, Mother Jones smuggled out messages to her friends, stories to reporters, and on one occasion herself, for a bottle of beer.

The court-martial began on 7 March at the Oddfellows Hall (the largest public building available) in Pratt. The trial lasted a week, during which Mother Jones gained widespread publicity despite the best attempts of the military authorities to keep the press at bay. One journalistic outlet remained mute because the local Associated Press stringer doubled as an officer in the National Guard and, putting his military duties first, sent no dispatches. A reporter for the *Charleston Kanawha Citizen* was briefly detained by the National Guard after interviewing Mother Jones. He then published her ringing statement, "It is not the first time that I have had to measure steel with the minions of the ruling class. I have never yet raised the white flag, and I shall fight so that the red flag of industrial freedom shall not perish on the bosom of young Columbia."[34] The *New York Call* quoted her as saying, "We are not afraid to testify, but we demand that our rights as citizens of this republic be recognized. . . . I maintain that no body of men in West Virginia has the power to suspend the Constitution of the United States."[35]

Drawing on her religious upbringing and centuries of literal self-sacrifice by radicals, she positioned herself as a martyr. She told a *New York Times* journalist, "I am 80 years old and I haven't long to live anyhow. . . . Since I have to die I would rather die for the cause to which I have given so much of my life. My death would call the attention of the whole United States to conditions in West Virginia. It would be worth while for that reason."[36] A Philadelphia daily reported her as being "ready for the eternal sleep," saying, "I will die gladly," and challenging the authorities to "string me up to your tree. . . . That is the only way that you can still my voice."[37]

Predicting her apotheosis reminds us of how frequently Mother Jones infused her speeches with religious imagery. She told West Virginia miners that "the labor movement, my friends, was a command from God Almighty." She then related the story of the parting of the Red Sea for the Jews escaping from Egypt, telling how "when the army of the pirates followed them, the Dead Sea [sic] opened and swallowed them up, and for the first time the workers were free." She concluded, "That can well be applied to the state of West Virginia."[38] Mother Jones saw her own life as a mission, claiming, "I have got a contract with God Almighty to stay with you until your chains are broken."[39] The miners shared this hallowed task, for she told them they were "doing God's holy work" and promised, "I can see victory in the heavens for you. I can see the hand above you guiding and inspiring you to move onward and upward. . . . We must redeem the world."[40] Reminding them of their guilt—of their fall from grace—she worried about their ability to complete the task God had set them. She told them, "You are to blame" for low pay and poor working conditions because "you don't stand in your union," a reminder that Paint Creek had been organized in 1902 and the miners had failed to retain their organization.[41]

Before her own guilt or innocence could be established by court-martial, the United Mine Workers initiated habeas corpus proceedings to test the constitutionality of martial law. The union argued that the civil courts were open in Charleston, where she had been arrested, and she should therefore be tried there. The state supreme court split, but a majority ruled against the union, and the defendants remained in custody in Pratt. This was the third and final habeas corpus case the union had championed and lost. The decisions recognized the governor's right as commander in chief of the state militia to declare martial law and bypass civil courts in the exercise of justice.

A public spectacle of the highest order, the trial attracted reporters from around the country. Charged with conspiring to steal a machine gun and murdering two mine guards in the attempt, the defendants refused to enter their pleas as a protest against the legality of the court. When asked how she pled to the charge of complicity in the murder of a mine guard, Mother Jones said, "I have no defense to make. Whatever I have done in West Virginia, I have done it all over the United States, and when I get out, I will do it again."[42] She then maintained an uncharacteristic silence for the rest of the trial. The defense lawyer, Capt. Charles R. Morgan, sought clemency for his client, telling the court,

> Old age—very old age, sometimes causes flinging discretion just a little bit to the winds, and, I leave it to you gentlemen, if there has been a single item of evidence introduced here that this old woman, who has been here, and has been so courteous and so patient to you all—if she has done a single act in the furtherance of this conspiracy with which she is charged.[43]

He proceeded to dismiss the evidence against her by casting doubts on the reliability of the prosecution witnesses and recalling some of the discomforts she faced in the Kanawha Valley. It was left to the judge advocate to rule and send his verdicts to the governor.

What happened next is shrouded in mystery. The court sealed the charges and sent them to the new governor, Henry D. Hatfield, installed just two weeks before. That document has never been found, so the verdict against Mother Jones remains unknown. Hatfield's actions suggest that the judge advocate found her guilty. The governor released the majority of the defendants and transferred eleven to civilian jails. He left Mother Jones incarcerated in the boardinghouse in Pratt in which she had been detained since 13 February. Her release came on 7 May 1913, apparently because the West Virginia authorities were concerned about the implications of keeping her imprisoned while a Senate investigative committee examined conditions in Paint Creek.

The strike itself ended after Hatfield intervened. Acting as a broker between the union and the operators, the new governor convinced both sides to accept a nine-hour day, bimonthly pay, and checkweighmen appointed by the miners. By the end of April 1913 the strike was over. For many union members and socialists the agreement was a betrayal of the miners, and it earned Hatfield the sobriquet "political rattle snake" from Mother Jones.[44] West Virginia socialists distributed leaflets in the strike zone calling for miners to ignore the agreement, insist upon recognition of the union, and continue fighting for their original demands. Socialist newspapers attacked Hatfield mercilessly, and initially it appeared that the miners would refuse to end the strike. The governor responded by ordering the miners to return to work or face deportation from the state. He then suppressed the socialist newspapers, autocratically closing two of them (the *Labor Argus* and the *Huntington Socialist and Labor Star*), imprisoning journalists and editors, and impounding the presses. State socialists appealed to the national party for assistance, while other newspapers ignored the governor's action. Eugene Debs traveled to West Virginia, interviewed Hatfield, and, on the basis of that talk, exonerated the governor of wrongdoing. In the wake of Debs's report, socialists left the party in droves and joined the IWW. For her part, Mother Jones traveled to Colorado for another confrontation with John D. Rockefeller, Jr. This time her actions would bring her face-to-face with the industrialist, with unexpected consequences.

9

Massacre at Ludlow

IF 1912 HAD WITNESSED a level of drama unprecedented in Mother Jones's career, the year 1914 demonstrated history's uncanny ability to repeat itself. The scene shifted once more from West Virginia to Colorado, where Mother Jones was again arrested, deported, and jailed at the hands of authorities strengthened by martial law. The flow of events was depressingly familiar to Mother Jones. Mine operators perceived her agitation as a root cause of the unrest leading up to the 1913–14 Colorado coal strike. They blamed her for unsettling supposedly contented workers and for encouraging violence. She paid the price for her reputation as the most dangerous woman in America by being imprisoned twice and deported from the strike zone three times. Her efforts and the work of other union organizers brought the repressive measures employed by and for operators to the attention of legislators in Washington, D.C. In this respect the Colorado conflict differed from West Virginia: politicians seeking to understand its causes focused a national spotlight on the strike almost as soon as it erupted.

Having been released from "the iron hands of capitalism" in May 1913, Mother Jones traveled to the nation's capital. After recuperating from her three-month incarceration in Pratt, West Virginia, she began to plan for the future. One of her first acts was to express her gratitude to the readers of the socialist newspaper *Appeal to Reason* for the support she received from them while in "the military bastile." She urged them to continue fighting and "to carry on the battle for my imprisoned colleagues" because "the workers must be aroused."[1]

She returned to Colorado in late summer 1913 to do just that. Mother Jones found the state much as she had left it in 1904. Colorado coal could only compete nationally if mined cheaply, which meant long hours for low pay. A few large corporations retained control of the coal industry and made labor organizers exceedingly unwelcome. Compared to West Virginia the coal regions were less mountainous but experienced greater extremes of climate. Business interests continued to dominate state politics and made enforcing protective legislation impossible. Miners' collective grievances echoed those of West Virginia: they complained of low pay, dangerous working conditions, long days, and poor housing. Company stores controlled local markets and charged exorbitant prices for food and other supplies; corporate checkweighmen underreported the amount of coal brought out of the mines, and pay packets were commensurately smaller; and any effort to organize met with resistance and even job loss.

Not everything remained the same, however. After a doomed strike in 1910 in the northern fields, operators had replaced ethnically British miners with recent immigrants, and the influx of new workers continued. The operators hoped that a diverse work force would limit union organizing, but subsequent events proved that calculation wrong. The just-concluded

A Typical Mining Tunnel, courtesy Library of Congress Prints and Photographs Division

West Virginia conflict signaled a shift in federal approaches to local strikes, making them the subjects of Congressional inquiries.

One example of the trend toward national investigations occurred in 1913 when the Senate Subcommittee on Education and Labor launched an inquiry into conditions before and during the Paint Creek strike. This action, proposed and pushed by Senator John Worth Kern of Indiana, led to hearings in Charleston and in Washington. During the proceedings Kern used a telegram from Mother Jones to good effect. He brought her case before the Senate during a debate leading to the investigation. Senator Nathan Goff of West Virginia, defending the coal operators on the floor of the Senate, asserted that Mother Jones was not in prison. Kern then stood up and read to the Senate the telegram she had secretly sent him. In it, Mother Jones asked the government to analyze conditions in the mining regions of West Virginia. Kern's reward, she promised him, would arrive when "children yet unborn will rise and bless you."[2]

Mother Jones did not testify before the subcommittee, though she did attend parts of the Senate debate leading to its creation. Though there is no hard evidence to support the supposition, it is likely she was released precisely because of the impending investigation. Accompanied by labor leaders from the Mountain State, she heard Senator William Borah of Idaho refute Goff's assertion that martial law had been declared constitutionally.

A Mining Tunnel Collapse, courtesy Library of Congress Prints and Photographs Division

Borah, who would soon earn her praise and with it her forgiveness for his role in the trial of IWW leader "Big Bill" Haywood, argued that other states facing similar crises should not follow the example set by West Virginia. He warned the Senate of the importance of opposing the precedent of allowing governors to "close the doors of the courts and deny the right of trial by jury."[3] Mother Jones shared his analysis of martial law as leading to tyranny and therefore inimical to the constitution.

Mother Jones then embarked on a speaking tour to raise awareness of the events in West Virginia. She related her experiences during the strike, telling an audience in Pittsburgh how she entered the Paint Creek strike zone and was told by a miner, "If you go up there mother, you will come back on a stretcher." She went anyway, and, as she told her listeners, "I spoke there. I didn't come out on a stretcher. I raised hell." She noted, "I shall never forget the last day of the trial. It seemed to me as if the flag of liberty was gone and in its stead the flag of Russia waved." Then, invoking the work of journalist and social critic John Kenneth Turner, who had recently published an exposé of conditions in Mexico under Porfirio Díaz, she continued, "I want to say that the brutality there is worse than darkest Russia and barbarous Mexico."[4]

Mother Jones traveled constantly as if to make up for lost time after her three-month imprisonment in West Virginia. In September 1913 she visited Colorado and found conditions there to her liking. The state was once more in ferment as coal miners contemplated a strike, and Mother Jones added her voice to those who advocated a walkout. From Denver she wrote to Senators Borah and James Edgar Martine of New Jersey to express her appreciation for their work on behalf of the West Virginia miners, telling them that "Colorado miners join with me in tendering sincere congratulations for the splendid manner in which you handled the workers' cause."[5] She then traveled into southern Colorado, to Trinidad, to attend the state miners' convention and urge them to take their future into their own hands. On 16 September she called for a strike in order to redeem the union in the eyes of the southern-field miners betrayed in 1903. In that year, miners in the northern field had returned to work, leaving the miners in the south to fend for themselves with disastrous consequences. She tried to reassure her listeners that the mistakes of that earlier strike would not be repeated. She asked the delegates to vote for a strike and therefore to

> be true to your fellow men and stand loyally to the cause of the worker. No power on earth can dissolve us and we will get what we want if we are loyal. If you go ahead and do right, victory is yours.

The United Mine Workers of America will never leave the state of Colorado until the banner of industrial freedom floats over every mine in the state. It is up to you, my boys, to gain victory. I will be with you and your [union] officers will be with you.[6]

Mother Jones knew that the previous defeat still stung but believed that the union had learned the lesson of remaining united. Another battle in the class war was about to be joined.

Given the depth of their unhappiness with living and working conditions, the miners needed little prodding and voted to strike. As in 1903 the strength of the turnout surprised labor leaders and mine operators alike. Though the UMWA had only a few hundred members in the state, the mines closed in rapid succession. Mining families evicted from their company-owned houses moved into tent colonies established by the union. There were thirteen of these in all, the largest at Ludlow. Many of the tents had been transported from West Virginia by the union; following in their wake were Baldwin-Felts guards brought to Colorado by mine operators envious of the West Virginia operators' firepower. Local law enforcement officials gave the guards deputy sheriffs' badges in an effort to justify their presence and the violence that followed them.

Colorado governor Elias Ammons made several attempts to avert and then to settle the strike. At each turn, however, he was stymied by the operators. In August, at the urging of the union, Ammons sent Edwin Brake, his deputy commissioner of labor, to Trinidad in an effort to avert the strike. Not only did Brake fail, but his arrival coincided with the murder of a union organizer, George Lipiatt, in front of the hotel where Brake was staying. The two Baldwin-Felts guards who killed Lipiatt were never indicted, a sign of things to come. Ammons also drafted a letter pledging the operators to abide by Colorado's existing mining legislation, but he allowed them to rewrite it, and the union refused to sign the revised version. What Ammons did not know was that behind the scenes the operators had agreed to unite to defeat the union.

At first the strike was peaceful, but a month into it, with Mother Jones mobilizing support, raising the morale of strikers' families, and probably encouraging confrontation if not bloodshed, violence erupted. Baldwin-Felts guards shot randomly into the tent colonies in an effort to intimidate the miners and their families. Traveling in an armored car with a Gatling gun mounted on its roof the guards killed one miner and injured two children at the Forbes colony on 17 October. A week later they shot and killed four miners in Walsenberg. Shortly after this incident Mother Jones traveled to the town and asked the miners, "What is the matter with you?

Are you afraid? Do you fear your pitiful little bosses? Are you great, strong men, with so much latent power in you, afraid of your masters or the Baldwin-Felts thugs hired by your masters? I can't believe it. I can't believe you are so cowardly, and I tell you this, if you are, you are not fit to have women live with you."[7] Attacking their manhood certainly caught the attention of her audiences.

As winter neared, the conflict appeared no closer to a settlement than it had been in September. Fearing anarchy and alarmed by reports of violence in the coalfields Governor Ammons declared martial law on 28 October 1913. He ordered the National Guard to disarm anyone not authorized to carry weapons, restrict the mine guards to the property of the operators, protect those who wanted to work, and prevent the importation of strikebreakers. The miners saw this as a possible victory, though the militia sided with the operators and even enlisted former Baldwin-Felts guards. Mother Jones remained unrepentantly optimistic, traveling to El Paso, Texas, in a failed effort to negotiate with the government of Mexico to stem the flow of replacement workers crossing the border. Before departing she wrote UMWA vice-president Frank Hayes, "We are still battling away out here, and, considering the obstacles we are up against, we have the situation well in hand."[8]

Her own fame proved to be an unexpected obstacle. Mother Jones had gained a national reputation as a successful agitator whose rhetoric occasionally crossed the line from demanding solidarity to urging the use of violence. No shrinking violet, she broadcast her intentions to all who would listen. She quickly became a target of state-sponsored corporate intimidation: the National Guard and its leader, Adjutant General John Chase, made no attempt to hide their desire to assist the operators by keeping her away from the strike zone.

Returning to Trinidad from the border with Mexico, Mother Jones resumed her agitation among striking miners and their families. Her work on this occasion was short-lived: a contingent of National Guard soldiers boarded her train as it arrived at Trinidad depot on the morning of 4 January 1914 and arrested her. The soldiers escorted her to a nearby hotel for breakfast, and, keeping union officials seeking an audience with her at arm's length, they marched her back to the depot in time to catch a train to Denver. She reportedly told the soldiers, "I did not think you would dare go this far," and her subsequent efforts to leave the train and give a speech as planned at Walsenberg ended in failure. As the train pulled away from the station, she leaned out of the window of her carriage and sarcastically informed the crowd gathered to meet her, "I expect to visit you again, when Colorado is made part of the United States."[9]

Upon arriving in Denver she learned that General Chase had issued an order forbidding her to enter the strike zone until the conflict ended. Reacting as a bull does to a red flag she immediately proclaimed her intention of returning to Trinidad, telling reporters, "I'll go back. They can't keep me from my boys." Of the National Guard she said, "I am not afraid of all the troops in the State."[10]

The deportation of Mother Jones was not an isolated incident but part of a pattern of intimidating union organizers, a tactic used by Colorado authorities to crush the strike. In the northern field, vigilantes mobilized by the Taxpayers League forcibly—and illegally—removed seven strike leaders from the Oak Hill mines. These men telegrammed their representative, Edward Keating, in Washington, D.C., to ask, "Will the United States government allow a federal officer to take the law into his own hands, establish mob rule, and deprive men of their rights guaranteed by the laws of the United States?"[11] Keating called for a federal investigation similar to the inquiry then under way into conditions in West Virginia. The risk of confrontation heightened as union officials in Colorado "advised all strikers to arm themselves in order that they might resist any attempt of deportation."[12] Union leaders began interviewing witnesses to the deportations, as evidence for Keating. They telegrammed the Colorado political delegation in Washington demanding to know "whether the equal protection of the law is to be [no] longer denied to citizens and others without investigation and action by congress."[13]

Mother Jones kept her promise and returned to Trinidad. A week after being deported from the town she reentered wearing a disguise and leaving her train before it came to the station. Within hours the militia found her, and she was "arrested shortly before noon by a detail of state troops, hurried out of the hotel, placed in an automobile and whirled through the streets, with a cavalry escort galloping at full speed in front and behind the machine."[14] Instead of being deported, she was imprisoned in a local Catholic hospital, Mt. San Rafael. In a statement explaining his decision to order her incarceration, Gov. Ammons noted, "This state is paying $5,000 a day for the preservation of order in the strike regions and I don't propose that she shall make that expenditure useless." Anticipating criticism on the grounds of her sex and age, he continued, "Simply because she is a woman and an old one that is no excuse for her actions and is no reason why she should be permitted to stir up trouble," a clear expression of the authorities' belief that outside agitators upset otherwise contented miners. Ammons promised, "She will be released whenever she announces her willingness to leave the strike region. She can go to any town in the state and talk her head off so long as she keeps away from the strike district."[15]

Despite threats by miners to forcibly release her, she remained in custody for two months. She stayed, as she later described it, "in a small room with white plastered walls, with a cot, a chair and a table, and for nine weeks I stayed in that one room, seeing no human beings but the silent military. One stood on either side of the cell door, two stood across the hall, one at the entrance to the hall, two at the elevator entrance on my floor, two on the ground floor elevator entrance."[16] She told a congressional subcommittee that while in the hospital "I never got a line, never got a newspaper, never had a book. I never saw a human being, only Mr. [Horace] Hawkins," the union attorney.[17] Her release arrived the day before the Colorado supreme court was to hear her habeas corpus appeal, suggesting that the state knew she would win her freedom.

While Mother Jones languished in her hospital prison, the strike continued, and the two sides engaged in an ugly propaganda war. The operators claimed every violent incident had been initiated by the union and reiterated the refrain about outside agitators unsettling their contented and well-remunerated work force. Colorado UMWA leaders responded by creating a press bureau to counter the operators' disinformation campaign. The first act of this new body was to release copies of miners' wage statements showing how poorly they were paid.

After her discharge from the Trinidad hospital Mother Jones wrote to her old friend Terence Powderly, onetime leader of the Knights of Labor and a Catholic. She complained to him of the "cold blooded hypocrisy" of nuns who "permitted their religious institution to be turned into a military prison" and condemned the moral cowardice of sisters and priests "owned body and soul by the Rockefeller interests."[18] She also planned her travel to Trinidad and announced to the press, "I fully expect to be arrested and returned to prison when I reach the strike zone." She connected her experiences in Colorado with events in West Virginia, stating bluntly, "No Governor or President can make me abandon my constitutional rights as a citizen to go where I please. So long as I live I shall refuse to submit to military despotism. If they do not arrest me at once I shall go ahead caring for the strikers' women and children and encouraging the men to resist tyranny and robbery by the coal operators."[19] The miners' struggle thus took on a transcendent significance, with Mother Jones at the center defending the Constitution. As she boarded her train in Denver en route to Trinidad on 22 March she told reporters, "I certainly expect to be rearrested the moment I step from the train," and anticipated that she would be forced to "go back to the hospital since the soldiers have the bayonets and I have nothing but the constitution."[20]

This time her prediction was only half accurate. She was indeed arrested as the train approached Walsenberg; asked by a militia officer, "Will you take my arm, Madam?" she replied, "No I won't . . . you take my suitcase." Instead of the relative comfort of the hospital, she was held in the Huerfano county jail in Walsenberg, which she called "an outrage."[21] The jail had been declared unfit for prisoners by a state investigation a decade beforehand, and conditions had not improved. Here, she wrote in her autobiography, "I was put in the cellar under the courthouse. It was a cold, terrible place, without heat, damp and dark. I slept in my clothes by day, and at night I fought great sewer rats with a beer bottle."[22] Unlike at Mt. San Rafael, she did receive books, newspapers, and her mail.

For Governor Ammons and General Chase the arrest of Mother Jones was a case of enforcing the law. Ammons claimed that her presence would "result in bloodshed," while Chase saw it as a necessary response to her provocations.[23] The militia leader told the press, "I understand that Gov. Ammons' orders are just the same as they were before—that Mrs. Jones is to be imprisoned until she is ready to leave the strike zone."[24] This time she remained behind bars for three weeks, and again her release by the military authorities coincided with an imminent habeas corpus hearing. She immediately traveled to Denver for consultations with union officials before journeying to Washington, D.C., where she testified before the House Subcommittee on Mines investigating the Colorado mining industry. Offering her proposals for ending the strike, she told the congressmen, "If I was president of the United States I would notify that governor immediately to dispose of those gunmen" and then tell John D. Rockefeller Jr., "You have got to make concessions to those people. You have got to stop robbing them. . . . Give those men the right to organize. Give them the right to have their coal weighed. Pay them every two weeks."[25]

Rockefeller also testified before the mines subcommittee. On 6 April he denied having any prior knowledge of the miners' grievances and proudly—some would say, arrogantly—informed the members that he had not intervened to end the strike or even attended any Colorado Fuel and Iron board meetings. Rockefeller defended the actions of his subordinates in Colorado on the grounds that they were protecting the "great principle" of the open shop. He compared his opposition to unions with revolutionary war resistance to British tyranny. His stand earned him the praise of businessmen around the country and a gift of ten thousand shares in CFI from his father. Just two weeks later, however, events in Ludlow exposed the emptiness of his pronouncements.

As Mother Jones traveled east, the strike entered a new, more bloody phase. The miners' union and the state of Colorado had both been experiencing financial difficulties because of the sheer length of the walkout. The UMWA had been forced to borrow funds from its own Midwest districts to support striking miners and pay the legal fees for arrested organizers. The state government had run out of money to pay the militia and sent them home, giving Gen. Chase a makeshift army of company employees and mine guards. In March a troop of these soldiers forcibly evicted families from the Forbes camp and destroyed the tents. Then they began to encircle the remaining camps, flooding them with electric light at night to break the morale of the strikers.

This policy of intimidation exploded into murder on Sunday, 19 April. As the strikers in Ludlow were preparing to celebrate Greek Orthodox Easter, a gun battle broke out. No one knows who fired the first bullet, but hundreds more quickly followed. Women and children hid in holes dug under their tents to avoid being caught in the cross fire, and the men massed on a small rise overlooking the camp. The miners exchanged fire with the mine guards dressed in militia uniforms until the strikers exhausted their supply of ammunition, at which point they vanished into the hills. What happened next was unimaginably brutal. The mine guards marched into the camp and began setting fire to the tents, taking prisoners, and executing in cold blood some of the strike leaders who had returned to help their families. The fire raged through the night; at dawn, the bodies of twelve women and children were discovered, asphyxiated in the burrows under their tents. When all the bodies had been recovered a total of twenty people were dead, most of them women and children.

In the aftermath of the murders a guerilla war broke out in earnest. Miners seized control of the town of Trinidad and an area some fifty miles wide around it. Mines were attacked and torched, while mine operators traveled in fear of their lives. Protest meetings around the country condemned the slaying of innocent people. Resolutions castigated the mine operators generally and John D. Rockefeller Jr. specifically. Testifying soon afterward in Washington, Mother Jones claimed she could have prevented the murders, telling the mines subcommittee, "I always look after those women and children, and I think if I had been in Colorado now and the governor had left my hands loose, this tragedy would not have taken place."[26] She hoped that "the burning up of homes, and women and children in there," would help bring the strike to an end by recalling everyone to their shared humanity.[27] She blamed Ammons for the killings and reiterated her desire for the federal government to ban the use of private guards to break strikes. Asked what the miners wanted, she said

Aftermath of the Ludlow Massacre (April 1914), courtesy Library of Congress Prints and Photographs Division

union recognition. In response to the argument that the union wanted to coerce operators into creating "closed shops" forcing all miners to join the UMWA, she retorted that Rockefeller opposed unions because "he can do all the robbing and stealing he wants to do in the open shop."[28]

As the situation in Colorado worsened, President Woodrow Wilson sent Martin Foster, a congressman from Illinois and member of the mines subcommittee, to interview Rockefeller about negotiating a settlement. The financier remained unrepentant and unyielding, claiming that any compromise on his part would lead inexorably to union recognition and a loss of control over his property. According to one of his most trusted advisers, Frederick T. Gates, only "the officers of the Colorado Fuel and Iron Company were averting chaos, anarchy, proscription, and confiscation."[29] Facing this intransigence, Wilson ordered federal troops into the state on 29 April 1914. Their arrival and the disbanding of the faux National Guard quieted the situation.

The Ludlow Massacre revived a long-running hatred of the concentration of wealth in the hands of a few families. Centered in New York City, the Morgans, Astors, Belmonts, Goulds, Carnegies, Guggenheims, Vanderbilts, and Rockefellers seemed to many Americans to exercise an unparalleled, and unwanted, power over the economy. Renowned for their callous business methods, the Rockefellers personified this aristocracy. Their wealth rested on Standard Oil, a corporation that had gained a monopoly on the oil-refining business by unscrupulously buying or destroying its competitors. By 1908 the *Wall Street Journal* reported that the family had earned more than $929 million in profits over the previous twenty-five years. The *Appeal to Reason* used this figure to estimate that the Rockefeller wealth exceeded that of all of the royal families of Europe combined. And Junior, as John D. Rockefeller Jr. was commonly known, stood to inherit the bulk of it.

Junior owned a controlling interest in Colorado Fuel and Iron and became a target for Americans venting their fury after Ludlow. His office at 26 Broadway and his mansion in Tarrytown were bombarded with critical letters and protesters. In early May, sixteen people picketed the entrance to his mansion. Restrained from entering by the "four guards [who] were on duty at each gate, . . . armed with clubs and guns," they settled for posting a handbill reading in part, "Rottenfeller has a bible class because he is an ass," a reference to his weekly attendance at Sunday school.[30] Two days later, "several strange men" and a woman with a black bag tried to enter the grounds of the Rockefeller estate but were rebuffed by guards.[31] These were not isolated incidents, and protests continued in Tarrytown and on Broadway. On at least one occasion threats of physical violence were yelled at the buildings, and the Rockefeller family adopted a siege mentality.

At about this time Mother Jones arrived in New York seeking an interview with Junior. Ever willing to share her thoughts, she told reporters "she believes that he means well and has only been misled by bad advisers. She is confident, she asserts, that she can get him to agree to a conference with a representative of the miners."[32] She wrote to inform him of her presence in New York City "for the purpose of directing public opinion in mining conditions in Colorado" and offered to visit him in his office to give him "the exact facts in the entire matter."[33] Rockefeller's office rejected her missive, delivered by registered mail, and she sent it to the *New York Call* for publication, hoping to shame him into action for ignoring an old woman. Rockefeller evaded her on this occasion, and she traveled to Lake Forest, Illinois, on a tip from Upton Sinclair that Junior was with family members there. Unable to track him down and tiring of her wild goose chase she visited her friend Caroline Lloyd, sister of Henry Demarest Lloyd, to whom she complained of being "over worked." Nonetheless she prepared to journey west because "I never know when they will lock me up to stay. The Pirates are after me."[34]

At the end of May Mother Jones did indeed travel west, to Seattle. There she delivered an address at the inaugural Labor Memorial Day celebration, held to honor victims of the Ludlow Massacre. Union members wearing badges bearing a picture of Mother Jones paraded through the streets of the city, while the guest of honor rode in an open automobile with the day's organizer and six children. In her speech Mother Jones praised her audience for participating in "a great war with a bunch of high-class burglars and looters," which would end in "the emancipation of the mine workers and the nationalization of the mines."[35] She urged them to fight because "individual freedom" would not "drop down from the clouds" and, by standing firm, "the fight can be won, and will be won, but the struggle will be long and education, agitation and class solidarity must all play a part in it."[36] From Seattle she tried to visit Canada to speak to striking miners in Nanaimo but was denied permission by an immigration official who told her, according to her autobiography, "'You can't go' . . . like he was Cornwallis." When he claimed that her presence in the strike zone would cause a disturbance, she replied that she had a perfect right to enter Canada and told him, "You'll have to state your reasons to my uncle." Her uncle, it transpired, was Uncle Sam, who "cleaned Hell out of you once and he'll do it again."[37] In fact, the UMWA successfully appealed the ruling to the Canadian government, and she was allowed to board a steamer for British Columbia. Her first visit to the Harris family's adopted country since she had left in 1859 had turned into a replay of the American Revolution.

Mother Jones felt confident in leaving Colorado because federal troops calmed the situation. The focus of the strike had shifted from open conflict to a debate over the value of Wilson's chosen solution, a presidential commission to examine miners' grievances and recommend further action. Speaking to a UMWA special convention in Trinidad in September 1914, Mother Jones advised the delegates to accept the president's proposal. She placed them in the vanguard of a great historical movement in which "industrial despotism will have to die and you, my boys, must use your brains, you must study and think. The sword will have to disappear and the pen will have to take its place."[38] She extolled the president for standing up to Rockefeller, "the greatest moneyed power in the world . . . [who] controls the whole of New York City and New York" and who "owns the mines, the industries and the railroads clear through the nation."[39] Admitting that Wilson's proposal "is not all we want but Christ did not get all he wanted," she begged the miners to agree to the presidential commission "in the name of the women and children of Ludlow."[40]

In this case the union followed socialists in calling for the nationalization of the mines. James Lord, head of the AFL mining department, met with Wilson's adviser on labor matters, the future Supreme Court justice Louis Brandeis, to ascertain the legality of such a move. Apparently Brandeis advised against it, for when Lord and Mother Jones visited Wilson in

October 1914 they "urged that if the operators declined to accept the plan of settlement proposed the President should close the mines."[41] Even in this watered-down form the idea drew a sarcastic editorial from the *New York Times*, which belittled Mother Jones as a danger to property owners who had the temerity to "think that property in this country can be enjoyed under the law."[42] But the debate about government ownership reached into Wilson's cabinet, and Mother Jones kept up the pressure, telling Philadelphia unionists in November that Rockefeller should settle the strike in five days or see the government move in. She warned him that "we are ready to make war with you" and asked if he was "building palaces" on the bodies of the Ludlow victims. She wondered if he "hear[d] the voices of the children crying who were shot in the trenches by the uniformed murderers and then [had] the oil of John Rockefeller thrown over them to burn them to a crisp."[43]

The Colorado strike brought Mother Jones before a national audience just as the West Virginia conflict had done. At a New York City meeting denouncing U.S. foreign policy the speakers praised Mother Jones and called her "the greatest woman the democratic impulses of the century had developed."[44] For Rockefeller, on the other hand, the coal strike had the opposite effect. His role in directing the actions of Colorado Fuel and Iron would only later become public knowledge, but he found himself roundly condemned for the restrictions on individual freedoms his policies encouraged. Like many others, Mother Jones spoke out against the creation of "a Rockefeller government in this country." She foretold of an age of freedom and prosperity for working people, for "the laboring man is tired of working to build up millions so that millionaires' wives may wear diamonds."[45]

Standard Oil developed during the period in history known as the Gilded Age, when the United States exhibited enormous wealth alongside incomprehensible poverty. The years following the Gilded Age have conventionally been styled the Progressive Era, and historians have until recently drawn a sharp line, around the year 1901, between the two time periods. The Gilded Age was supposedly filled with devious and avaricious "robber barons" like John D. Rockefeller Sr., who employed unscrupulous business methods to consolidate wealth. They did this on the backs of millions of Americans, many of them recent immigrants living in squalor and misery. After 1901 things slowly changed for the better. Earnest reformers, disgusted by the contrasts they saw around them or read about in the muckraking press, cleaned up politics and, led by the trust-busting Theodore Roosevelt, brought corporate interests to heel.

John D. Rockefeller Sr. and Junior, courtesy Library of Congress Prints and Photographs Division

Recent research contradicts this picture and suggests that the boundary between the nineteenth and the twentieth centuries has been drawn too sharply. Instead of Progressives creating social stability around consensus on the future direction of the country, the number and frequency of strikes suggest a divisive assertiveness on the part of organized labor. Moreover, if there was no unanimity about the future, continuities with the years before 1870 are indicative of even greater complexity. Governmental and corporate power continued to grow, one legacy of the Civil War, and bureaucracies expanded to mobilize people and expand production. Expert commissions did become more important after 1901, but even that accelerated a trend evident before the turn of the century.

If one thing did change after 1901 it was the desire of capitalists for positive publicity. The Rockefellers exemplified this shift: John D. Rockefeller Sr. did not care what others thought of or said about him, but Junior wanted to be respected, if not loved, by the American public. Ludlow smashed his hopes for carving a new image for himself and the family name into the popular imagination. Central to that project had been creating the Rockefeller Foundation to direct the family's philanthropic giving, but the federal government simultaneously charged Standard Oil under antitrust legislation. This contradiction percolated in the collective consciousness. When Junior testified about his apparent distance from events in Colorado he was attempting to present himself as a benevolent if remote owner. That facade would come crashing down when he testified before the U.S. Commission on Industrial Relations, appointed by President Taft in 1912 to investigate the upsurge in violent confrontations between capital and labor. Chaired by Kansas City reformer Frank Walsh, the commission began taking testimony in 1913 and amassed evidence on a wide variety of labor relations questions.

In January 1915 Mother Jones traveled from Denver to Washington, where she proposed to "let Rockefeller know and the government in Washington that the working people are demanding to be heard."[46] She attended hearings at which Junior defended the Rockefeller Foundation from Walsh's charge that it was an autocratic institution devised to deflect public attention from the unethical actions of the corporations the family owned. Before the session, Junior invited her to "come down to my office and talk over the Colorado situation with me" on the grounds that she knew the miners "better than I or my associates possibly could and we would be very glad to have your point of view."[47] When the hearing began Rockefeller received a roasting from Walsh, who demanded to know if it was "just and socially desirable" that the total remuneration paid to the fifteen thousand miners in the employ of Colorado Fuel and Iron was "only ten times the income of" John D. Rockefeller Sr.[48]

Rockefeller's charm offensive swung into action. On 28 January Mother Jones accepted Junior's invitation and paid a visit to 26 Broadway. Rockefeller told reporters afterward that she had explained the miners' grievances and

> I told her that I realized that it was my duty as a director of the company to know more about them. I assured her that I believed that as a matter of principle the things of which she complained were wrong. Of course there should be free speech, free assemblage, independent stores, public schools, and all that. We found that on all matters which we discussed we were in agreement.[49]

Mother Jones fell for his good-guy act, telling reporters that "he has been misunderstood" and "no one has wronged him more than I have." Regretting that she "used to call him a high class burglar," she asserted, "I am sure he means to do right."[50] Clearly she had enjoyed her moment in his spotlight. One journalist who interviewed her shortly afterward compared her to "a very young miss, just arriving home again after attending her first ball [who] caught her breath excitedly as she went over the glory of it all again."[51]

The implication of her naïveté was clear. Her friends knew Mother Jones had been taken in, much as she had accused John Mitchell of being fooled by Theodore Roosevelt's charm in 1902. Upton Sinclair telegraphed her, "We are sure you will not let yourself be overcome by the sweet odor of the American Beauty rose."[52] This and other admonitions convinced Mother Jones to curb her enthusiasm. While she stood by her new view of Junior, she warned him, "Good intentions are alright as paving blocks, but what we want is performance—and we want it now."[53] She then castigated his proposed company representation plan, designed to give miners a voice at work and to avoid the necessity of recognizing the UMWA. She saw this as a way for Rockefeller to pay "only lip service to democracy in industry."[54] As time passed Mother Jones became convinced she had been taken for a ride, and her invective against Junior became less forgiving. Speaking to striking dressmakers in New York in February, she asserted that the Colorado conflict had "ended in our forcing John D. Rockefeller to admit that we were right."[55] By August 1915, less than eight months after her amicable meeting with him, Mother Jones called Junior an "insulting rat" and "the greatest murderer this nation had ever produced," who, had she been president of the United States, would have been subpoenaed, arrested, and taken to Washington in handcuffs to settle the Colorado strike.[56]

Driving her change of heart were dramatic revelations regarding Junior's role behind the scenes during the Colorado strike. When Frank Walsh announced that the Commission on Industrial Relations would resume public hearings in May 1915 he issued a statement "that Mr. Rockefeller was the real directing head of the Colorado Fuel and Iron Company throughout the struggle with the striking miners."[57] Rockefeller immediately denied the charge, but Walsh's investigators had uncovered documents from Rockefeller's office showing not only that Junior had enjoyed considerable and timely information about the state of affairs in Colorado during the strike but that he had regularly communicated with his subordinates there. Walsh stepped up his attacks, telling the press that "the men who led the Colorado strike were fighting for liberty 'against an enemy as powerful and menacing as any ever faced by our revolutionary forefathers.'" He blamed Rockefeller personally for conditions most people "deemed un-American and intolerable."[58] Much of the anti-union propaganda and intimidation, including the tactics leading to the Ludlow Massacre, had been conceived by Rockefeller. This contradicted Junior's January testimony, and another public relations disaster loomed.

Junior, recognizing that the time for action had arrived, had his bags packed and traveled to Colorado. Accompanied by a retinue of newspaper reporters he visited the site of the Ludlow tent colony, danced with miners' wives, and announced a new grievance-resolution scheme. He earned positive press and seemed to have deflected the charges. So confident was he that he was clearing the family name that he even denied receiving shares in CFI as a reward for his January 1915 testimony, claiming falsely to be "in ignorance of the transaction."[59]

The Commission on Industrial Relations invited Mother Jones to testify about the Colorado strike. She took the opportunity to speak volubly, occasionally on the topic of the strike but mostly to recap her career as a labor organizer from, as she claimed, 1877. Ignoring conventions of space and time, "she proceeded," according to a *New York Times* reporter, "in her quaint way without being tied down to geography or continuity of events." Her mingling of fact and fiction made for testimony that was alternatively moving and entertaining, for "at times her narrative became tragic and again and again was pricked out with witty and sharp comment that started a round of laughter."[60]

Two themes dominated her testimony. First, she reported that violence in labor conflicts only erupted after the companies brought in armed guards or state militia. Respectable union members, according to

Mother Jones, always wanted to maintain the peace, but local authorities frequently bowed to pressure from capitalists to intimidate workers into ending strikes. She testified to witnessing businessmen express their anger at the Pennsylvania Railroad by committing "acts of violence" and "participating in the riots" during the 1877 strike. Much of the damage to company property, she reported, was caused by "a lawless element" who had traveled to Pittsburgh "during the panic of 1873" in search of work. On the other hand, "the employees of the railroad and others went to the mayor of the city and asked him if he would not swear them in as deputies to preserve the property and have the law enforced." She contrasted the destruction in Pittsburgh with the situation at Arnot, Pennsylvania, in 1899–1900, where "there were no deputies and no gunmen and no militia brought in there, and there was no violence." Because of this, she said, "the men were orderly and they themselves took care of the property."[61] She made similar claims about the strikes in West Virginia and Colorado. The moral was clear: honest, decent workingmen could be trusted to maintain the peace even when engaged in industrial war. Only the bosses cultivated violence during strikes.

Also reverberating through her testimony was an unalloyed humanism. She regularly referred to the inherent virtue of all people, no matter how apparently cruel or unfeeling. Everyone shared a common humanity and could be redeemed, a lesson from her Catholic upbringing. Of National Guard soldiers she testified, "I think they are human beings like all the rest of us," and, "They are good boys when you get at them right."[62] She said she could talk to Baldwin-Felts guards by finding common ground because, as she told them, "you have yourselves mothers and wives and children probably."[63] Of newspaper reporters she testified, "I know they have to make their living."[64] Even Judge Jackson, who had tried her in West Virginia in 1902 and "was looked upon as a terrible fellow by the whole labor world," illustrated her contention that all people have "a human side." He had responded to her appeal on behalf of a fellow prisoner who fell ill by suspending his sentence.[65] She told how individuals in positions of authority aided her: the sheriff at Arnot who refused to deputize mine guards, a guardsman in Pratt who slipped her reading material, a soldier in Walsenburg who brought her the mail, railroad conductors who treated her kindly, an engineer who warned her of impending violence in Trinidad, and others. The character sketches dotted throughout her testimony contributed to her weaving a tapestry of hope grounded in the natural goodness of all people.

Opposition to the use of militia and martial law by authorities remained a common thread in her own work after the Colorado strike. In

1915 New York debated a new constitution. Mother Jones joined other labor leaders in attacking it for rejecting proposed amendments for pensions and a workers' compensation fund; she also condemned the constitution for failing to subordinate military power to civil authority, "a condition, in the face of the opposition of the laboring classes in the country, which was the cause of the revolutionary war."[66] The constitution, opposed by various groups on the grounds that it centralized power in the hands of the governor and ignored the will of the majority of the people, was soundly rejected when put to a vote. For once, Mother Jones had lined up on the winning side in a political contest.

10

Streetcars and Steel

VIOLENCE SEEMED TO FOLLOW Mother Jones. Even when she pursued peace or counseled patience the gun battles and murders rampant in some strikes attached themselves indelibly to her name. This was unfair. Though she did occasionally recommend violent confrontation, the threat of bloodshed carried greater value to Mother Jones than actual hostilities. After the Ludlow Massacre she had advised miners not to seek revenge, and in West Virginia she would do the same during a strike in 1921. Preaching class war did not mean neglecting realistic appraisals of the power of the enemy. And the enemy—the "pirates"—had plenty of firepower to defend their wealth, political influence, and control of the legal system. Mother Jones urged confrontation as a strategy to awaken the workers to their grievances and intimidate the bosses into submission.

Paradoxes abounded in Mother Jones's attitude toward conflict, but two constants remained: she worked hard to avoid internal labor union rifts; and she knew that the threat of violence provided strategic opportunities to demonstrate the potential power of workers. Two vignettes from 1916 illustrate these tendencies. Mother Jones advocated union–movement unity and strove to exacerbate class division. She wanted to end institutional factionalism and implored workers' organizations to unite for revolutionary change. This desire was evident when, at the United Mine Workers' convention in January 1916, "her unpolished oratory raised the 1,500 miner delegates to a fury of enthusiasm" for ending a long-running feud between leaders and locals over "charges of graft and extravagance against union leaders."[1] In this case the principals shook hands at her urging, though the issue came to a divisive vote anyway. Nine months after this conciliatory gesture New York City police blamed her for inciting violence by relatives of striking streetcar workers. She told the women to assist their husbands and brothers in any way necessary to win the strike and to demonstrate the power of the working class. Immediately after her speech some of her audience members destroyed a trolley car. The newspapers declared her guilty of causing the riot, but she publicly refused to apologize for her words or to condemn the women.

The New York strike was one of many stoppages involving workers in what had become, and would remain for a short while, one of the country's most important industries: urban railways moving people through the increasingly crowded cities of the United States. Americans relied heavily on public transport as their primary means of travel. Electrified trolleys, or "streetcars," provided carriage for city dwellers until the advent of subways and then automobiles in the early twentieth century. As late as the 1920s trolleys remained crucial to the smooth functioning of American cities. Frequently owned by private electric companies, they became part of a contemporary debate about whether utilities should be in the hands of capitalists or controlled by the government. Reeling under the combined pressure of competition from other forms of transportation and the need for investment to meet increased usage, streetcar companies pushed their employees to work longer hours. Consequently there were approximately two hundred strikes nationwide between 1901 and 1917. Often bitter and occasionally violent, these confrontations left nearly one hundred people dead, second only to the number of fatalities during mining strikes.

Mother Jones claimed she tried to organize streetcar workers whenever she rode the trolley. By her own estimate she had been organizing streetcar motormen and conductors from 1870, though the historical evidence dates only from 1905. Her strategy, she told the 1909 UMWA convention, was "to get on the cars early in the morning and talk to them and show the necessity of getting together."[2] This was union organizing at its most basic and potentially its most powerful, meeting workers one-on-one. She told an audience in Pittsburg, Kansas, how, because of her earlier efforts to unionize Chicago trolleymen, "I ride everywhere in Chicago because those boys know what is what." She said she only rode in Kansas City when it was absolutely necessary because the streetcar companies had successfully resisted unions, and therefore "every time you take a ride on it, you go to work and back on a scab car, and [with] a scab crew."[3] Nevertheless, like coal mining, streetcars supplied a constant source of potential union members, but unlike her widely publicized efforts among miners, her work with streetcar employees remained mostly sub rosa and gained little press attention.

This changed in 1916 when she made streetcar workers her particular target and threw herself into strikes in El Paso, Texas, and the New York metropolitan area. She traveled to Texas at the invitation of the trolleymen's union after attending the Arizona Federation of Labor conference in Bisbee. She came to El Paso in a fighting mood, telling striking streetcar employees that "I don't know of a more joyous death than in fighting the battles of you laboring men."[4] Playing on the well-known connection between streetcars and utility companies she urged the women in a crowd of three thousand people to support the strike by using candles instead of electricity. She claimed, "We want no Sunday school people. We want practical men and women. I do not belong in the church or the parlor or the clubroom. I belong on the firing line. At the same time, I do not believe in murder or violence. The day of brute force and violence has passed. We must get what we want by other means."[5] Those "other means" included encouraging workers to flex their economic muscles by boycotting non-union merchandise, telling them to "look to see if the things you buy from your merchants have the union label."[6]

Mother Jones's brief sojourn in the Lone Star State made no lasting impression, but subsequent efforts in New York generated plenty of drama and press coverage. This strike occurred when streetcar companies began requiring crews to sign contracts pledging them to remain non-union. Beginning in Mount Vernon, adjacent to the then-independent city of the Bronx, members of the Amalgamated Association of Street and Electric Railway Employees rejected these "yellow-dog" contracts. In September 1916 the carmen of Westchester County struck to retain the right to remain in the Amalgamated Association.

The strike grew more and more contentious as its first month drew to a close. The Mount Vernon Common Council repealed an ordinance requiring crews to accumulate fifteen days' experience in the city before operating streetcars without supervision. This law had originally passed after lobbying by the union, and its repeal signaled a political counterattack. Revoking it would enable the company to hire strikebreakers. The union retaliated by importing Mother Jones, who addressed women relatives of the strikers in front of New York City's Mozart Hall. Here, at the scene of several mid-nineteenth-century women's political conventions, she exhorted them to take matters into their own hands and "get the 'scabs' off the cars." She told the women, "You are too sentimental," and condemned them for "staying at home thinking of dress and trinkets, when you ought to be out raising hell."[7] She told them, "This is the fighting age. Put on your fighting clothes. America was not discovered by Columbus for that bunch of bloodsucking leeches who are now living off of us."[8] The effect was instantaneous: the women attacked a trolley car stopped in front of the hall, surrounding it and throwing paving stones through the windows. They then entered the car and ripped up the seats. Powerless to stop them, police at the scene called for reinforcements, who rescued the crew, broke up the crowd, and arrested six women, along with three men who had joined in.

The use of strikebreakers contributed to the rioters' anger, but newspapers had no doubt about who had triggered the destruction. Calling her "a notorious apostle of violence," the New York Times editorialized sarcastically that, while "it would be a pity to interfere with the diversions of so gentle and fragrant a personage as 'Mother' Jones," this outburst justified legally restraining "her charter of speech."[9] Mother Jones remained unrepentant, telling a crowd of five thousand strikers the next day that "they say I started the riot. Well, I'm not going to say whether I did or not. . . . I'm not going to make any apology." Fighting was necessary because "if the police are organized to shed our blood we are going to organize to shed the other side's blood."[10] This type of language came close to inciting violence. She seemed to encourage bloodshed while actually calling for being organized, a possible euphemism for being armed. But despite Mother Jones's intervention and support from many sympathizers who tried to keep it going, the New York streetcar workers' strike collapsed in the face of intransigence by the companies.

More successful for the workers involved was Mother Jones's appearance in Bloomington, Illinois, in July 1917. Her old friend John H. Walker, then president of the Illinois Federation of Labor, invited her to this central Illinois commercial and agricultural community to assist employees of the Bloomington and Normal Railway who had been on strike since May. Before then they had been working ten-hour days for six or seven days a week, earning a modest $50 month. The strike had entered a stalemate before Mother Jones arrived on 5 July. Much like her New York speech, she reminded workers of their duty to their class and to their families. She counseled expanding the strike, and the next day, strikers closed the lines of other streetcar companies in and around the city. According to the Chicago Daily Tribune, "One car was taken from the rails and placed across the railroad tracks, several conductors and motormen were badly beaten, and one man, said to have been in the crowd which was attacking the cars, was shot through the neck." Electric company employees closed the power plant after fearing an attack, and "the city is without light or power, except for the municipal plant which furnishes lights for the streets."[11] The governor sent a contingent of National Guard soldiers from Chicago to calm the area, and negotiations between union and companies resulted in workers winning an eight-hour day and a six-day week along with a pay raise, their first in three years. Mother Jones would continue to work with streetcar unions. She attended their 1918 convention in Salt Lake City, where she convinced delegates to commit funds to help striking miners in Michigan and to pass "resolutions denouncing the methods of Michigan mine operators," which were forwarded to President Woodrow Wilson.[12]

The Utah resolution was not the first time Mother Jones had asked Wilson for assistance. As she traveled around the country during the election year of 1916 she endorsed him for reelection, telling working people that she could see a socialist society in the distant future but that Wilson, a Democrat, represented the best deal for labor over the short-term. She preferred his policies, including appointing her old friend William B. Wilson as the first secretary of labor, to those of the Republicans. In November 1916, after he had secured reelection, Mother Jones attended a White House reception as one of 401 delegates from the AFL convention then meeting in Baltimore, entreating the president "to be good to my boys."[13] He did her the courtesy of listening, winning her respect and support.

Mother Jones found the Democrats to her liking in 1916. She earned the wrath of the socialists by campaigning in Indiana for Democrat John Worth Kern, who was seeking to retain his seat in the Senate. She did so, she told friends, to thank Kern for his efforts on her behalf while she had been imprisoned in Pratt, West Virginia, in 1913. She neither endorsed nor canvassed for Eugene Debs, then running for Congress from the district around his hometown of Terre Haute, Indiana. Debs was trounced by the Republican candidate despite receiving support from the national Socialist Party, and Mother Jones parried criticism that she had contributed to his loss. She wrote to a prominent Ohio socialist that "I had nothing to do with Debs's campaign." She asserted defensively and inaccurately that "the socialists in their whole lives never gave me a dollar." Still angry about the Barnes affair, she continued, "They are not running my affairs and they don't own me and they had better learn to quit slandering people if they are going to revolutionize the nation. They had better revolutionize their own brains first."[14]

Her distance from the socialists, if not from socialism, increased because of her admiration for Woodrow Wilson. Shocking many of her old friends, she supported the war effort when the United States entered World War I in April 1917. Here again she found herself opposing Debs, who urged socialists to campaign for peace and to keep the United States out of what he labeled an imperialist war. Mother Jones shared Debs's sense of the arrival of a great, world-altering crisis, but she saw the war as an opportunity "to clean the kaiser up." Speaking at the UMWA 1918 convention, she urged working people to join "the Home Guards" so that, at war's end, "we will have the guns and we will turn them on the common enemy." This unequivocal call to arms represents one of the few times Mother Jones urged workers to engage in systematic violence in anticipation of capitalists using "their army to crush the workers and destroy the future of the nation."[15]

Tempering Mother Jones's support for Wilson was her interest in the welfare of working people. The war offered labor unions an unprecedented opportunity for growth when the federal government, in its quest for uninterrupted industrial output to ensure a smooth flow of supplies for the war effort, regulated prices, set wages in many industries, and took control of the railroads and telegraphs. It also enforced existing state labor laws guaranteeing collective bargaining for miners and banning company stores. Labor unions, shielded from discrimination by the government, expanded: the AFL added over a million new members, reaching a total of 3.5 million by the end of 1918.

Mother Jones spent most of the war in West Virginia, where she ignored national labor relations policies and fomented industrial conflict. She organized miners in the New River field, previously non-union but a fertile area for the UMWA thanks to wartime protections. These had been obtained in return for a ban on strikes, which Mother Jones promised to honor, telling the 1918 UMWA convention, "What we must do is to settle down to one thing—no more strikes in the mines, not a single strike. Let us keep at one strike, a strike to strike the Kaiser off the throne."[16] In the Mountain State she contradicted herself by urging strikes, causing the governor, a state senator, and various mine operators to appeal to federal and union officials to silence her or remove her from the state. Though reports of her speeches have not survived, clearly she was encouraging miners to see the global conflict as an opportunity to fight for higher wages and better working conditions, advising them to take advantage of their strong bargaining position by striking if necessary.

The end of the war in 1918 was followed by a brief period of optimism and then fear for the future. Much of the postwar anxiety focused on the red menace supposedly caused by the presence of socialists and communists in the United States. Generating these fears was the Russian Revolution of November 1917, when a communist faction called the Bolsheviks seized power under the leadership of Lenin. Mother Jones caught the mood of the times by calling herself a Bolshevik. Speaking to striking furniture makers in Rockford, Illinois, in April 1919 she exclaimed, "I am a Bolshevist," defining it somewhat generally as "rule of the majority."[17] At this moment in American history such a declaration guaranteed publicity, possibly a jail term, and even, as happened to a handful of Americans and many foreign nationals, deportation to Russia. Paranoia about communism and efforts to detect so-called subversives led to the suspension of civil rights as the federal government and local authorities arrested hundreds of people for seditious behavior. The Red Scare followed hard on the heels of the war and gave employers an excuse to roll back labor's wartime gains. As soldiers returned from the front, unemployment increased and employers sought to cut costs. The stage had been set for renewed industrial conflict.

Mother Jones once again enlisted the past to aid her cause. She claimed that Jesus and the American revolutionaries had been communists because of their desire for social change. She scandalized the reading public by calling Washington, Lincoln, and Patrick Henry "Reds," saying the Bolsheviks were doing God's work. The war and the revolution in Russia meant "labor slaves used to eat the crumbs from the masters' tables. Now they take their chairs."[18] Speaking in Peoria, Illinois, in April 1919 she explained how, "when I was in Washington, I heard the word Bolsheviki and I wondered what it meant, so I went to the library to find out and I found that Bolsheviki stood for the majority taking over the industry." Such a state of affairs, in reality a political situation in which "soviets" (workers' councils) took power, seemed perfectly natural to her because "the industry belongs to us. We run them. [Industries] don't belong to the [capitalist]. He stole them. He is a high class burglar." To clarify her meaning she continued, "Our boys are coming home in their uniforms. We sent them abroad to shoot the Kaiser. Let me tell you, we are going to get some Kaisers here at home." Invoking the labor theory of value she compared workers to the hands of a wristwatch, which would be "nice looking" but useless without the hands, those "tools that move the nation" for whom "a new civilization is coming."[19]

Her millennial language echoed events in 1919. Heightening the authorities' fear of revolution was an upsurge in labor unrest. That year saw a greater proportion of the American work force on strike than any other twelve-month period in U.S. history. Nearly one-fifth of all workers went on strike at some point during the year. One of the largest and most violent of those strikes involved workers in the steel industry, and Mother Jones was there. She spent much of 1919 organizing on their behalf.

Fewer commodities were as important to the American economy as steel or as hazardous to produce. The U.S. Steel Corporation, formed in

1901 by the merger of the largest companies in the industry, produced most of the steel manufactured in the United States. Controlled by Judge Elbert Gary, Charles Schwab, and other capitalists, its managers fiercely opposed unions. Conditions in steel mills were a brutal combination of heat, exhausting physical labor, extreme danger from large machinery and molten metals, and long working days. Workers endured twelve-hour shifts six days a week, with one twenty-four-hour shift on Sundays to enable night laborers to change over to daytime work. The challenge for organized labor lay not in formulating or publicizing steelworkers' grievances—those were widely known—but in overcoming the vertical integration of the industry and the fragmentation of its work force, which encompassed occupations from patternmaking to bricklaying.

To meet this difficulty the AFL agreed to support the work of the National Committee for Organizing Iron and Steel, an initiative of the Chicago Federation of Labor. Created after a successful drive to unionize meat packers, the National Committee undertook the Herculean task of convincing twenty-four separate unions to cooperate. Under the leadership of Chicago Federation of Labor president John Fitzpatrick and Pittsburgh-based organizer and former Wobbly William Z. Foster, the National Committee set about coordinating the separate unions organizing workers in the steel industry. The UMWA, the largest constituent of the AFL, agreed to assist, and its acting president, John L. Lewis, assigned Mother Jones to Pittsburgh in February. Though a center of the steel industry, western Pennsylvania was not the most important region for the organizing drive, and it is probable that Lewis, who did not like her, sent Mother Jones there to get her out of his way or to divert her from the looming coal strike.

Regardless of his motives, Lewis could surely have guessed that her work in Pennsylvania would generate excitement and publicity. It did both. Mother Jones, as was her wont, perceived her work as having world-historical importance. She had long claimed to be close to steelworkers, whose strike in 1915 she had called "a part of the great industrial conflict" promising to reshape the world.[20] In her 1919 Peoria address she proclaimed, "Friends, fellow workers, we are living today in the greatest age the world has ever passed through in human history. The whole world is ablaze with revolt."[21] The impending steel strike indicated that "the cyclone was coming. We must get ready for it."[22] In August she was arrested for speaking without a permit in Homestead, the infamous steel suburb of Pittsburgh. A crowd of steelworkers followed her to jail intent on rescuing her and only dispersed after she advised them to go home. She could also counsel violence, though, calling the authorities of the steel region a "brutal autocracy," urging the men to fight back, and complaining

William Z. Foster and
Other Steel Strike Leaders,
courtesy Library of Congress
Prints and Photographs
Division

about another speaker who cautioned strikers to be peaceful. At this she wondered, "Imagine what a statement to make to men who are going to strike. I wonder if Washington was peaceful when he was cleaning hell out of King George's men." Instead of harmony, she promised, "we're going to have hell. Strikes are not peace. We are striking for bread, for justice, for what belongs to us."[23]

As workers' expectations rose and pressure for a strike mounted, Mother Jones and three other organizers were arrested and briefly jailed, one battle in an escalating war of words and deeds between the National Committee and the steel bosses. Foster and Fitzpatrick tried to convince employers to negotiate, but the steel companies continued to retract the gains made by labor during World War I and refused to recognize the organization. Economic conditions favored their counterattack, just as the Red Scare aided anti-union drives. Unemployment rose, providing employers with a reserve army of labor with which to smash unions and enforce the open shop. The National Committee appealed to President Wilson for assistance, and he urged both sides to wait for a presidential commission to investigate conditions in the steel industry; but the steel bosses refused, and conflict appeared inevitable.

The strike began on 22 September 1919, authorized by a strongly favorable vote by steelworkers. The National Committee demanded recognition of the various unions as collective bargaining agents, an eight-hour working day with overtime pay, a guaranteed day off every week, and abolition of the twenty-four-hour shift. Mother Jones traveled from steel center to steel center, bolstering morale, garnering support, and reminding steelworkers of the significance of their action. In one week in October, for example, she traveled to Chicago "to 'buck up'" wavering strikers.[24] She spoke in South Chicago, Gary, Hammond, Waukegan, and Joliet. In Gary, a new city named in honor of the president of U.S. Steel, she promised, "We're going to change the name and we're going to take over the steel works and we're going to run them for Uncle Sam." She reminded striking steelworkers that they were fighting against "the damned gang of robbers" and urged them to "clear hell of every damned scab you can lay hold on. We'll hang the bloodhounds to the telegraph pole. Go out and picket." Connecting union activism to religion, she exhorted them, "For Christ's sake, be men and women," telling them, "Christ was the world's greatest agitator, but I defy any one to tell me Christianity reigns." She told the policemen in her audience that they had gone to Europe "to clean up the Kaiser" and wondered, "Ain't you men enough to come over and help us get the Kaisers at home?" She then proclaimed, "If Bolshevist is what [I] understand it to be, then I'm a Bolshevist from the bottom of my feet to the top of my head."[25]

Steel industry employers proved to be unrelenting foes. Manipulating the media, they blamed every outbreak of violence on the unions and tarred them with the charge of communism. Though Foster publicly disavowed his IWW past, newspapers published the steel bosses' claims that he was in the pay of Russian communists and had a secret agenda to undermine the government and foment revolution. Mother Jones calling herself a Bolshevik did not help matters. Starting just a month after the strike had begun, pro-business newspapers regularly printed reports about how the effort was on the verge of collapse. Despite the exertions of Mother Jones and the other organizers for the National Committee, strikers slowly returned to work. The action continued into 1920, but a cold winter and an understandable fear of losing their jobs undermined the resolve of those still out. After one last effort to open negotiations with the steel owners, the National Committee called off the strike on 8 January 1920; twenty-two workers had been killed and countless others injured. The strike had highlighted the power of capitalists in the postwar labor relations environment, but it also showed how steelworkers could unite to challenge the owners.

After the steel strike collapsed, Mother Jones traveled to California to recover her health. She visited old friends, including some in prison, before returning once more to West Virginia. In April 1920 she arrived in the Mountain State to assist in an ongoing union drive. This time, with most of the state effectively unionized during World War I, the UMWA concentrated on three non-union southern counties of Mingo, Logan, and McDowell. Though she felt that these were "stirring times," Mother Jones also allowed doubt about the future to creep into her letters. She told John H. Walker that "I don't know what the outcome is going to be," an unprecedented admission at the commencement of a drive. Her health was also a bother. She confided to him that "I am not as well and strong as I was when I saw you last."[26] Contributing to her pessimism was her mistrust of the president of the union, John L. Lewis.

To Mother Jones and many of her friends Lewis represented a new generation of union leaders more interested in consolidating their own power at union headquarters than in waging the class war. He was a disciple of business unionism, the idea that labor should fight within the system for realistic material gains rather than social reform. It did not help that one of Lewis's rivals for the presidency was John H. Walker. Lewis controlled the executive board and the union journal, giving him the leverage to gradually remove his challengers from the union. That the UMWA had won an important victory through the federal wages commission in early 1920 failed to impress Mother Jones. She feared that her legacy of a fighting union was vanishing beneath the compromises and quotidian concerns of the Lewis faction.

Organizing miners remained, after all, her occupation and her avocation. Mother Jones persisted through ill-health in West Virginia and continued to speak and travel in the three non-union counties. Military intelligence agents on the lookout for "Red" subversion followed her and transcribed some of her speeches. Her old themes came through clearly: she urged Mingo County miners to show "that spirit of manhood" to end capitalist tyranny and remind the world that "an injury to one working man is an injury to all."[27] She tried to enlist soldiers returning from the front on the grounds that, when they came home, "they didn't find any democracy but an increased autocracy. . . . Now we are after the robbers, the Kaisers at home."[28] She appealed to miners' pride ("You yourselves are men of honor, high-principled men") and their guilt ("Damn you, you are not fit to live under the flag. . . . You call yourselves Americans. Let me tell you America need not feel proud of you").[29] Her aim, as always, was forging class unity or, as she put it, "to get you solidified."[30] She continued to delight in historical references, asking, "Will you come back to the days of Patrick Henry, Jefferson, Lincoln, or will you stay with Schwab and Rockefeller?"[31] She also invoked patriotism, suggesting that "the bosses have no answer to give when you stand up and say that you are an American, and you are not going to enslave me. Join the Union and don't be afraid of anybody."[32]

The difficult, frustrating, and occasionally disillusioning work in West Virginia was happily interrupted by an invitation to return to Mexico.

Following the end of World War I and the settlements forged at Versailles and other postwar conferences, international meetings once more became commonplace. Mother Jones participated in one of these in January 1921 when she traveled to Mexico City as an AFL delegate to the Pan-American Federation of Labor. Journeying with West Virginia UMWA organizer Fred Mooney, she arrived on 9 January. Before their train even reached the capital, however, a line of taxis forced it to stop. Striking jewelry factory workers insisted on treating "Madre Yones" to a ceremonial entrance into Mexico City, festooning her with crimson carnations and blue violets as they drove her in procession to the capital. The Mexican government paid all of their expenses in honor of her work on behalf of the *revoltosos* in 1910. She had become an international celebrity, and some of the trappings of fame were made available to her: two servants and a taxicab were ready for her at any time in Mexico City, luxuries she guiltily enjoyed.

Before the conference started she told a contingent of journalists how increasing unemployment heralded the likelihood of the soviet system of government taking over in the United States. At a speech to the conference she told the assembled delegates, "It is a great age; it is a great time to live in." Samuel Gompers, no doubt fearful of what she might say, handed his chairman's gavel to another delegate before she started to speak. She did not disappoint, proclaiming, "Some people call us Bolsheviks, some call us I.W.W.s, some call us Reds. Well, what of it! If we are Red, then Jefferson was Red, and a whole lot of those people that have turned the world upside down were Red."[33] Mother Jones saw grounds for hope on the horizon, "because the world's workers have produced the enormous wealth of the world, and others have taken it; therefore, when the war was over, soldiers began to ask what was this war for, and why did we give up our wives and join the army. There is discontent everywhere, no matter where you go."[34] The conference itself represented grounds for optimism, for "when the workers solidify the world will rise, my friends. As long as you permit the capitalists to keep you divided, calling each other names and poisoning each other, you are going to make no progress."[35] She even found kind words for the AFL, calling it "the one institution that is leading the nations upward and onward to the final goal."[36] She concluded her address by reminding delegates, "You are here to unlock the doors to the coming age," and urging them to "stand together, let nothing divide you, and make every part of this hemisphere a fit place for men and women and children to live in."[37] It was classic Mother Jones.

The government of Mexico made an apartment available to Mother Jones for her use after the conference, but she did not linger. She fell ill soon after returning to West Virginia, writing to John H. Walker from

Charleston in April 1921 that "I have not been well John, since I came back from Mexico, I have had rheumatism so much, and it is kind of playing on me."[38] She did return to Mexico for three months at the end of April 1921, visiting the Yucatán to see her old friend Felipe Carillo Puerto, then provincial governor. She stayed in her apartment in Mexico City and traveled to give speeches, as much as her health would allow her. She wrote to John Fitzgerald and Ed Nockles of the Chicago Federation of Labor about her visit to Orizaba, a manufacturing center where she "got new hope for the future." When she spoke at a municipal building used by labor unions she was astonished to find that "there was no uniformed police there, either at the entrance or inside of the building. This was something marvelously new to me, because with us in the United States, in the great American Republic, you know the outside and inside would have been multiplied by the uniformed representatives of the high class burglars."[39] But dampening her optimism was the presence of what she called "sewer-rats" or "so-called revolutionists . . . that are doing their best to destroy the Labor movement."[40] Her visit to Mexico reinforced her perception that factionalism undermined movements for social change.

From the relative comfort of her apartment in Mexico City, Mother Jones had been monitoring events in West Virginia. What she learned worried her. She wrote to Walker, "I'm afraid they are going to lose out in Mingo [County] because they haven't had the man to handle the strike at the beginning." She believed that the absence of strong leadership was the consequence of business unionism. As she put it to her old friend, "They like to have a slate and they think more of 'my individual friend' than they do of the destinies of thousands of men, women and children."[41]

Mother Jones did not fully recover her health, and she found herself feeling tired and generally unwell. She briefly visited West Virginia in early August, giving an emotional address in which she seemed to counsel violent confrontation with the operators after the assassination of Sid Hatfield on 1 August. Hatfield, the pro-union police chief of Mingo County, was killed by a mine guard to avenge his role in an earlier gun battle during which seven Baldwin-Felts guards died. Violence escalated to the extent that Mother Jones made another speech on 24 August, this time urging miners not to kill the pro-operator sheriff of Logan County, Don Chafin. At this conciliatory speech she told the miners she had received a telegram from President Harding advising them to disband and promising to remove all Baldwin-Felts guards from the state. For once her fictionalizing was revealed. Fred Mooney, who had accompanied her to Mexico, and another union organizer doubted the authenticity of her telegram. They drove to Charleston and telephoned the White House. Harding's secretary told them that the president had sent no such missive: Mother Jones had been exposed, and her credibility suffered a terrible blow. Her subterfuge had convinced some miners to turn back temporarily, but the revelation of her sham telegram damaged her reputation, and the miners' march on Logan County proceeded.

At the end of August miners and mine guards engaged in a three-day shoot-out. The Battle of Blair Mountain, as this engagement became known, was the largest armed confrontation in the United States since the Civil War. This time President Harding did intervene, sending federal troops backed by airpower to end the fighting. The miners retreated, and the conflict moved to the courts, where the UMWA lost repeatedly and its leaders suffered the indignity of being called Reds and having their patriotism questioned. The operators won, and the three southernmost West Virginia coal counties remained non-union. Their cheap coal forced other operators in the state to smash the union.

The frustration Mother Jones felt at what she saw as the destruction of the UMWA by John L. Lewis poured out at the 1921 convention. She began by warning the leadership that it needed to stop "wasting a whole lot of time and money" and unite to force Congress to ban the use of armed guards and injunctions against union activities. She pleaded for a return to "the old times of Patrick Henry and Jefferson and Lincoln."[42] At a second address to the convention three days later, she reminded delegates of their responsibilities, telling them that union income "isn't your money; it is the money of the children and the women. You are giving the money to the capitalists, the hotels, street cars and pool rooms," and that, as "the fighting army of the working class of America," they had a duty to support the miners of West Virginia.[43]

Despite promising to do so, Mother Jones did not return to West Virginia. She fell ill, finally stopping in Springfield, Illinois, to recover with the Walkers, who put her under the care of a doctor after an attack of rheumatism. Compounding her disillusionment was continued UMWA infighting as Lewis sought to take control of the union by discrediting his three main rivals, Frank Farrington, Alexander Howat, and John H. Walker. As she wrote to William Green, the secretary-treasurer of the miners' union, "It is not alone the physical sickness that is breaking me down, but it is the thoughts of the internal trouble among ourselves within our own ranks. I dread the future of the organization, from what I see now."[44] Her own future, full of ill-health and uncertainty, also appeared bleak, but she continued to fight for the causes close to her heart.

11

Mother Jones of America

MOTHER JONES SPENT THE FINAL decade of her life suffering from rheumatism, censuring the union movement, and seeking to protect the legacy of her life's work. The ratification of constitutional amendments legalizing woman suffrage and banning alcoholic drinks pained her. She spent an amazing amount of time traveling, particularly for a woman in her late eighties and early nineties. Prolonged illnesses in 1922 and 1925, which earned extensive newspaper coverage because she seemed near to death, slowed her considerably. Regardless of her poor health she kept abreast of the labor movement and traveled to hot spots whenever able. She also devoted her time to aiding fellow organizers imprisoned by what she saw as the capitalist-controlled legal system.

Mother Jones felt her sicknesses deeply. While assisting a UMWA organizing drive in West Virginia in 1920, she wrote to John H. Walker, president of the Illinois Federation of Labor and one of her closest friends, that "I have just as great a desire to keep on fighting," but confessed to "not feeling as well John as I used to" and feared she would not "be able to do the work I have been."[1] She wrote with uncharacteristic pessimism to another longtime friend, UMWA secretary-general William Green, that the future "looks so dark to me."[2] On several occasions Mother Jones worried she would not recover. In December 1923, during a particularly harsh winter, she told Walker how she was "suffering severely with rheumatism" and feeling "awfully nervous," leading her to believe she would never "get over that attack."[3] Despite the ministrations of a doctor, Mother Jones soon complained, "It looks as if [I] will not get well again."[4] She often wintered in California in an effort to gain some relief from her rheumatism, but in 1925 she wrote Walker from Los Angeles that "I have given up all hopes of regaining my health. I am going back to stay at Powderly's" in Washington, D.C., where she would "get to see some of the old timers occasionally. While that does not bring back my health, still it does away with the blues."[5] She returned to California one last time in early 1927 "owing to the condition of my health," but sickness overtook her while en route to Washington, and she was hospitalized for a month.[6] These periods of immobility dented her usual optimism and brought her close to depression.

By the time she had reached her eighty-third year in 1920, Mother Jones considered Washington her home. Terence and Emma Powderly kept a bedroom for her in their house outside the city. As early as June 1920 Powderly, the former leader of the Knights of Labor and by then a government immigration official, wrote to her while she was in West Virginia that "if you don't feel just exactly right switch off and come home at once."[7] It must have been a great comfort, after three decades of virtually nonstop traveling, to have found stability like this. Powderly wrote how he and Emma "talk of you every day and express regret that you did not remain at home until fully recovered and strong enough to take up the burden again."[8] Mother Jones, who had no desire to stop organizing, finally had a refuge when she needed one. In her letters she responded positively to the idea of a permanent residence, writing in 1921 to Powderly, "I am coming home when the spring comes."[9] With the Powderlys she found companions who had shared her suffering in the cause of labor and who affirmed her role as Mother Jones. She wrote to Emma Powderly in February 1923, "I miss home very much and all the old friends about it," and to Terence Powderly in May of the same year, "I'll be home sometime soon."[10] After Terence Powderly died in June 1924 she began to split her time between Emma Powderly and her friends Lillian and Walter Burgess, who owned a farm near Silver Spring, Maryland. It was there in 1930 that she would celebrate her "centennial" and, six months later, die.

Home, whether with the Powderlys or the Burgesses, comforted Mother Jones at a time when she believed the labor movement was self-destructing. She neither liked nor trusted John L. Lewis as he slowly eliminated his rivals for the UMWA presidency. Her animosity toward Lewis was buttressed by John H. Walker, who battled Lewis for leadership of the union into the 1930s. Walker shared Mother Jones's concerns about the direction of the workers' movement and wrote to her in November 1922 that Lewis and his allies were "out to assault and destroy everybody

Mother Jones at Home in Hyattsville, Maryland (1929), courtesy Library of Congress Prints and Photographs Division

in every position in the labor movement."[11] Lewis's tactics, Walker wrote a month later, showed "the inhuman cruel and unscrupulous nature of that gentleman," proving "how little he cares for the labor movement. . . . It means nothing to him except as it may serve his own personal purposes."[12] Walker subsequently offered Mother Jones his opinion that Lewis was "brutal" and lacked "human feeling or decency."[13]

Mother Jones agreed wholeheartedly with Walker's characterization of Lewis and his associates, adding her own grievances. She remained angry at Fred Mooney and Frank Keeney for exposing her telegram from President Harding as a forgery and thwarting her attempt to avert the

Battle of Blair Mountain. She blamed them for her ill-health at the end of 1922, reminding Walker, "You know I helped to build up West Va[.] I waded creeks to get [to] meeting[s.] I faced machine guns[.] I spent months in Military Prisson." She complained inaccurately that she had been forced to argue her own case in court because "the miners never spent a Dol[lar] for a Lawyer for me" and that all the money she earned she gave away or spent during the course of her organizing. Her main point was that "Lewis never did that."[14]

Embedded in her criticisms of Lewis and the union movement of the 1920s was a broader concern about an apparent shift in tactics from confronting owners and fomenting social revolution to fighting for modest material gains. She feared that the UMWA had become a business union concerned only with improving wages and living standards for its members. Though Mother Jones exaggerated the extent to which the union movement had changed, there was a grain of truth in her charge that it had become focused on incremental gains and relinquished any claim to a social agenda. Leaders like Lewis made demands they believed owners could realistically be expected to concede. The revolutionary programs associated with unions such as the Western Federation of Miners and the IWW seemed passé. *Realism* was the watchword of the new leaders, though they were actually following in the footsteps of John Mitchell and Samuel Gompers. Mother Jones derided conservatism in her quest for dramatic improvements in the lives of her "boys" and ultimately workers' control of industry. Because of this she ignored the extent to which wages and working conditions had been part of the UMWA agenda from its very beginning. She also overlooked the union's ongoing claim to act as the recognized collective-bargaining institution for all workers in the industry, a demand mine operators resisted fiercely in their desire for the "open shop."

As an organizer Mother Jones claimed to see beyond the immediate grievances of a particular strike. Uniting workers into a single class by convincing them of their power had been her objective, one she feared the union movement was abandoning. She wrote in 1921 to her friend William Green of the UMWA how "it makes me tremble at the thoughts of men fighting each other when a great principle is at stake. This is the time we should have harmony" to oppose the common enemy.[15] She damned the 1920s as "a pie-counter age" in which union officers showed "a much deeper desire for the odor coming from the flesh pot of capitalism than they have for . . . the future of the nation."[16] Self-aggrandizement and factionalism heralded the end of the labor movement, she thought, and "the wrecking force will be from within."[17]

Despite her anger at Lewis and her expressions of alarm at the direction he was taking the UMWA, she showed how much she valued unity at the February 1922 miners' union convention. Here, on her final appearance at the annual meeting of miners' delegates, she attempted to end a divisive clash between Lewis and his enemies. Miners' delegates were debating Lewis's treatment of Kansas leader Alexander Howat instead of discussing upcoming wage negotiations. Howat had been jailed for ordering Kansas miners to strike in defiance of a state law banning strikes and requiring miners to enter arbitration to settle grievances. Lewis saw Howat, not unreasonably, as a rival for the presidency and used Howat's illegal strike call as a pretext for removing him from the union. Though she admired Howat's stand and spoke in his defense, Mother Jones called on the delegates to return to the issue of wage negotiations and to stop wasting time and money on internal battles. She urged them to honor the memory of "the men who laid the foundation of this great organization" and respect "the bones of the men who marched miles in the dead of night to get you together."[18] She admonished the delegates, "Now, boys, settle it, and stop this howling like a lot of fiends." She spoke of her admiration for Howat and advised the convention to take up his case at a later date and "settle down to business today."[19]

Contemporary newspaper reports credited Mother Jones with restoring order at what had been, until her intervention, a tumultuous gathering. The *New York Times* reported how she silenced Howat's supporters and, ironically, enabled Lewis to win a close vote to expel the Kansas leader.[20] Mother Jones maintained that she was motivated by the best interests of working people, something she claimed to be uniquely qualified to understand because "I have no ax to grind—I am not looking for any office."[21] In a pie-counter age she refused to join the feast. As she told the delegates in 1922, she remained neutral because "I don't get myself under obligations to any officer; I keep my hands clean and can fight any of them."[22] She believed that her independence, her desire to avoid internal disputes, and her love of organizing furnished her with political neutrality and permitted her to criticize every side.

Her mistrust of institutions, and especially of union organizers and leaders who did not see the world as she did, remained a constant in Mother Jones's life. In 1905 she had written to William B. Wilson, a founder of the UMWA and destined to be U.S. secretary of labor from 1913 to 1921, about what she considered incompetent and untrustworthy organizers. She called them succinctly "those Traitors."[23] Nearly two decades later she complained to Green that members "are betrayed by the very men they pay."[24] Mother Jones positioned herself as a self-appointed benevolent matriarch who, standing above the fray, could see beyond the distractions of the moment. Her vision never wavered: she wanted class war for the sake of working families and demanded wages sufficient to allow women to remain at home raising children. As she wrote to Green in 1921, "The destinies of thousands of men[,] women and children are of far more interest to me than all the office holders within [the union's] ranks."[25]

Mother Jones believed that union leaders who refused to use their organizations as forces for social change exhibited a cowardly concern with their own high salaries and comfortable lives. They had, she thought, forgotten what it was like to toil in a mine or a factory and were exploiting those whose dues funded their incomes. As she put it to Walker, "The fellow who gets fourteen thousand a year and expenses, will hardly take any chances."[26] She complained to Robert Watchorn, the first UMWA secretary, about a poor miner who won election to union office wearing patched trousers and old shoes and who, after twelve years as an official, had "a fine home, automobiles," and a wife "decorated with diamond rings." Such behavior dishonored "the men and women who are moulding in their graves that took the thorns out of the pathways of those office-holders of today."[27] Mother Jones was beginning to see herself as one of those early leaders and resented being ignored by the union movement. She feared for her place in history.

The growing evidence of her own mortality accelerated her dread of being lost to posterity. Early in the 1920s she wrote about her own death. She told Terence Powderly while preparing her autobiography that "I don't want as much as ten cents in my possession when I travel to the grave" and distanced herself from the "heathenism" of a "fine coffin."[28] She admitted she wanted "the tributes paid while we live" but began to contemplate burial in the miners' cemetery at Mount Olive, telling John Walker, "When I pass away the boys at Mt. Olive will see that I am laid to rest with the boys that gave up their lives some twenty seven years ago in Verdon [sic] Illinois."[29]

Her version of history played a key role in how Mother Jones shaped her legacy, particularly her obsession with martyrdom. She placed her own agitation in a direct line from Jesus to the American revolutionaries, invoking Columbus and the Pilgrims along the way to demonstrate the justice of her cause. Her right to free speech came "from Patrick Henry, and Jefferson, and Adams, and Washington."[30] She most admired Patrick Henry for his willingness to die for the cause of liberty, a death she sought for herself. As she told the mine workers' convention in 1902, "I say with [Henry], 'Give me liberty or give me death, for for liberty I shall die, even if they riddle my body with bullets after I am dead.'"[31] As was the case for the Virginia revolutionary, however, fate refused to deliver the type of death she desired. Mother Jones had the misfortune of living into old age and seeing many of her friends and colleagues preceding her to the grave; as she put it, "Most all the old warriors are gone or dead."[32]

Mother Jones hoped to remind people of her life and legacy by celebrating the centenary of her birth in Chicago, telling leaders of the Chicago Federation of Labor (CFL), "I want to live to be 100 and come to Chicago to celebrate the anniversary."[33] Mother Jones shaped her reputation by telling and retelling stories about her contributions to the union movement. In the last decade of her life she attempted to fashion how she would be remembered. As she pondered her place in history, Mother Jones bemoaned how the union movement seemed to neglect, deny, and even denigrate its early leaders. At the height of her anger toward John L. Lewis she complained to Walker that "down all of history the workers have crowned their Trators [and] crucified her Saviors."[34] She regretted how contemporary labor leaders failed to show labor's pioneers "some appreciation of what they did," of how they had sacrificed families, material comfort, and even their lives for the sake of the organization.[35] Responding to this lament William Green assured her, "The work you have done will live. Nothing can destroy it."[36] Mother Jones also found comfort in the company of Terence Powderly, with whom she remembered "the stormy days of the past" and regretted that "there is no one in the labor movement that understands its struggle more clearly than we do."[37] She wrote in confessional mode to West Virginia governor Ephraim Morgan how "I regret war more than I have words to utter,—the terrific mistake that was made in West Virginia." She told him that she admired his stand against the mine operators and proposed that only "practical, fundamental, patriotic education" could bring about positive social change.[38]

Mother Jones could not shield her legacy from the political and social transformations of the 1920s. Most dramatically, the status of women changed when passage of the Nineteenth Amendment legalized woman suffrage nationally. Women had been voting in some western states before then, but women's contributions to World War I and the long-running pressure of organized suffrage groups paid off after generations of challenging and violating nineteenth-century moral and sexual codes. By the end of the century reformers like Emma Goldman and Margaret Sanger called for amending divorce laws and disseminating information about birth control, while dance halls and amusement parks facilitated an unprecedented mingling of the sexes. Above all a growing chorus demanded the vote for women.

Mother Jones perceived these developments as distractions from the hard work of fomenting class war in the quest for a just and equitable society. She had long championed organizing women workers, who had grown as a proportion of the paid work force from 15 percent in 1870 to about 21 percent by 1910. As early as July 1901 she helped "several hundred servant girls [who] have signified their intention of becoming charter members of the first servant girls' union of Chicago," and she regularly mobilized women into mop and broom brigades in support of striking miners.[39] Clearly, she did not believe that women should be docile and dependent, but she did take a traditional view of women's role in the family.

Mother Jones benefited from the freedoms of movement and action women were making for themselves, but she despised what she sneeringly called "the modern woman of today."[40] She maintained that women's primary roles should be wife and mother, writing in 1915 that "the mission of women is to develop human hearts and minds along charitable and sympathetic lines."[41] Women who ignored this imperative earned her wrath, including suffragists who, she said, neglected their duty by "playing parlor politics instead of raising the children of the nation."[42]

Mother Jones did not shy away from criticizing women. She particularly disliked upper-class women who abandoned their children to wet nurses and nannies. She expressed nothing but contempt for wealthy women who cared only for "idleness, fads, extravagance and display of wealth."[43] After a visit to the Colony Club, an exclusive women's club in New York City, she reported to journalists that "I saw the biggest bunch of women parasites and scandal cats ever gotten together under one roof." She noted how "five hundred dollar hats, wonderfully feathered, adorned [the] empty heads of women who know nothing of how the other half lives." Her condemnation traveled from their "flabby bodies . . . clothed in the richest of silks" to what she considered their ignorance, for "not a single one of these parasites know anything useful."[44] Ever attuned to fashion and willing to supply her own interpretation of its meaning she told elite women in Toledo, "You wear high collars to support your jaw and keep your befuddled brains from oozing out of your mouths."[45] To an audience of upper-class suffragists gathered in her honor in 1914 she claimed, without regard for either their sensibilities or their politics, that women voters in Colorado hurt workers in the state. She told them they "got the vote without knowing anything about the civic conditions" and therefore exercised the franchise blindly by voting as their husbands instructed them.[46]

In her speeches to miners Mother Jones often told a story about seeing a wealthy woman driving with her poodle seated beside her. She said, "I watched the poodle—every now and again the poodle would squint its eye at her and turn up its nose when it got a look at her." Putting words in the mouth of the canine companion she imagined it saying, "You corrupt, rotten, decayed piece of humanity, my royal dogship is degraded sitting beside you."[47] Mother Jones seemed particularly angry that wealthy women insulated themselves from life's realities, including raising children. If rich women would "raise their own babies their hearts would open and their feelings would become human."[48]

Mother Jones usually opposed extending the franchise to women. She told an audience of miners in Princeton, West Virginia, in 1920, "I am not a suffragette, for I have been suffering all my life."[49] She claimed that suffrage organizations distracted women from the struggle for class consciousness, telling miners, "I don't care about your woman suffrage and the temperance brigade or any other of your class associations."[50] She believed that "labor has not yet learned the lesson of lining up its women. The plutocrats have learned it. They give their women suffrage, prohibition, and other fads to keep their minds busy."[51] After the Ludlow Massacre she complained unfairly that women voters in Colorado "never raised their voice against this infamy."[52] She criticized suffragists who heckled President Woodrow Wilson in 1917, calling them "idiots" and telling reporters, "They ought to be in jail or the insane asylum, I can't decide which." They were behaving, she decided, "like a bunch of naughty little girls" and were "an insult not only to the president, but to the entire country."[53]

Countering these complaints about the futility of women voting were occasional hints that there was a place for women at the ballot box. Prior to excoriating the wealthy women of Toledo she exonerated all women from the charge of neglecting public life—in this case for ignoring the use of injunctions against union organizers—on the grounds that "women are not responsible because they have no vote."[54] This implied that enfranchising women would allow them to exercise their public duties. Her sporadic approval of woman suffrage seemed not to have represented a change of heart but, rather, suggested a casual inconsistency. In 1910, for example, she linked the powerlessness of the Milwaukee brewery girls (and by extension all women workers) to their being disenfranchised. She wrote that, "had they the vote . . . their case would likely have attracted more attention from all sides." In the ballot box, on this occasion, lay salvation.[55]

If inconsistent on the matter of suffrage, Mother Jones remained steadfast in her conviction that women needed to participate in strikes. She contradicted the distinction between public and private spheres even as she demanded women stay at home raising children. She told striking New York City shirtwaist makers, "The woman must fight in the labor movement beside [the] man. Every strike that I have ever been in has been won by women."[56] She argued in 1911 that working-class women understood this, for "the women in the industrial field have begun to awaken to their condition of slavery." As evidence she spoke of how "in New York and Philadelphia the women . . . gave battle fearlessly. They were clubbed, they were jailed, they were insulted, but they bore it all for a principle they believed in. Never can a complete victory be won until the woman awakens to her condition."[57] She recognized how male workers restricted women, admonishing miners in 1914 that "the trouble with you has been that you have never allowed your women to come into your meetings and take a share in discussing these great questions."[58] She promised that if women gained full access to "economic fights . . . we could clean it up tomorrow."[59]

One way to understand the inconsistencies—as they appear from the outside—in Mother Jones's approach to the place of women in American society is to see them in the context of her own life. Though she worked for a living as a paid organizer known for her ability to mobilize women and bring men into the union, she retained a nostalgic view of her role in the Jones household in Memphis. Moreover, the experience of working alongside children in the factories of the Deep South stayed with her. She believed, "It is in the home where the child is nursed, where character is formed, and where everything depends upon the early training, that the true work of reform can be done."[60] She had complete faith in maternal nurturing. As she put it in 1921, "If you raise the child properly we would have no murders and we would not have to resent war, because nobody would go to war. There would be more time in the home to develop the coming generations, plant the human feeling in their breast and show them their duty."[61] Mother Jones proved herself to be as conservative on the appropriate role for women as she was radical on the question of social change.

She vehemently opposed ratification of the Eighteenth Amendment and the Volstead Act banning the production, distribution, and consumption of intoxicating liquors. She denounced prohibition as a prime example of elitist legislation, asking in 1923, "Why should ambassadors of foreign countries and people of wealth be privileged to enjoy choice liquors while the laboring class are denied the use of beer and wines?"[62] The hypocrisy and injustice of a law easily evaded by the rich angered her, as did the obvious attack on a working-class culture in which alcohol played an important role. Mother Jones participated in the masculine culture of the saloon, where she met and organized miners and other workers in defiance of socially prescribed limits on women. She often promised audiences a "jag" (or binge) when their lives improved, telling West Virginia miners in 1912, "I would rather drink than let the banker drink," and advising them, "I don't mind you taking a drink, I know you need it."[63]

As with the issue of woman suffrage, the animosity Mother Jones displayed toward temperance advocates ran through her speeches. Mother Jones saw prohibition as another distraction from the main issues she believed working people should care about. Writing in 1900 she criticized "temperance parasites" who "warn the miners against wasting their money for drink," taking away one of the few pleasures enjoyed by workingmen seeking respite from occupational hazards.[64] She complained that "in the steel mills, men working beside roaring blast furnaces in waistline attire, the excessive heat wasting away their bodies, have to be contented to drink water to quench their thirst. The same is true of workers in other industries."[65] She did not believe prohibition could last, predicting inaccurately in April 1923, "Before I am another year older I expect to see light wines and beer returned to the people of the United States."[66]

Though the success enjoyed by suffrage and prohibition advocates reinforced her mistrust of politics, Mother Jones briefly participated in the proceedings of the Farmer-Labor Party. This third party originated in Chicago in 1920 at the impetus of her friend John Fitzpatrick, head of the Chicago Federation of Labor. In her autobiography she claimed to have "rejoiced to see the formation of a third political party," but her correspondence told another story.[67] She expressed doubts about its viability from the very beginning, writing to Walker in March 1920, "I wouldn't have much to do with that political movement if I were you. . . . I don't think, John, it will have the effect that the boys thought it would—However, let us hope for the best."[68] She was afraid that the radical impulse had expired, writing to Kansas City journalist Ryan Walker that the socialist movement in his town was "practically dead" because the "old timers" who sustained it "are all going over to the [Farmer-]Labor party."[69] Perhaps, she hoped, the new party might revive class war.

If so, her wish would not be granted. Despite her misgivings she attended and spoke glowingly to the Farmer-Labor Party's 1923 convention, calling it "the most important [gathering] since the Revolutionary War." In her speech to the delegates she advised them to "organize and use your heads" to defeat employers and eliminate "crooked labor leaders." She concluded with her expectation that "the producers, not the meek, shall inherit the earth. Not today perhaps, nor tomorrow, but over the rim of years my old eyes can see the coming of another day."[70]

Her uplifting rhetoric disguised contempt for what she found at the convention. She told Walker that the Farmer-Labor Party attracted "high-brows and know it all[s], who had no more conception of the death struggle that we are in than a lot of school children."[71] Her fear that the party represented merely another opportunity for "pie counters" to take advantage of working people was confirmed when William Green verified her hunch that "a woman delegate there who . . . was a member of the Communist party" was traveling around Illinois collecting funds for herself under false pretences.[72]

Mother Jones attended the Farmer-Labor Party convention because it was convenient for her to do so: she spent much of the first half of 1923 in Chicago writing her autobiography. The idea for this project, she said, came from the famous defense lawyer Clarence Darrow, with whom she had cooperated on the 1905 Idaho trial of Western Federation of Miners leaders. She asked Walker in December 1922, "I wish you would see Darrow about that book he has wanted me [to] write . . . [because] now I am ready for I cannot do anything else."[73] She traveled to Chicago in March 1923 and moved in with Ed Nockles, secretary of the CFL, to draft the manuscript. She found the task onerous, telling Emma Powderly, "I am getting so D— tired writing this book."[74] Her publisher, Charles H. Kerr, hired Chicago journalist Mary Field Parton to keep Mother Jones on track by writing down her reminiscences and, in all likelihood, drafting the first version of the work. The result displeased Mother Jones enormously: not only did it fail to make any money—she had hoped to donate the profits to the defense of imprisoned union leaders—but "the book is not printed as I wrote it anyway, and I have never been satisfied with it."[75]

Her autobiography did not enjoy the success Mother Jones anticipated because it captured neither her personality nor her rhetorical style. Newsworthy and noteworthy, Mother Jones had been attracting attention ever since her arrest and imprisonment in the 1902 West Virginia coal strike. She knew how to use the press, and much of her fame derived from reports of her speeches and interviews. Traveling from Indianapolis to Colorado in 1915, for example, she offered a set of epigrams to a *Chicago Daily Tribune* journalist while stopping in the Windy City; her list found its way onto the front page of the newspaper's 15 February edition. On another occasion a report of her appearance at a CFL meeting recorded that "damns and darns punctuated" the proceedings as Mother Jones, "in untempered English," opposed injunctions against picketing.[76]

A startling indication of her growing fame occurred in 1919 when she visited the Illinois mining town of Zeigler. Here, "they turned two machine guns on me" when she had tried to organize miners a decade before, but now "I went in on a special train and was met at the depot by the Mayor," himself a miner, and stayed at his house.[77] She had become famous, and her reputation transcended the union movement. Beginning in 1926 her exploits were recalled periodically in a *Chicago Daily Tribune* column looking back at the recent past. In October 1926, for example, an article under the heading "10 Years Ago Today" recalled the "riot" of women during the New York streetcar strike.[78] In July of the following year the newspaper commemorated the twenty-fifth anniversary of her appearance before Judge John Jackson in Parkersburg, West Virginia.[79] She also had become a cultural icon who appeared in other people's memoirs. Florence Jaffray Harriman from the Commission on Industrial Relations called Mother Jones "at first glance a sort of benign little body . . . known for forty years down every mine shaft in America" and famous for "raising hell."[80] Woodrow Wilson's secretary Joseph P. Tumulty recalled in his autobiography how, during World War I, Mother Jones had been a regular visitor to the White House, where she came to inform the president "in her vigorous, emphatic way" about "labor conditions in the coal field."[81] She changed her party allegiance after the 1920 election, and when she visited with and then endorsed Calvin Coolidge for president in 1924 newspapers

President Calvin Coolidge, Mother Jones, Grace Coolidge, and Theodore Roosevelt Jr. at the White House (1924), courtesy Library of Congress Prints and Photographs Division

published her statement that "he is fair. His policies are sound and I am convinced that he is the right man for the White House."[82]

Mother Jones had long sought the assistance of U.S. presidents, beginning in 1897 when she had traveled to Washington to visit President McKinley to obtain the release of an imprisoned American Railway Union activist. In 1906, at Clarence Darrow's suggestion, she had embarked on a speaking tour to assist "Big Bill" Haywood, Charles Moyer, and George Pettibone in their trial for murdering former Idaho governor Frank Steunenberg. Likewise her efforts to raise public awareness of and funds for the *revoltosos* indicated her desire to combat injustice by speaking and writing on behalf of the people she considered victims of a legal system controlled by capitalists. These examples were only the tip of the iceberg: Mother Jones tried to free the men imprisoned for bombing the *Los Angeles Times* building in 1910; assisted Tom Mooney, charged with bombing a Preparedness Day parade in 1916; wrote in 1920 to President Wilson seeking a pardon for Eugene Debs, imprisoned in Atlanta for speaking against World War I; and lent her name to groups fighting in 1927 for the release of Nicola Sacco and Bartolomeo Vanzetti, two Italian immigrant anarchists charged with murder.

Mother Jones Outside the White House (1924), courtesy Library of Congress Prints and Photographs Division

In addition to these high-profile prisoners, Mother Jones assisted many others behind the scenes. A case in point is Mr. Dolla, a young miner whose first name has been lost to history. Dolla found himself caught up in a violent strike in Pennsylvania in 1923. Mother Jones informed CFL president John Fitzpatrick of her plans to "get that poor helpless wretch out of jail and take him to his wife and children." She wrote Fitzpatrick that "we are working to find who the members of the Pardon Board are in order to be able to approach them." She also hoped to exert pressure in a different direction, for "I know a newspaper man here who is very close to the Governor and I think I will be able to do a little successful work."[83] In January 1924 she met with Secretary of Commerce (and future president) Herbert Hoover and with Pennsylvania governor Gifford Pinchot, a former Progressive ally of Theodore Roosevelt, asking for their assistance. She also wrote to West Virginia's Ephraim Morgan suggesting an exchange of prisoners, which he politely declined. She was optimistic of a quick release for Dolla nonetheless, writing to Fitzpatrick in February, "Things look bright for that boy in Pa."[84] The wheels of justice turned slowly, however, and her determination was not rewarded until July 1924 when Cornelia Bryce Pinchot, the governor's activist wife, wrote from Harrisburg to inform her that Dolla had been freed. Mrs. Pinchot also mentioned that "I did enjoy meeting you in Washington last winter," an indication that Mother Jones made a favorable impression on the Keystone State's first couple.[85] Mother Jones replied, "I have no words to convey how deeply I appreciate the interest you and Governor Pinchot have taken in the family of this poor boy. It was so good of you to restore the provider to the mother and children."[86] Her correspondence and occasional fragments in the press illustrate how Mother Jones helped numerous other workingmen in this way.

Despite her debilitating rheumatism and the comforts of the Powderly home, Mother Jones continued to travel as much as possible. In summer 1926 she spoke to striking dressmakers in Chicago, her final act of union organizing. She followed the labor movement closely and watched with interest the demise of the Farmer-Labor Party after its poor showing in the 1924 election, but Mother Jones became increasingly wrapped up in her own past. By 1926 travel was exceedingly difficult because of ill-health, though she did see old acquaintances from Ruskin Community, the utopian experiment she had visited in the 1890s, who lived in Alliance, Ohio. Here, Susana DeWolfe and Samuel Steiner helped her to participate in the Alliance Labor Day parade, which would prove to be her last public appearance. After staying in Chicago for the 1927–28 winter, Mother Jones returned to Washington, D.C., her travels at an end.

During the summer of 1929 her occasional visits to the Maryland farmhouse of her friends Walter and Lillian Burgess turned into a permanent arrangement. She spent most of her time in bed, but Mother Jones did manage to participate fully in her "centenary" celebrations on 1 May 1930. Her original plan to travel to Chicago for the event proved unrealistic, though as late as January of that year she told reporters, "I will be one hundred years old May 1 . . . and I am going to Chicago on that day, where the Chicago Federation of Labor intends to have a celebration in honor of my century of life."[87] The next month she fell ill, and her friends feared death was at hand, but by April she had rallied sufficiently to be excited about her forthcoming birthday and realistic enough to recognize she would have to remain in Maryland. The American Federation of Labor prepared to host parties in her honor across the country, and she anticipated addressing the nation in a radio speech.

Planning for the celebration began by obtaining the cooperation of county authorities to accelerate construction of a paved road connecting the farmhouse with the District of Columbia, facilitating the arrival and departure of guests. An influx of letters, telegrams, and flowers at the Burgess home began in mid-April, filling the house and spilling out onto the front porch with reminders of how famous Mother Jones remained. On 1 May policemen directed traffic along the new road and helped with crowd control as visitors arrived at carefully staggered intervals. On the lawn a band from the nearby Soldiers Home played Irish and American songs to entertain the overflow crowd while they waited for Mother Jones to appear.

Around midmorning Walter Burgess and a neighbor assisted Mother Jones from her bedroom to the lawn in front of the house, which had been decorated with bunting for the occasion. She sat under an apple tree wearing a black silk dress and greeting the many politicians, labor leaders, and admirers who came to the Burgess home to see her. They paid homage to her, chatted with her, admired the flowers she received, and read the telegrams that continued to arrive from around the country. They also shared her enormous birthday cake, topped by one hundred candles, supplied by the Building Trades Council of Washington, D.C.

Mother Jones marshaled her energy for one last speech, saying "in a ringing voice" that "America was not founded on dollars but on the blood of men who gave their lives for your benefit." She lamented the neglect of the labor theory of value that had driven so much of her organizing and rhetoric, thundering, "Power lies in the hands of labor to retain American liberty, but labor has not yet learned how to use that power." She touched on the theme of gender, noting, "A wonderful power is in the hands of women, too, but they don't know how to use it. Capitalists side track the women into clubs and make ladies of them. Nobody wants a lady, they want women. Ladies are parlor parasites."[88] She also made a brief newsreel in which she recounted how she had spent her life helping workers take control of "the civilization that Christ handed down to man."[89]

Though by now an invalid who did not leave her bed after the 1 May celebrations, the ninety-three-year-old Mother Jones followed events in the world around her as best she could. The day after her birthday she exchanged telegrams with John D. Rockefeller Jr., who wished her "my heartiest congratulations on your one hundredth birthday" and praised "your fearless adherence to your duty," which, he claimed, "is an inspiration to all who have known you." In reply Mother Jones thanked Junior, particularly because "knowing all the responsibilities on your shoulders it was a human act to think kindly of me at this time."[90] She then told journalists that "I can't tell him that the past is buried and we are friends again but I want him to know I appreciate his message." Combining her Catholic upbringing with her agitator's sensibility, she continued, "I forgive them, but I don't forget."[91] In September she sent money to John H. Walker to assist his fight for presidency of the UMWA against John L. Lewis. She did so, she told a reporter, "to help defend the miners against leaders who are thinking more of themselves than they are of my boys."[92]

She hoped to live to see Lewis "licked" but began to fear the worst. In mid-September she told a United Press reporter, "Sometimes I wish I could jump out of bed, get dressed, and go out and fight, but I know I'm all through."[93] She ingested only milk and cocoa and prepared to die in the Burgess farmhouse. In October, with the newspapers reporting that she had stopped eating, William Green, now president of the AFL, paid her a visit before leaving for the federation convention in Baltimore. Other friends did likewise, no doubt expecting to bid her farewell for the last time. Reports of her imminent demise continued through October and November, but Mother Jones had a strong constitution. Finally, at 11:55 p.m. on 30 November, she died in her sleep, attended by Lillian Burgess. The final journey of Mother Jones, to the miners' cemetery in Mount Olive, Illinois, began.

Above: Mother Jones Lying in State in the Oddfellows Hall, Mt. Olive, Illinois (1930), by kind permission of the Illinois Labor History Society, Germer Collection

Below: Mother Jones's Funeral Service, Mt. Olive, Illinois (1930), by kind permission of the Illinois Labor History Society, Germer Collection

Conclusion

A Life in Motion

AT THE END OF HER DAYS Mother Jones could remember almost a century of hard labor and heartbreak. But she had done what few people could hope to do: she had shaped her own life. Her trademark dresses, Irish brogue, earthy language, and toughness combined to create a stir wherever she went. Her rousing speeches and determined organizing made her an effective representative of labor unions. Associated with West Virginia and Colorado for her agitation during strikes in those states, she carved out a national reputation for herself. Her understanding of the labor theory of value and her attachment to class war gave her an honored place in radical politics and drove her to educate workers about their rights. Her origins, however, could hardly have been more humble or more anonymous.

Born into a family of farmers in Cork, Ireland, in 1837, Mary Harris witnessed incredible hardships growing up. The Harris family, like so many others, suffered through the terrors of the potato famine in the 1840s and decided to leave the country. Young Mary saw the evidence of disaster all around her. Abandoned houses, sickened people, coffins and corpses, and fear drove hundreds of thousands to emigrate and scarred the landscape. Immigration brought only partial respite. Her new life in Canada exposed her to nativist prejudice and social inequality. She would have heard anti-Catholic sentiments and seen how her father, an unskilled laborer, could barely support his family while others enjoyed luxury and plenty. She was educated as a teacher in a public normal school and turned her back on the Catholic faith. In the growing city of Toronto she saw women entrepreneurs who inspired her to teach in Monroe, Michigan, and later go into business for herself in Chicago. In Memphis, Tennessee, though, none of her previous experiences could have prepared her for the horrors of losing her entire family to a yellow fever epidemic. Returning to Chicago after the death of her ironworker husband and their four children she opened a dressmaking business only to have it destroyed in the Great Fire of 1871.

At that point, having been defeated twice in her efforts to create a conventional life, Mary Jones became Mother Jones. Though the actual details are unclear, she seems to have remembered the lessons of being married to a union man and began to take an active interest in the labor movement. At some point between 1871 and 1890 she moved closer to becoming a labor organizer by attending meetings, talking with and to people, and perhaps even proselytizing on behalf of a streetcar workers' union. Though her own version is replete with exaggerations, distortions, and fabrications, her interest in workers' organizations grew as she tried to reconstruct her life.

Mary Harris Jones moved physically—Cork, Toronto, Monroe, Chicago, Memphis, and back to Chicago—primarily because of events she could not control: the potato famine, the yellow fever, and the Chicago fire. After the destruction of her shop in Chicago she spent two decades in a wilderness she never explained. She claimed to have been in Pittsburgh in 1877 at the height of an important strike, when federal troops protected private property. The historical record tells a different story because there is no evidence that Mary Jones was in Pittsburgh in 1877. Had she been a strike leader, as she insisted, she would in all likelihood have followed this up with further agitation, but in fact she appeared only when Coxey's Army took to the roads of America in 1894. For most of the Gilded Age, Mary Jones remained elusively quiet. She may have been helping with anti-Chinese immigration protests in California; she could have been working as a prostitute; she may even have held a series of factory jobs. What we do know is that she helped lead a Kansas City contingent of Coxey's Army when unemployed people marched on Washington, D.C. She did travel through the South, for her writings about textile mills and rope factories read like eyewitness accounts. She also organized a rally for Eugene Debs in Birmingham, Alabama, and journeyed to Ruskin Community, the utopian village in Tennessee.

There can be no doubt that in the 1890s she found her way into the United Mine Workers of America. She began organizing miners for the 1897 strike in Pennsylvania, and she proved to be very good at it. Her toughness carried her through the damp and dangerous conditions all labor organizers—walking delegates, in the language of the day—confronted. Blessed with a nimble mind and a keen sense of humor, she could defuse potentially volatile situations. Her desire to fight for change meant she endured many hardships in the field, including intimidation, arrest, imprisonment, and deportation from strike zones. Her oratorical skills and her ability to summarize the hopes and fears of working people in her speeches gave her immense power.

One issue to which Mother Jones returned frequently was child labor. In 1903 her anger at employees who encouraged children to work in factories and mines boiled over. In that year she took a group of mill children and their parents on a march from Philadelphia to Oyster Bay—"Mother Jones's Industrial Army," as it was initially called—which attracted national attention. This particular piece of street theater garnered mixed reviews, as some journalists praised her for giving the issue the prominence it deserved while others condemned the march as a publicity stunt for New York City socialists. Her condemnation of child labor rested on moral and practical grounds. She wanted children to enjoy childhood, and she believed that the republic needed healthy, educated adults who had not been stunted by early working lives. This critique matched her desire for a society in which all people were treated fairly. It also reinforced her conventional views on the place of women in society, for she believed that women needed to spend their days raising children and keeping the home a safe haven from the corrupting influence of the world beyond its doors.

The march demonstrated what most already knew: Mother Jones preferred to lead alone. She had no time for internal institutional squabbles, as she labeled the political maneuvering of union leaders. She decided after the Colorado strike of 1903–4 to work for the socialists, though she quickly found herself enmeshed in intra-organizational rivalries. Mother Jones wanted to focus on the job at hand, as she perceived it: fighting for meaningful social change through the instrument of class war. Her awareness of poverty amid wealth and of the exploitation of workers infused her speeches, her writings, and her travels. The pirates who commanded the ship of capitalism needed to be taught a lesson, ideally by being forced to walk the plank. To her mind, petty jealousies over positions within organizations distracted the workers' champions from the fight for a better future.

In 1905 the perfect instrument for fighting the class war seemed to present itself: the Industrial Workers of the World. For a brief moment the forces of radicalism put aside their differences and gathered in Chicago to create a union for all workers. Mother Jones attended the first meeting and subsequent convention of the IWW, but the organization was soon beset with problems, and she left it. Her early role in the formation of this organization shows how she was regarded by other radicals as an important part of their world. She remained in contact with several leaders of the IWW, including Eugene Debs—a longtime friend—and William "Big Bill" Haywood. They, like Mexican *revoltosos* and numerous other radicals, benefited from her willingness to fight on behalf of those she deemed unjustly imprisoned.

In 1919, toward the end of her career as a labor organizer, she joined the national steel strike, though her star was waning. The president of the UMWA, John L. Lewis, sent her to Pittsburgh, far from the center of the action in northwestern Indiana, and even though Mother Jones was arrested, she was not as prominent as other labor leaders in this ultimately failed action. She did gain attention by announcing before, during, and after the strike, "I am a Bolshevist," a brave move at a time when Americans began to fear the specter of communism in Russia.

Mother Jones could not cheat death, though she did try to control its impact on her reputation. In this she was unsuccessful: Mary Harris Jones experienced a single physical death, but Mother Jones died three times. Her first death occurred on 30 November 1930 when the last breath left her recumbent body. Her second came just one day later, on 1 December, when a widely circulated Associated Press obituary presaged the taming of her reputation and the waning of her fame. The opening sentence identified her as a "militant crusader for the rights of the laboring man," but the article presented her as an anodyne organizer whose transgressions had been limited to using foul language.[1] It depicted her as a longtime ally of the AFL who had been "opposed to socialism, the I.W.W. and bolshevism" and who found violence "silly." The obituary quoted an interview from 1913 in which Mother Jones suggested, "If labor would eliminate violence and capital would eliminate injunctions the battle would be practically over. We then could go on sanely to arranging peace. Common sense, uninflamed, could step in."[2] The obituary contained nothing about her arrests or imprisonments and nothing about her being court-martialed. It omitted any mention of her work for the Socialist Party or of Mother Jones calling herself a "bolshevist". Her dedication to class war, her desire for revolutionary social change, and her pragmatic approach to the strategic use of violence had vanished. This was a false portrait befitting a time when labor militancy and radicalism were being condemned as dangerous foreign imports and circumscribed for threatening the status quo.

The third death was the one Mother Jones feared the most: the rapid disappearance of her name from labor lore and popular culture. Mother Jones had worried about her historical reputation, fearing she would be forgotten. As a woman in a man's world she knew she could not expect to become a union officer, and she abhorred institutional factionalism anyway. Moreover, the Mother Jones effect could be frustratingly short-lived, as she learned in 1903 when northern Colorado miners returned to work after she left the strike zone. Nonetheless, she hoped that her name would enter the history books.

That it did not immediately do so was a result of the nature of her work and her approach to it. Attracting union members was a slow, exacting, and often dangerous business of meeting with workers individually or in small groups to encourage them to tell their colleagues about the advantages of joining the union. The mass meetings Mother Jones addressed occurred only after weeks, or even months, of preparation. Bringing members into a union was like trying to keep sand on a beach: successive waves of employer intimidation, oppression, and anti-union propaganda, or even a loss of nerve on the part of new members, could quickly reverse all the hard work.

To make matters worse, Mother Jones had not experienced the type of death she desired. In several speeches she compared her work with that of Christ and made it clear she wished to die a similar death. Being martyred would, she felt sure, cement her place in the pantheon of labor leaders devoted to social change. In Montgomery, West Virginia, for example, she told an audience of miners, "I know a lot of you will go off and condemn me, but you condemned Christ, you condemned every man and woman that ever dared to raise their voice in behalf of truth and justice, and you will do the same with me."[3] In her autobiography she claimed to have told police during the 1916 New York streetcar strike, "If they want to hang me, let them. . . . And on the scaffold I will shout 'Freedom for the working class!'" She then informed them, "When I meet God Almighty I will tell him to damn my accusers."[4] After Frances Selling, an organizer in the 1919 steel strike, was killed by police while trying to help a steelworker, Mother Jones wondered sadly why Selling had been martyred and not herself. Murder at the hands of capitalists would, Mother Jones felt sure, assure her role in the history books.

But Mother Jones earned her place in history without being martyred. The 1960s witnessed a revival of interest in Mother Jones, and her name reentered popular culture. She came to be seen as an exemplary female agitator, and posters attributing to Mother Jones the epigram "Pray for the dead and fight like Hell for the living" began to dot the landscape. In 1976 a new investigative magazine appropriated the name Mother Jones for its masthead. Mother Jones had become a labor movement icon once again, this time as a revolutionary worth emulating. Several biographies aimed at juvenile audiences, to whom she illustrated how a woman could overcome tremendous personal tragedy and defy convention to lead a useful life in the service of others, appeared. In 1992 the U.S. Department of Labor inducted her into its Hall of Fame, and she is in an unrelated virtual Labor Hall of Fame on the Web. A documentary film of her life starring historian Elliott Gorn appeared in 2007, accompanied by a Web site dedicated to her memory.

The Mother Jones revival is driven by fascination with her life and career, the development of women's history, and the human need for exemplary forebears. Mother Jones provides us with a fascinating and important example of a woman who shaped her own life in spite of social constraints and expectations, in part by inverting them and using them to her own advantage. Developing out of Mary Harris, the Irish Catholic immigrant who survived several terrible disasters, Mother Jones created an independent, useful role for herself as a union organizer and agitator for meaningful social change.

Notes

INTRODUCTION

1. *New York Times*, 8 December 1930, p. 21.
2. *Chicago Daily Tribune*, 9 December 1930, p. 28.
3. Quoted in Archie Green, "The Death of Mother Jones," *Labor History* 1, no. 1 (Winter 1960): 8.
4. Philip S. Foner, ed., *Mother Jones Speaks* (New York: Monad Press, 1983), 493.

CHAPTER I

1. Edward M. Steel, ed., *The Speeches and Writings of Mother Jones* (Pittsburgh: University of Pittsburgh Press, 1988), 95, 178.
2. Ibid., 221.
3. *Autobiography of Mother Jones* (Chicago: Charles H. Kerr, 1925), 15–16; and for the unlikelihood of this happening, see Elliott J. Gorn, *Mother Jones: The Most Dangerous Woman in America* (New York: Hill and Wang, 2001), 47–48.
4. See, for example, *Autobiography of Mother Jones*, 11; and *New York Times*, 1 June 1913, p. 40.
5. Steel (*The Speeches and Writings of Mother Jones*, 259) speculates that she was born in 1837, but Gorn (*Mother Jones*, 9) uses parish records in Cork to prove her date of birth.
6. Djuna Barnes, *Interviews*, ed. Alyce Barry (Washington, DC: Sun and Moon Press, 1985), 98.
7. Steel, *The Speeches and Writings of Mother Jones*, 109.
8. Ibid., 108, 144.
9. Barnes, *Interviews*, 104.
10. Philip S. Foner, ed., *Mother Jones Speaks* (New York: Monad Press, 1983), 536.
11. Steel, *The Speeches and Writings of Mother Jones*, 30.
12. Ibid., 83.
13. Ibid., 102.
14. Ibid., 130.
15. Barnes, *Interviews*, 97.
16. Steel, *The Speeches and Writings of Mother Jones*, 74.

17. *Autobiography of Mother Jones*, 11.
18. Edward M. Steel, ed., *The Correspondence of Mother Jones* (Pittsburgh: University of Pittsburgh Press, 1985), 107.
19. Barnes, *Interviews*, 101.
20. Steel, *The Speeches and Writings of Mother Jones*, 163, 9; Barnes, *Interviews*, 102.
21. Steel, *The Speeches and Writings of Mother Jones*, 26.
22. Ibid., 60.
23. Steel, *The Correspondence of Mother Jones*, 122.
24. Barnes, *Interviews*, 103.

CHAPTER 2

1. Edward M. Steel, ed., *The Speeches and Writings of Mother Jones* (Pittsburgh: University of Pittsburgh Press, 1988), 141.
2. Ibid., 41.
3. Philip S. Foner, ed., *Mother Jones Speaks* (New York: Monad Press, 1983), 504; and see Elliott J. Gorn, *Mother Jones: The Most Dangerous Woman in America* (New York: Hill and Wang, 2001), 30–31.
4. Foner, *Mother Jones Speaks*, 499.
5. Bessie Louise Pierce, ed., *As Others See Chicago: Impressions of Visitors, 1673–1933* (Chicago: University of Chicago Press, 2004), 144.
6. Ibid., 146.
7. Steel, *The Speeches and Writings of Mother Jones*, 5.
8. Ibid., 231.
9. *Autobiography of Mother Jones* (Chicago: Charles H. Kerr, 1925), 12.
10. Djuna Barnes, *Interviews*, ed. Alyce Barry (Washington, DC: Sun and Moon Press, 1985), 101–2.
11. *Autobiography of Mother Jones*, 12.
12. Ibid., 12–13.
13. Pierce, *As Others See Chicago*, 192–93, 197.
14. Foner, *Mother Jones Speaks*, 370.

CHAPTER 3

1. Philip S. Foner, ed., *Mother Jones Speaks* (New York: Monad Press, 1983), 274.
2. Edward M. Steel, ed., *The Speeches and Writings of Mother Jones* (Pittsburgh: University of Pittsburgh Press, 1988), 252.
3. Ibid., 162.
4. *Autobiography of Mother Jones* (Chicago: Charles H. Kerr, 1925), 13–14.
5. Foner, *Mother Jones Speaks*, 404–5.
6. *Autobiography of Mother Jones*, 14–15.
7. Foner, *Mother Jones Speaks*, 444.
8. *Autobiography of Mother Jones*, 17.
9. Steel, *The Speeches and Writings of Mother Jones*, 170.
10. *Autobiography of Mother Jones*, 17–18.
11. Ibid., 19.
12. Ibid., 17.
13. Steel, *The Speeches and Writings of Mother Jones*, 196.
14. *Autobiography of Mother Jones*, 20.
15. Edward M. Steel, ed., *The Correspondence of Mother Jones* (Pittsburgh: University of Pittsburgh Press, 1985), 313, 63.

CHAPTER 4

1. Philip S. Foner, ed., *Mother Jones Speaks* (New York: Monad Press, 1983), 510.
2. Quoted in John H. Keiser, *The Union Miners Cemetery: A Spirit-Thread of Labor History* (Chicago: Illinois Labor History Society, 1980), 10.
3. Edward M. Steel, ed., *The Speeches and Writings of Mother Jones* (Pittsburgh: University of Pittsburgh Press, 1988), 310.
4. Ibid., 87.
5. Foner, *Mother Jones Speaks*, 137.
6. Steel, *The Speeches and Writings of Mother Jones*, 66.

7. Ibid., 286.
8. Ibid., 20–21.
9. Ibid., 71.
10. Foner, *Mother Jones Speaks*, 91.
11. Ibid., 78–79.
12. Edward M. Steel, ed., *The Correspondence of Mother Jones* (Pittsburgh: University of Pittsburgh Press, 1985), 52.
13. Ibid., 214.
14. Quoted in Elliott J. Gorn, *Mother Jones: The Most Dangerous Woman in America* (New York: Hill and Wang, 2001), 64.
15. *Autobiography of Mother Jones* (Chicago: Charles H. Kerr, 1925), 117.
16. *San Francisco Call*, 12 May 1904, p. 14.
17. *Autobiography of Mother Jones*, 119.
18. Ibid., 119, 120–21.
19. Ibid., 124.
20. Steel, *The Speeches and Writings of Mother Jones*, 97.
21. Foner, *Mother Jones Speaks*, 249.
22. Steel, *The Correspondence of Mother Jones*, 184.
23. *Autobiography of Mother Jones*, 29.
24. *Appeal to Reason*, 28 September 1895, quoted in John Graham, ed., *Yours for the Revolution: The "Appeal to Reason," 1895–1922* (Lincoln: University of Nebraska Press, 1990), 54.
25. Steel, *The Speeches and Writings of Mother Jones*, 35.
26. Ibid., 37.
27. Ibid., 132.
28. Foner, *Mother Jones Speaks*, 518.
29. Ibid., 460.
30. Steel, *The Speeches and Writings of Mother Jones*, 76.
31. Steel, *The Correspondence of Mother Jones*, 45.
32. Ibid., 21.
33. Steel, *The Speeches and Writings of Mother Jones*, 8.
34. Steel, *The Correspondence of Mother Jones*, 87.

CHAPTER 5

1. *Autobiography of Mother Jones* (Chicago: Charles H. Kerr, 1925), 27.
2. Edward M. Steel, ed., *The Speeches and Writings of Mother Jones* (Pittsburgh: University of Pittsburgh Press, 1988), 19, 32.
3. Ibid., 16.
4. Philip S. Foner, ed., *Mother Jones Speaks* (New York: Monad Press, 1983), 249.
5. Ibid., 110.
6. Ibid., 92.
7. Steel, *The Speeches and Writings of Mother Jones*, 94.
8. Ibid., 295.
9. Ibid., 294.
10. Ibid., 180.
11. *New York Times*, 14 August 1900, p. 10.
12. *New York Times*, 23 September 1900, p. 1.
13. *New York Times*, 25 September 1900, p. 1.
14. *New York Times*, 20 September 1900, p. 1.
15. *Chicago Daily Tribune*, 23 September 1900, p. 2.
16. *New York Times*, 27 September 1900, p. 2.
17. *Autobiography of Mother Jones*, 90–91; see *Chicago Daily Tribune*, 17 October 1900, p. 9.
18. *Autobiography of Mother Jones*, 91.
19. *New York Times*, 14 October 1900, p. 1.
20. Edward M. Steel, ed., *The Correspondence of Mother Jones* (Pittsburgh: University of Pittsburgh Press, 1985), 21.
21. *Chicago Daily Tribune*, 1 November 1901, p. 7.
22. *New York Times*, 7 June 1902, p. 2.
23. Steel, *The Correspondence of Mother Jones*, 32–33.
24. Foner, *Mother Jones Speaks*, 79.
25. Steel, *The Speeches and Writings of Mother Jones*, 86.

26. Ibid., 16–17.
27. *Chicago Daily Tribune*, 25 July 1902, p. 1.
28. Quoted in Edward M. Steel, "Mother Jones in the Fairmont Field, 1902," *Journal of American History* 57, no. 2 (September 1970): 290–307, at 301.
29. Ibid.
30. Steel, *The Correspondence of Mother Jones*, 45.
31. *Chicago Daily Tribune*, 25 July 1902, p. 6.
32. Ibid., 1.
33. Ibid.
34. *New York Times*, 26 July 1902, p. 8.
35. *Chicago Daily Tribune*, 26 September 1902, p. 3.
36. *The Letters of Theodore Roosevelt*, vol. 3, ed. Elting Morison (Cambridge, MA: Harvard University Press, 1951), 357.
37. *Autobiography of Mother Jones*, 63.
38. Ibid., 69–70.
39. Ibid., 59.
40. Ibid., 59–60.
41. Ibid., 60.

CHAPTER 6
1. Edward M. Steel, ed., *The Correspondence of Mother Jones* (Pittsburgh: University of Pittsburgh Press, 1985), 42.
2. *New York Times*, 19 October 1902, p. 8.
3. *Chicago Daily Tribune*, 27 March 1903, p. 7.
4. Steel, *The Correspondence of Mother Jones*, 43–44.
5. Philip S. Foner, ed., *Mother Jones Speaks* (New York: Monad Press, 1983), 97.
6. Ibid., 98.
7. Ibid., 93.
8. Edward M. Steel, ed., *The Speeches and Writings of Mother Jones* (Pittsburgh: University of Pittsburgh Press, 1988), 4.
9. Ibid.

10. Ibid., 5.
11. Foner, *Mother Jones Speaks*, 98.
12. Ibid., 93.
13. *Autobiography of Mother Jones* (Chicago: Charles H. Kerr, 1925), 71.
14. *Chicago Daily Tribune*, 22 August 1902, p. 5.
15. *Autobiography of Mother Jones*, 74.
16. *New York Times*, 8 July 1903, p. 5.
17. The banners are in *New York Times*, 24 July 1903, p. 5; the tableaux props are in *New York Times*, 8 July 1903, p. 5.
18. *Autobiography of Mother Jones*, 73.
19. *New York Times*, 10 July 1903, p. 1.
20. *New York Times*, 11 July 1903, p. 1.
21. Ibid.
22. *New York Times*, 12 July 1903, p. 1.
23. *Autobiography of Mother Jones*, 76.
24. *Winona Republican-Herald*, 23 July 1903, p. 2.
25. *New York Times*, 14 July 1903, p. 2.
26. *New York Times*, 16 July 1903, p. 5.
27. *New York Times*, 15 July 1903, p. 1.
28. *New York Times*, 17 July 1903, p. 5.
29. *New York Times*, 14 July 1903, p. 2.
30. *New York Times*, 17 July 1903, p. 5.
31. *New York Times*, 18 July 1903, p. 7.
32. *New York Times*, 20 July 1903, p. 10.
33. *Chicago Daily Tribune*, 22 July 1903, p. 4.
34. Steel, *The Correspondence of Mother Jones*, 45.
35. *New York Times*, 24 July 1903, p. 5.
36. Ibid.
37. Ibid.
38. *Chicago Daily Tribune*, 24 July 1903, p. 3.
39. *New York Times*, 27 July 1903, p. 10.
40. Ibid.
41. Ibid., 3.
42. *New York Times*, 31 July 1903, p. 6.
43. Steel, *The Correspondence of Mother Jones*, 47.
44. *Winona Republican-Herald*, 23 July 1903, p. 2.

45. Steel, *The Correspondence of Mother Jones*, 46.
46. Ibid.
47. Ibid., 48.
48. *New York Times*, 2 August 1903, p. 6.
49. *Chicago Daily Tribune*, 6 August 1903, p. 6.
50. *New York Times*, 9 August 1903, p. 2.
51. Steel, *The Correspondence of Mother Jones*, 55; Steel, *The Speeches and Writings of Mother Jones*, 61.
52. Steel, *The Speeches and Writings of Mother Jones*, 61.

CHAPTER 7
1. Edward M. Steel, ed., *The Speeches and Writings of Mother Jones* (Pittsburgh: University of Pittsburgh Press, 1988), 33.
2. Edward M. Steel, ed., *The Correspondence of Mother Jones* (Pittsburgh: University of Pittsburgh Press, 1985), 49.
3. Quoted in Dale Fetherling, *Mother Jones the Miner's Angel: A Portrait* (Carbondale: Southern Illinois University Press, 1974), 59–60.
4. *Chicago Daily Tribune*, 9 November 1903, p. 2.
5. Steel, *The Correspondence of Mother Jones*, 50.
6. *Chicago Daily Tribune*, 12 November 1903, p. 4.
7. Philip S. Foner, ed., *Mother Jones Speaks* (New York: Monad Press, 1983), 106.
8. Ibid.
9. *Chicago Daily Tribune*, 26 November 1903, p. 1.
10. *Ogden Standard*, 29 March 1904, p. 7.
11. *Chicago Daily Tribune*, 27 November 1903, p. 10.
12. Foner, *Mother Jones Speaks*, 115.
13. *Eastern Utah Advocate*, 5 May 1904, p. 7.
14. Steel, *The Correspondence of Mother*

Jones, 52.
15. *New York Times*, 8 August 1904, p. 40.
16. Eugene V. Debs, *Unionism and Socialism* (Terre Haute: Standard Publishing, 1904), 24.
17. Steel, *The Correspondence of Mother Jones*, 83.
18. Ibid., 52.
19. Quoted in Joyce L. Kornbluh, ed., *Rebel Voices: An I.W.W. Anthology* (Ann Arbor: University of Michigan Press, 1968), 8–9.
20. Quoted in Nick Salvatore, *Eugene V. Debs: Citizen and Socialist* (Urbana: University of Illinois Press, 1982), 206.
21. Steel, *The Speeches and Writings of Mother Jones*, 22–23.
22. Steel, *The Correspondence of Mother Jones*, 61.
23. Steel, *The Speeches and Writings of Mother Jones*, 142–43.
24. Ibid., 74.
25. Foner, *Mother Jones Speaks*, 137.
26. Steel, *The Speeches and Writings of Mother Jones*, 27.
27. Ibid., 74.
28. Ibid., 73.
29. Quoted Kornbluh, *Rebel Voices*, 7–8.
30. Ibid., 8–9.
31. Steel, *The Speeches and Writings of Mother Jones*, 52.
32. Foner, *Mother Jones Speaks*, 139.
33. Steel, *The Speeches and Writings of Mother Jones*, 52.
34. Quoted in Leon Litwack, ed., *The American Labor Movement* (Englewood Cliffs, NJ: Prentice Hall, 1962), 42.
35. Steel, *The Speeches and Writings of Mother Jones*, 78.
36. *Eastern Utah Advocate*, 8 June 1905, p. 7.
37. Foner, *Mother Jones Speaks*, 255.
38. *Deseret Evening News*, 25 October 1901, p. 3.
39. Steel, *The Speeches and Writings of*

Mother Jones, 81.

40. *New York Times*, 1 June 1913, p. 40.

41. Ibid.

42. Steel, *The Correspondence of Mother Jones*, 62.

43. Ibid., 64.

44. Ibid., 58.

45. *New York Times*, 14 March 1906, p. 3.

46. Steel, *The Speeches and Writings of Mother Jones*, 276–77.

47. Ibid., 278.

48. Ibid., 32.

49. Ibid., 25.

50. Ibid., 288.

51. Ibid., 286.

52. Steel, *The Correspondence of Mother Jones*, 72–73.

53. Ibid., 98.

54. *New York Times*, 20 January 1906, p. 2.

55. *San Francisco Call*, 19 July 1908, p. 36.

56. Steel, *The Correspondence of Mother Jones*, 76.

57. Ibid., 78.

58. Ibid., 83.

59. Ibid., 84.

60. Ibid., 97.

CHAPTER 8

1. *New York Times*, 4 August 1910, p. 2.

2. *Chicago Daily Tribune*, 4 August 1910, p. 7.

3. Edward M. Steel, ed., *The Speeches and Writings of Mother Jones* (Pittsburgh: University of Pittsburgh Press, 1988), 294.

4. Ibid.

5. Ibid., 295.

6. Edward M. Steel, ed., *The Correspondence of Mother Jones* (Pittsburgh: University of Pittsburgh Press, 1985), 78, 84.

7. *Autobiography of Mother Jones* (Chicago: Charles H. Kerr, 1925), 148.

8. Philip S. Foner, ed., *Mother Jones*

Speaks (New York: Monad Press, 1983), 418.

9. *Autobiography of Mother Jones*, 154, 156.

10. Quoted in Melody Bragg, *Window to the Past: 1912–1913 Mine Wars and Mother Jones* (Glen Jean, WV: Gem Publications, 1990), 7.

11. Ibid., 7–8.

12. Steel, *The Speeches and Writings of Mother Jones*, 98.

13. Foner, *Mother Jones Speaks*, 491.

14. Ibid., 492.

15. Steel, *The Speeches and Writings of Mother Jones*, 91.

16. Foner, *Mother Jones Speaks*, 421.

17. Steel, *The Speeches and Writings of Mother Jones*, 64.

18. Ibid., 98.

19. Ibid., 60.

20. Ibid., 102.

21. Ibid., 111.

22. Foner, *Mother Jones Speaks*, 396.

23. Steel, *The Speeches and Writings of Mother Jones*, 86.

24. Ibid., 89.

25. Ibid., 110.

26. Ibid., 95; emphases in the original.

27. Ibid., 107.

28. *New York Times*, 19 November 1912, p. 7.

29. Quoted in Bragg, *Window to the Past*, 15.

30. Ibid., 16.

31. Ibid., 8.

32. Steel, *The Speeches and Writings of Mother Jones*, 112.

33. Ibid., 113.

34. Edward M. Steel Jr., ed., *The Court-Martial of Mother Jones* (Lexington: University Press of Kentucky, 1995), 34.

35. Ibid., 35.

36. *New York Times*, 11 March 1913, p. 1.

37. Steel, *The Court-Martial of Mother Jones*, 35.

38. Steel, *The Speeches and Writings of Mother Jones*, 91.

39. Ibid., 60.

40. Ibid., 73, 96.

41. Ibid., 86.

42. Steel, *The Court-Martial of Mother Jones*, 100.

43. Ibid., 275.

44. Steel, *The Correspondence of Mother Jones*, 137.

CHAPTER 9

1. Edward M. Steel, ed., *The Correspondence of Mother Jones* (Pittsburgh: University of Pittsburgh Press, 1985), 116.

2. Ibid., 115.

3. *New York Times*, 16 May 1913, p. 2.

4. *Eastern Utah Advocate*, 22 May 1913, p. 1.

5. Steel, *The Correspondence of Mother Jones*, 118.

6. Edward M. Steel, ed., *The Speeches and Writings of Mother Jones* (Pittsburgh: University of Pittsburgh Press, 1988), 128.

7. Philip S. Foner, ed., *Mother Jones Speaks* (New York: Monad Press, 1983), 237.

8. Steel, *The Correspondence of Mother Jones*, 120.

9. *Chicago Daily Tribune*, 5 January 1914, p. 1.

10. *New York Times*, 5 January 1914, p. 6.

11. *Chicago Daily Tribune*, 5 January 1914, p. 1.

12. *Chicago Daily Tribune*, 6 January 1914, p. 2.

13. *Chicago Daily Tribune*, 7 January 1914, p. 2.

14. *Tooele Transcript* (Utah), 16 January 1914, p. 2.

15. *Chicago Daily Tribune*, 13 January 1914, p. 2.

16. *Autobiography of Mother Jones* (Chicago: Charles H. Kerr, 1925), 182.

17. Foner, *Mother Jones Speaks*, 384.

18. Steel, *The Correspondence of Mother Jones*, 122.

19. *New York Times*, 17 March 1914, p. 9.

20. *Chicago Daily Tribune*, 23 March 1914, p. 1.

21. *New York Times*, 24 March 1914, p. 1.

22. *Autobiography of Mother Jones*, 185.

23. *Chicago Daily Tribune*, 23 March 1914, p. 1.

24. *Chicago Daily Tribune*, 24 March 1914, p. 15.

25. Foner, *Mother Jones Speaks*, 389, 391.

26. Ibid., 387.

27. Ibid., 394.

28. Ibid., 395.

29. Quoted in Ron Chernow, *Titan: The Life of John D. Rockefeller, Sr.* (New York: Random House, 1988), 580.

30. *New York Times*, 11 May 1914, p. 4.

31. *New York Times*, 13 May 1914, p. 22.

32. *New York Times*, 11 May 1914, p. 4.

33. Steel, *The Correspondence of Mother Jones*, 127.

34. Ibid., 128.

35. Foner, *Mother Jones Speaks*, 248.

36. Ibid., 249.

37. *Autobiography of Mother Jones*, 198.

38. Steel, *The Speeches and Writings of Mother Jones*, 151.

39. Ibid., 154.

40. Ibid., 155.

41. *New York Times*, 29 October 1914, p. 10.

42. Ibid.

43. Foner, *Mother Jones Speaks*, 261.

44. *New York Times*, 24 April 1914, p. 6.

45. Ibid., 10.

46. Steel, *The Correspondence of Mother Jones*, 133.

47. *Chicago Daily Tribune*, 27 January 1915, p. 6.

48. Ibid.

49. *Chicago Daily Tribune*, 28 January 1915, p. 1.

50. Ibid.

51. *Chicago Daily Tribune*, 28 January

1915, p. 8.
52. Foner, *Mother Jones Speaks*, 264.
53. Ibid., 266.
54. Ibid.
55. *New York Times*, 7 February 1915, p. 9.
56. Steel, *The Speeches and Writings of Mother Jones*, 159, 161, 165.
57. *New York Times*, 27 April 1915, p. 4.
58. *New York Times*, 1 June 1915, p. 18.
59. *New York Times*, 13 October 1915, p. 8. For evidence of the gift, see Chernow, *Titan*, 586, where Junior received "another eighty thousand shares of CFI stock," giving him control of the company.
60. *New York Times*, 14 May 1915, p. 14.
61. Foner, *Mother Jones Speaks*, 404–5.
62. Ibid., 407, 428.
63. Ibid., 419.
64. Ibid., 407.
65. Ibid., 410.
66. *New York Times*, 10 October 1915, p. 22.

CHAPTER 10
1. *Urbana (Illinois) Daily Courier*, 20 January 1916, p. 1.
2. Edward M. Steel, ed., *The Speeches and Writings of Mother Jones* (Pittsburgh: University of Pittsburgh Press, 1988), 33.
3. Ibid., 162.
4. Philip S. Foner, ed., *Mother Jones Speaks* (New York: Monad Press, 1983), 284.
5. Ibid., 286.
6. Ibid.
7. *Chicago Daily Tribune*, 6 October 1916, p. 1.
8. *New York Times*, 6 October 1916, p. 1.
9. *New York Times*, 7 October 1916, p. 10.
10. Ibid., 20.
11. *Chicago Daily Tribune*, 6 July 1917, p. 1.
12. *Carbon County (Utah) News*, 18 September 1918, p. 2.

13. *New York Times*, 19 November 1916, p. 1.
14. Edward M. Steel, ed., *The Correspondence of Mother Jones* (Pittsburgh: University of Pittsburgh Press, 1985), 161.
15. Steel, *The Speeches and Writings of Mother Jones*, 187, 191.
16. Ibid., 188.
17. *Urbana Daily Courier*, 9 April 1919, p. 4.
18. Ibid.
19. Steel, *The Speeches and Writings of Mother Jones*, 198–99.
20. Ibid., 157–58.
21. Ibid., 194.
22. Ibid., 195.
23. Ibid., 202–3.
24. *Chicago Daily Tribune*, 21 October 1919, p. 2.
25. *New York Times*, 24 October 1919, p. 2.
26. Steel, *The Correspondence of Mother Jones*, 200.
27. Steel, *The Speeches and Writings of Mother Jones*, 212.
28. Ibid., 213.
29. Ibid., 216.
30. Ibid., 225.
31. Ibid., 229.
32. Ibid., 231.
33. Ibid., 233.
34. Ibid., 234.
35. Ibid., 235.
36. Ibid., 236.
37. Ibid., 237.
38. Steel, *The Correspondence of Mother Jones*, 223.
39. Ibid., 227.
40. Ibid., 229.
41. Ibid., 230.
42. Steel, *The Speeches and Writings of Mother Jones*, 239, 248.
43. Ibid., 252.
44. Steel, *The Correspondence of Mother Jones*, 236.

CHAPTER 11
1. Edward M. Steel, ed., *The*

Correspondence of Mother Jones (Pittsburgh: University of Pittsburgh Press, 1985), 204, 201.

2. Ibid., 236.
3. Ibid., 295.
4. Ibid., 303.
5. Ibid., 318.
6. Ibid., 331.
7. Ibid., 203.
8. Ibid.
9. Ibid., 236.
10. Ibid., 271, 279.
11. Ibid., 262.
12. Ibid., 263.
13. Ibid., 266.
14. Ibid., 264–65.
15. Ibid., 236–37.
16. Ibid., 237.
17. Ibid., 222.
18. Edward M. Steel, ed., *The Speeches and Writings of Mother Jones* (Pittsburgh: University of Pittsburgh Press, 1988), 255.
19. Ibid., 258.
20. *New York Times*, 20 February 1922, p. 10.
21. Steel, *The Correspondence of Mother Jones*, 275.
22. Steel, *The Speeches and Writings of Mother Jones*, 255–56.
23. Steel, *The Correspondence of Mother Jones*, 55.
24. Ibid., 242.
25. Ibid., 238.
26. Ibid., 197.
27. Ibid., 278.
28. Ibid., 279.
29. Ibid., 279, 321–22.
30. Steel, *The Speeches and Writings of Mother Jones*, 218.
31. Ibid., 19.
32. Steel, *The Correspondence of Mother Jones*, 194.
33. Ibid., 335.
34. Ibid., 329.
35. Ibid., 241.
36. Ibid., 243.
37. Ibid., 246.
38. Ibid., 239.
39. *Deseret Evening News*, 6 July 1901, p. 4.
40. Steel, *The Speeches and Writings of Mother Jones*, 133.
41. Ibid., 304.
42. Ibid., 219.
43. Ibid., 304.
44. *Chicago Daily Tribune*, 5 February 1915, p. 3.
45. Philip S. Foner, ed., *Mother Jones Speaks* (New York: Monad Press, 1983), 98.
46. *New York Times*, 23 May 1914, p. 3.
47. Steel, *The Speeches and Writings of Mother Jones*, 63.
48. Ibid., 305.
49. Ibid., 225.
50. Ibid., 95.
51. Foner, *Mother Jones Speaks*, 290.
52. Steel, *The Speeches and Writings of Mother Jones*, 246.
53. *Chicago Daily Tribune*, 16 September 1917, p. 5.
54. Foner, *Mother Jones Speaks*, 97.
55. Steel, *The Speeches and Writings of Mother Jones*, 292.
56. Foner, *Mother Jones Speaks*, 137.
57. Steel, *The Speeches and Writings of Mother Jones*, 45.
58. Ibid., 132.
59. Ibid., 142.
60. Foner, *Mother Jones Speaks*, 255.
61. Steel, *The Speeches and Writings of Mother Jones*, 236.
62. *Chicago Daily Tribune*, 8 February 1923, p. 12.
63. Steel, *The Speeches and Writings of Mother Jones*, 64, 113.
64. Ibid., 270.
65. *Chicago Daily Tribune*, 8 February 1923, p. 12.
66. *Chicago Daily Tribune*, 27 April 1923, p. 6.
67. *Autobiography of Mother Jones* (Chicago: Charles H. Kerr, 1925), 238.
68. Ibid., 197.
69. Ibid., 212.
70. Foner, *Mother Jones Speaks*, 364.

71. Steel, *The Correspondence of Mother Jones*, 206.

72. Ibid., 286.

73. Ibid., 264.

74. Ibid., 284.

75. Ibid., 322.

76. *Chicago Daily Tribune*, 7 April 1924, p. 14.

77. Steel, *The Correspondence of Mother Jones*, 192–93.

78. *Chicago Daily Tribune*, 6 October 1926, p. 10.

79. *Chicago Daily Tribune*, 25 July 1927, p. 10.

80. *New York Times*, 25 November 1923, p. 3.

81. *New York Times*, 18 December 1921, p. 85.

82. *Chicago Daily Tribune*, 27 September 1924, p. 9.

83. Steel, *The Correspondence of Mother Jones*, 297.

84. Ibid., 310.

85. Steel, *The Speeches and Writings of Mother Jones*, 311.

86. Ibid., 312.

87. *Chicago Daily Tribune*, 15 January 1930, p. 1.

88. *Chicago Daily Tribune*, 2 May 1930, p. 23.

89. *New York Times*, 12 May 1930, p. 30.

90. Steel, *The Correspondence of Mother Jones*, 346.

91. *Chicago Daily Tribune*, 4 May 1930, p. 1.

92. *New York Times*, 6 September 1930, p. 16.

93. *New York Times*, 14 September 1930, p. 16.

CONCLUSION

1. *Chicago Daily Tribune*, 1 December 1930, p. 1.

2. Ibid., 4.

3. Edward M. Steel, ed., *The Speeches and Writings of Mother Jones* (Pittsburgh: University of Pittsburgh Press, 1988), 83.

4. *Autobiography of Mother Jones* (Chicago: Charles H. Kerr, 1925), 237.

Annotated Bibliography

Mother Jones has been the subject of many biographies, of which the best are Elliott J. Gorn, *Mother Jones: The Most Dangerous Woman in America* (New York: Hill and Wang, 2001), and Dale Fetherling, *Mother Jones the Miners' Angel: A Portrait* (Carbondale: Southern Illinois University Press, 1974). The former went to great lengths to explore and explode the many myths surrounding her career, beginning with the date of her birth; the latter focuses on her career as an organizer for the United Mine Workers but brings great depth to the subject. A very useful collection of articles on her death, burial, and legacy is Leslie F. Orear, ed., *Mother Jones and the Miners Cemetery* (Chicago: Illinois Labor History Society, 2002).

On the topic of her own life Mother Jones wrote the unreliable *Autobiography of Mother Jones* (Chicago: Charles H. Kerr, 1925). Fortunately, through the careful labors of historian Edward M. Steel, her speeches, writings, and letters have been published in two excellent edited volumes, *The Correspondence of Mother Jones* (Pittsburgh: University of Pittsburgh Press, 1985) and *The Speeches and Writings of Mother Jones* (Pittsburgh: University of Pittsburgh Press, 1988). From the same source, though more closely focused on one event in her life, is Edward M. Steel, ed., *The Court-Martial of Mother Jones* (Lexington: University Press of Kentucky, 1995). Also of use, though less accurate because more inclined to follow the myths she perpetuated about herself, is Philip S. Foner, ed., *Mother*

Jones Speaks (New York: Monad Press, 1983). In addition to these collected editions of her writings and speeches, of particular value is an interview with Mother Jones conducted on 7 February 1915 by novelist Djuna Barnes and available in Djuna Barnes, *Interviews*, ed. Alyce Barry (Washington, D.C.: Sun and Moon Press, 1985).

One of the ways this biography differs from others is a reliance on newspapers to explore specific moments in the life of Mother Jones. Prominent here are the *Chicago Daily Tribune* and the *New York Times*, but a host of others have proved both readily accessible and highly valuable because of electronic databases. Newspapers in Illinois, Utah, California, and other states are accessible and, even better, searchable online. The digitized total remains quite small compared to the number of newspapers published during Mother Jones's lifetime. Future researchers employing the same technology will unearth numerous pieces of the puzzle of her life, revising our understanding of Mother Jones.

To understand how Mother Jones used language and imagery, see the writings of Mari Boor Tonn, particularly "Effecting Labor Reform through Stories: The Narrative Rhetorical Style of Mary Harris 'Mother' Jones," in *Constructing and Reconstructing Gender: The Links among Communication, Language, and Gender*, ed. Charles E. Morris III and Stephen H. Browne (Albany: State University of New York Press, 1992), 406–28; and "Militant Motherhood: Labor's Mary Harris 'Mother' Jones," in *Readings on the Rhetoric of Social Protest*, ed. Lynn A. M. Perry, Lynn H. Turner, and Helen M. Sterk (State College, Pa.: Strata Publishing, 2001), 283–93. The place of Mother Jones in popular culture is explored in Archie Green, *The Death of Mother Jones* (Urbana: University of Illinois Institute of Labor and Industrial Relations, 1960); and John H. Keiser, *The Union Miners Cemetery: A Spirit-Thread of Labor History* (Chicago: Illinois Labor History Society, 1980).

For excellent introductions to the world in which Mary Harris grew up, see Maire Cruise O'Brien and Conor Cruise O'Brien, *Ireland: A Concise History*, 3rd ed. (New York: Thames and Hudson, 1985); and, more specifically, David Dickson, *Old World Colony: Cork and South Munster, 1630–1830* (Madison: University of Wisconsin Press, 2005), and Janet Nolan, *Servants of the Poor: Teachers and Mobility in Ireland and Irish America* (Notre Dame: University of Notre Dame Press, 2004). For the famine, see the classic essays in R. Dudley Edwards and T. Desmond Williams, eds., *The Great Famine: Studies in Irish History, 1845–52* (1956; reprint, Dublin: Lilliput Press, 1994).

On the myths and legends that informed some of Mother Jones's rhetoric and fired her imagination as a child, see Seamus Deane, *A*

Short History of Irish Literature (London: Hutchinson, 1986); E. Estyn Evans, *Irish Folk Ways* (New York: Devin-Adair, 1957); Marie Heaney, *The Names upon the Harp: Irish Myth and Legend* (New York: Arthur A. Levine Books, 2000); Richard Kearney, *Myth, History, Literary Tradition: Thomas Kinsella, John Montague, and Brendan Kennelly* (Dundalk: Dundalk Arts, 1989); John Mathews and Caitlin Mathews, *British and Irish Mythology: An Encyclopedia of Myth and Legend* (London: Diamond Books, 1995); Donald Morse and Csilla Bertha, eds., *More Real Than Reality: The Fantastic in Irish Literature and the Arts* (New York: Greenwood Press, 1991); Daithi O hOgain, *Myth, Legend, and Romance: An Encyclopedia of Irish Folk Tradition* (New York: Prentice Hall, 1991); Trina Robbins, *Wild Irish Roses: Tales of Brigits, Kathleens, and Warrior Queens* (Boston: Conari Press, 2004); and Brian Walker, *Dancing to History's Tune: History, Myth and Politics in Ireland* (Belfast: Institute of Irish Studies, Queen's University, 1996).

An excellent introduction to the religious milieu in which Mary Harris grew up is Patrick J. Corish, *The Catholic Community in the Seventeenth and Eighteenth Centuries* (Dublin: Helicon, 1981). Church history is often divided into two subjects, pastoral and liturgical. For an introduction to the first of these, see Emmet Larkin, *The Pastoral Role of the Roman Catholic Church in Pre-Famine Ireland 1750–1850* (Dublin: Four Courts Press, 2006), where the concept of the devotional revolution is fully explored. See also Brendan Bradshaw and Dáire Keogh, eds., *Christianity in Ireland: Revisiting the Story* (Blackrock, Co. Dublin: Columba Press, 2002), which includes Donal Kerr's chapter on the Church in the early nineteenth century; Irene Whelan, *The Bible War in Ireland: The "Second Reformation" and the Polarization of Protestant–Catholic Relations, 1800–1840* (Madison: University of Wisconsin Press, 2005); the essays in Stewart J. Brown and David W. Miller, eds., *Piety and Power in Ireland, 1760–1960: Essays in Honour of Emmet Larkin* (Belfast: Institute of Irish Studies, Queen's University of Belfast, 2000); and, on the state of the Catholic Church when Mary Harris grew up, S. J. Connolly, *Priests and People in Pre-Famine Ireland, 1780–1845* (Dublin: Four Courts Press, 2001).

For the Catholic Church in Canada, see Terence J. Fay, *A History of Canadian Catholics: Gallicanism, Romanism, and Canadianism* (Montreal: McGill-Queen's University Press, 2002); Mark George McGowan, *Michael Power: The Struggle to Build the Catholic Church on the Canadian Frontier* (Montreal: McGill-Queen's University Press, 2005), a biography of the bishop of Toronto at the time of the Irish potato famine; and Henry Horace Walsh, *The Christian Church in Canada* (Toronto: Ryerson Press, 1956). Also valuable are introductory histories by Mark A. Noll: *A History of Christianity in the United States and Canada* (Grand Rapids: William B.

Eerdmans, 1992) and *The Old Religion in a New World: The History of North American Christianity* (Grand Rapids: William B. Eerdmans, 2002). For the United States specifically, see Jay Dolan, *The American Catholic Experience: A History from Colonial Times to the Present* (Notre Dame: University of Notre Dame Press, 1992).

On Toronto and the effects of the famine immigrants, see Brian P. Clarke, *Piety and Nationalism: Lay Voluntary Associations and the Creation of an Irish-Catholic Community in Toronto, 1850–1895* (Montreal: McGill-Queen's University Press, 1993); and "Lay Nationalism in Victorian Toronto," in *Catholics at the "Gathering Place": Historical Essays on the Archdiocese of Toronto, 1841–1991*, ed. Mark George McGowan and Brian P. Clarke (Toronto: Canadian Catholic Historical Association, 1993), 41–52. Also valuable for understanding the barriers and prejudices Mary Harris may have faced are J. R. Miller's "Anti-Catholicism in Canada: From the British Conquest to the Great War," Murray Nicolson's "The Growth of Roman Catholic Institutions in the Archdiocese of Toronto, 1841–90," and Brian Clarke's "The Parish and the Hearth: Women's Confraternities and the Devotional Revolution among the Irish Catholics of Toronto, 1850–85," in *Creed and Culture: The Place of English-Speaking Catholics in Canadian Society, 1750–1930*, ed. Terrence Murphy and Gerald Stortz (Montreal: McGill-Queen's University Press, 1993), 25–48, 152–70, 185–203.

A good basic introduction to the history of immigration to the United States is Alan Kraut, *The Huddled Masses: The Immigrant in American Society, 1880–1921* (Wheeling, Ill.: Harlan Davidson, 1982). The transatlantic voyage is covered in Edward Laxton, *The Famine Ships: The Irish Exodus to America* (New York : Henry Holt, 1997). On the specific conditions facing immigrants from Ireland at the time of the famine, see the essays collected in Margaret M. Mulrooney, ed., *Fleeing the Famine: North America and Irish Refugees, 1845–1851* (Westport, Conn.: Praeger, 2003), and the compelling interpretation offered in Hasia R. Dinar, *Erin's Daughters in America: Irish Immigrant Women in the Nineteenth Century* (Baltimore: Johns Hopkins University Press, 1983). On working conditions in Canada, see the section of essays on preindustrial Canada in Laurel Sefton MacDowell and Ian Radforth, eds., *Canadian Working Class History* (Toronto: Canadian Scholars' Press, 2000). Particularly useful for understanding Mary Harris's migratory movements is Nora Faires, "Leaving the 'Land of the Second Chance': Migration from Ontario to the Upper Midwest in the Nineteenth and Early Twentieth Centuries," in John J. Bukowczyk, Nora Faires, David R. Smith, and Randy William Widdis, *Permeable Border: The Great Lakes Basin as Transnational Region, 1650–1990* (Pittsburgh: University of Pittsburgh Press, 2005), 78–119.

The best starting point for understanding the history of the Irish in America is Kevin Kenny, *The American Irish: A History* (Harlow: Longman, 2000). Also useful and insightful are David Noel Doyle, "The Remaking of Irish America, 1845–1880," in *Making the Irish American: History and Heritage of the Irish in the United States*, ed. J. J. Lee and Marion R. Casey (New York: New York University Press, 2006), 213–52, and Marjorie R. Fallows, *Irish Americans: Identity and Assimilation* (Englewood Cliffs, N.J.: Prentice-Hall, 1979). For Chicago, see the wonderful collection of documents in Bessie Louise Pierce, ed., *As Others See Chicago: Impressions of Visitors, 1673–1933* (Chicago: University of Chicago Press, 2004). To understand the environmental conditions Mary Harris encountered, Harold L. Platt, *Shock Cities: The Environmental Transformation and Reform of Manchester and Chicago* (Chicago: University of Chicago Press, 2005), is well worth reading.

For general histories of the American labor movement, see David Brian Robertson, *Capital, Labor and State: The Battle for American Labor Markets from the Civil War to the New Deal* (Lanham, Md.: Rowman and Littlefield, 2000), and Steve Babson, *The Unfinished Struggle: Turning Points in American Labor, 1877 to the Present* (Lanham, Md.: Rowman and Littlefield, 1999). A short (twenty pages), excellent overview is Leon Fink, *American Labor History* (Washington, D.C.: American Historical Association, 1997). For the general context, see Walter Licht's accessible *Industrializing America: The Nineteenth Century* (Baltimore: Johns Hopkins University Press, 1995), and Melvyn Dubofsky, *Industrialism and the American Worker, 1865–1920*, 3rd ed. (Wheeling, Ill.: Harlan Davidson, 1996).

On specific topics relevant to Mother Jones's career in the labor movement, see Richard Schneirov, *Labor and Urban Politics: Class Conflict and the Origins of Modern Liberalism in Chicago, 1864–97* (Urbana: University of Illinois Press, 1998), and the excellent *Death in the Haymarket: A Story of Chicago, the First Labor Movement, and the Bombing that Divided Gilded Age America* by James R. Green (New York: Anchor Books, 2007). The Knights of Labor, and especially the political activities of the fraternity, are admirably explored in Leon Fink, *Workingmen's Democracy: The Knights of Labor and American Politics* (Urbana: University of Illinois Press, 1983). An introduction to the streetcar industry is Scott Molloy, *Trolley Wars: Streetcar Workers on the Line* (Washington, D.C.: Smithsonian Institution Press, 1996); for the political significance of streetcar labor organizing, see Georg Leidenberger, *Chicago's Progressive Alliance: Labor and the Bid for Public Streetcars* (DeKalb: Northern Illinois Press, 2006).

For Coxey's Army, see the classic narrative by Carlos A. Schwantes, *Coxey's Army: An American Odyssey* (Lincoln: University of Nebraska Press,

1985). For a brief but insightful introduction, see the chapter on Coxey in Lucy G. Barber, *Marching on Washington: The Forging of an American Political Tradition* (Berkeley: University of California Press, 2002).

Two chapters in the life of Mother Jones that can only be approached tangentially are her supposed career as a prostitute and her experiences with the utopian Ruskin Community. For the first of these, two books provide a knowledgeable overview. For an introduction to prostitution in the West during Reconstruction, see Anne M. Butler, *Daughters of Joy, Sisters of Mercy: Prostitutes in the American West 1865–90* (Urbana: University of Illinois Press, 1985). A closer analysis is provided by Jan MacKell, *Brothels, Bordellos, and Bad Girls: Prostitution in Colorado, 1860–1930* (Albuquerque: University of New Mexico Press, 2004), which pays particular attention to mining towns such as Cripple Creek. The history of the Ruskin Community is explored in *A Socialist Utopia in the New South: The Ruskin Colonies in Tennessee and Georgia, 1894–1901* (Urbana: University of Illinois Press, 1996) by W. Fitzhugh Brundage.

Mother Jones became friends with many of the best-known labor leaders of her day. Two such were Eugene Debs and J. A. Wayland. For biographies of these two important influences on her career, see the compassionate and critical biography of Debs by Nick Salvatore, *Eugene V. Debs: Citizen and Socialist* (Urbana: University of Illinois Press, 1982), and the careful, interesting retelling of Wayland's life by Elliott Shore, *Talkin' Socialism: J. A. Wayland and the Role of the Press in American Socialism, 1890–1912* (Lawrence: University Press of Kansas, 1998). For Wayland's *Appeal to Reason* and its role in American radicalism, see John Graham, ed., *Yours for the Revolution: The "Appeal to Reason," 1895–1922* (Lincoln: University of Nebraska Press, 1990), which includes useful extracts from the newspaper. Another key friend, and one who assisted her materially in later life, was Terence Powderly, the leader of the Knights of Labor. His career has been carefully re-created by Craig Phelan in *Grand Master Workman: Terence Powderly and the Knights of Labor* (Westport, Conn.: Greenwood Press, 2000). A fine treatment of Mother Jones's nemesis in the United Mine Workers is the abridged version of Melvyn Dubofsky and Warren van Tine, *John L. Lewis: A Biography* (Urbana: University of Illinois Press, 1986).

If the name of Mother Jones became associated with any single state, it was West Virginia, a state analyzed carefully in Roger Fagge, *Power, Culture and Conflict in the Coalfields: West Virginia and South Wales, 1900–1922* (Manchester: Manchester University Press, 1996), which includes a chapter on the mine wars. For specific events and personalities, see Melody

Bragg, *Window to the Past: 1912–1913 Mine Wars and Mother Jones* (Glen Jean, W.Va.: Gem Publications, 1990).

Mother Jones engaged regularly with national figures. For an excellent analysis of the administration of one of her favorite bêtes noires, see Lewis L. Gould, *The Presidency of Theodore Roosevelt* (Lawrence: University Press of Kansas, 1991). Her sometime enemy John D. Rockefeller Jr. is admirably covered in the biography of his father by Ron Chernow, *Titan: The Life of John D. Rockefeller, Sr.* (New York: Random House, 1988), while her occasional ally Woodrow Wilson has found his biographer in John Milton Cooper Jr., *Woodrow Wilson: A Biography* (New York: Alfred A. Knopf, 2009).

Index